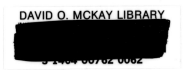
TOPICS IN THE STRUCTURE
OF RUSSIAN

An Introduction to Russian Linguistics

TOPICS IN THE STRUCTURE OF RUSSIAN

An Introduction to Russian Linguistics

David K. Hart

1996

Slavica Publishers, Inc.

Slavica publishes a wide variety of scholarly books and textbooks on the languages, peoples, literatures, cultures, history, etc. of the former USSR and Eastern Europe. For a complete catalog of books and journals from Slavica, with prices and ordering information, write to:

Slavica Publishers, Inc.
PO Box 14388
Columbus, Ohio 43214

ISBN: 0-89357-268-3.

Printed in the United States of America.

To LaRayne

CONTENTS

PREFACE

Students of Russian are often struck by the complexity of Russian grammar. In addition to having to learn numerous grammar and pronunciation rules, students must also learn a host of exceptions. The set of masculine noun endings for the genitive plural illustrates this well. Students learn that masc nouns ending in a hard consonant take the genitive plural ending -ов and that nouns ending in a soft consonant, except -й, take the ending -ей. Masc nouns ending in -й take the endings -ев or -ёв, depending on stress. Students must then remember that if the noun ends in a husher, whether soft or hard, then the ending is also -ей. For soft hushers this makes some sense, but for hard hushers this seems completely arbitrary and students may wonder about the reasons for this exception. Questions such as these occur naturally among language learners whose native language does not make extensive use of inflectional devices.

Students may wonder why the spelling rules exist, why there are fleeting vowels, why stress shifts around, or why consonants mutate in some verbal forms (чистить - чищу), in comparatives (сухой - суше) and elsewhere (книга - книжный). The aim of this book is to answer these and similar questions about Russian pronunciation and grammar and to show that many apparent irregularities can be explained through an understanding of the structure of Russian. It is hoped that when students become acquainted with the Russian grammatical system at a deeper level, they will find it easier to use the language in all of its aspects. Once it is understood why masc nouns ending in hushers take the genitive plural ending -ей, it is easier to remember this rule. Once students understand why the sounds г and ж alternate with each other, then pairs such as друг-дружный, могу-можешь make perfect sense. The text provides a description of the principal phonetic features of Russian, including descriptions of the most often encountered alternations. It introduces phonology, language history, morphology, and morphophonemics. The text concludes with a chapter devoted to stress. Since this book aims to introduce the science of Russian linguistics, terminology, formulae and quotes from works in Russian linguistics are used throughout the text.

Each chapter of this textbook introduces a fundamental problem in Russian grammar or pronunciation, and, with the exception of the final chapter, contains a section on dialectology. These sections give an overview of the most widespread deviations from the standard forms discussed in the main part of each chapter. Exercises are given periodically to check students' understanding of the text or to give students a chance to manipulate data so they may draw their own conclusions.

This book is intended for students who already have a firm grasp of Russian grammar and pronunciation. It could be used through a full year instruction if used with other material or in conjunction with a reading program. It fits well into the time constraints of two quarters or into a single semester if used as the only text.

I wish to express thanks to Professors Charles Gribble, Herbert Coats, and Raisa Solovyova for their thoughtful comments and recommendations on an earlier version of this text and to Professor Yuri Tretyakov of the Russian Academy of Sciences for his insightful criticisms and encouragement. I am also indebted to my students in our Structure of Russian course, whose insistence over the years on clarity of presentation has helped shape the organization and has influenced the content of this book. Full responsiblity for what follows, of course, rests with me. Finally I must thank LaRayne W. Hart, whose editing skills transformed much of the manuscript for this text into readable format and whose confidence in this book and its author has been vital to its completion.

David K. Hart, 1996

ABBREVIATIONS AND SYMBOLS

1st	first
2nd	second
3rd	third
4th	fourth
conj	conjugation
decl	declension
nom	nominative
acc	accusative
gen	genitive
prep	prepositional
dat	dative
instr	instrumental
sg	singular
pl	plural
masc	masculine
fem	feminine
neut	neuter
CSR	Contempory Standard Russian
MR	Modern Russian
OMN	Old Moscow Norm
[ ]	phonetic transcription
# #	phonological transcription
{ }	morphological/morphophonemic transcription
/	fleeting vowel
→	"becomes" or "is pronounced as"
=	prefix boundary
-	suffix boundary
+	ending boundary
#	word boundary
´	main stress
K	velar
Č	husher
~	"alternates with"

INTRODUCTION: Why Study the Structure of Russian

In addition to the many "why" questions we will try to answer in this course, one which should be clear is: why study this topic at all? After all, more time could be spent reviewing difficult grammar concepts, such as participles, constituent structure, and verbal aspect, or more time could be spent just in speaking. Why have a class devoted to learning more about the internal structure of the language? There are several answers to this question, and since the may not be very obvious it is a good idea to review them. First you should be aware that it is <u>not</u> a major objective of this text to help you improve in spoken fluency. This may come as a shock, since most of the Russian language courses you have taken up to this level probably do have spoken fluency as a major objective. You will continue to work on the spoken language elsewhere. So why have a class that concentrates on structure?

Some students say that they are not interested in grammar or linguistics. Grammar is boring, linguistics is too complex, and besides, who needs them? It is true that students who live in Russia can learn to speak Russian quite fluently without paying much attention to grammar. It has been found that most such students, however, find their ability to speak accurately leaves much to be desired. In order to speak accurately most students need to spend some time with grammar. As it turns out, the language doesn't exist without the grammar. However, as soon as we begin studying grammar--the rules of the language--we find all sorts of exceptions to the rules, difficulties in pronunciation and spelling, a myriad of endings to sort out, to say nothing of stress problems. Students are able to learn most of the rules involved and speak fairly well, although they may occasionally mix up some rules. Other curious students, sometimes in exasperation, ask "why?" Why are there spelling rules, why are there fleeting vowels, where do mutations come from, and so on. The structure course is meant to answer these and similar questions. Many of the problems we encounter are due to historical sound changes, so a look into the history of Russian is called for. Anyone with a bachelor's degree in Russian will be expected to know the answers to these kinds of questions. Even if you are not asked, you still should understand the questions and have an idea what the answers are. Many students have found that knowing why the spelling rules came into being helps keep them straight. Understanding what is regular allows you to identify what is irregular and needful of particular attention. In short, understanding the structure of the language will help you know the language better. One aspect of this is acquiring the habit of thinking precisely about what constitutes a language and formulating exactly what you know about Russian.

Most students taking a structure course are advanced undergraduate majors in Russian or students already in a graduate program. Students who continue their Russian studies in graduate school are usually required to choose a speciality: Russian literature, Russian linguistics, or Russian pedagogy. Obviously a structure course will provide an important introduction to students who choose to become linguists. For those who go on in literature or pedagogy, a basic linguistics course contributes valuable information about the language itself, its historical antecedents, and what makes up some of its lyrical qualities. Students who do not continue their education in Russian still find that the problem-solving strategies developed in a course such as this are valuable in all types of undertakings.

Though languages have been studied for thousands of years, theoretical linguistics is a fairly young science--just a few hundred years old. Most of the effort in this science has been devoted to describing languages and how languages change. Only within the last century have linguists turned to theoretical questions. We hope that answers to these questions will provide the framework in which applications may be made. Is it possible for a foreigner to learn Russian well in less than four years? Can a method be devised where difficult grammatical forms such as verbal aspect or stress be more naturally and quickly internalized? What exactly is being acquired when students acquire a foreign language? Can computers be made useful in the learning process? Can other devices be developed to aid in international communication and understanding? Can people who are dyslexic or victims of aphasia be helped in acquiring and using language? We don't know if these or any other applications will be possible through the science of linguistics. It would be a pity, though, if we didn't make the search. As one of mankind's most powerful instruments, language should be studied, understood, and attempts made to use it to improve lives.

SECTION 1: PHONOLOGY AND HISTORICAL PHONOLOGY

CHAPTER 1. Symbolizing Sounds: Phonetics

1.1 Writing Down Russian Sounds

If you were asked to describe Russian to someone who knew only English your description might include a reference to Russian's Cyrillic alphabet. You might point out that some of the Cyrillic alphabet's letters are similar to English letters and they represent the same sounds, such as Russian м and English M. Other Cyrillic letters represent the same sounds as in English but are written differently, such as Russian з and English z. Some Cyrillic letters resemble English letters but represent a completely different sound (Russian н, English H). And some letters, such as я, ю, ы, don't resemble English letters at all.

A little over a thousand years ago, when the ancestor of Russian was only spoken and not written, a method was devised to represent its sounds by written letters on paper. This system of symbols, known as the Cyrillic alphabet, is named after Cyril, a missionary of the Greek Orthodox Church who worked among the Slavs in the middle of the 9th century A.D.

In order to discuss the sounds of Russian in a medium such as a textbook, we need to use a system of symbols to represent each sound we hear. Unfortunately the Cyrillic alphabet is not completely adequate for this task; Russian has sounds that are not represented by any letter of the Cyrillic alphabet, and some of this alphabet's letters represent more than one sound. The very best system of representation would have every individual sound signified by a unique symbol. The Latin-based alphabet of English also falls short of this requirement. For example, English represents the sound "f" in three ways: f (fist), ph (phonology) and gh (enough). And the combination gh represents other sounds as well, for instance, "through" (no sound) and "ghastly" (g). An optimal system would avoid these ambiguities in representation; instead, each symbol would represent only one sound, and each sound would always be represented by the same symbol.

Consider the pronunciation of the following:

(1) a. молокó
   b. тётя
   c. читáть

As is well known, unstressed <u>o</u> is pronounced differently than stressed <u>o</u>, as illustrated in <u>молокó</u>. We can hear an <u>o</u> sound in <u>тётя</u>, yet no <u>o</u> is written. The final <u>т</u> in <u>читáть</u> is soft, but so are the two <u>т</u>'s in <u>тётя</u>. Clearly, Russian orthography does not follow the rule of one symbol for one sound.

*A 1. Which of the symbols used in (1) represent more than one sound?
   2. Which symbols in (1) represent only one sound?
   3. How many ways is soft <u>т</u> represented?

*B Using Russian letters or other symbols, write out the three words in (1) according to the way each word sounds. Each letter you use, however, should stand for just one sound. Thus every time you hear an <u>o</u>, you should use only one symbol for this   sound and that symbol can be used only for the sound <u>o</u>.

1.2 The Articulation of Consonants

Speech is composed of a wide variety of sounds, which are a part of three physiological processes: the production of sounds, the perception of sounds, and the assignment of meaning to those sounds. An important secondary activity related to speech, one which is critical to civilization, is representing the sounds of speech in writing. One of the main purposes of this chapter is to discuss how Russian orthography represents the sounds of Russian, to determine where the orthography is ambiguous, and to introduce a method of unambiguous representation. First, let's look at exactly what sounds Russians use and how they make them.

Sounds are created by means of an air flow which exits the lungs (лёгкие), passes through the the vocal chords (голосовы́е свя́зки), the mouth (рот), and the nasal cavity (по́лость но́са). The mouth, or more properly, the oral cavity (по́лость рта), contains several sound-varying devices: the tongue (язы́к), lips (гу́бы), teeth (зу́бы), hard palate (твёрдое нёбо), and soft palate (мя́гкое нёбо). Little noise is produced if the air stream passes from the lungs through the vocal chords and oral cavity with no obstruction; we hear a heavy breathing sound, or a sigh. When an obstruction to the air flow is created by means of one or more of the sound-producing devices just mentioned, then the air flow is interrupted and a noise can be heard. For example, by extending the edges of the tongue along the inner sides of the teeth and by extending the tip of the tongue toward the back of the front teeth and exhaling, we are able to make the sound s̲. By extending the tip of the tongue further, so it touches the back of the teeth, we stop the air flow. By retracting the tip of the tongue so the air flow continues, we make the sound t̲. For the sound t̲, we say that the device used to create this sound (in addition to the tongue), or the point of articulation (ме́сто артикуля́ции), is the teeth. Russian sounds can be grouped according to their points of articulation. For example, the lips, or the lips and teeth working together produce the following sounds: p̲, b̲, f̲, v̲, m̲. These sounds are called labials (губны́е) or labio-dentals (губно-зубны́е). For our purposes we will place the labials (p̲, b̲, m̲) and the labio-dentals (f̲, v̲) in one group and we will call this group the labials. In exercise *A you will become acquainted with the points of articulation used to produce consonants (согла́сные).

*A Here is a list of the consonant **letters** in Russian. Write out which consonants you think belong in each group given below.

б в г д ж з й к л м н п р с т ф х ц ч ш щ

1. Labial (губно́й): Either one or both of the lips are used.

2. Dental (зубно́й): The tongue either touches the back of the teeth or the air flow is directed against the back of the teeth.

3. Palatal (нёбный): The body of the tongue is raised nearly to touch the hard palate (the dome of the mouth) and air passes through the small opening between the tongue and the hard palate, creating a hushing sound.

4. Yod (йот): This palatal does not create a hushing sound, instead it is the gliding sound (глайд) <u>y</u> in English "<u>y</u>es" produced as the tongue is lowered.

5. Velar (задненёбный): The back of the tongue touches or nearly touches the soft part of the palate, either briefly stopping or restricting the air flow.

Another prominent member of the speech-producing organ is the alveolar ridge (альвео́ла). This is the hard ridge right behind the front upper teeth. This is the place of articulation of "t" for most American speakers. Note that the Russian "т" is not produced at the alveolar ridge, but at the back of the teeth. Thus, if we pronounce the word <u>тот</u> as we would the English <u>tote</u>, Russians hear an accent. Similarly, <u>нет</u>, <u>учи́ть</u>, and <u>тёплый</u> pronounced with an alveolar "t" rather than a dental "т" produces an English accent in these words, though it may not be obvious to native English speakers.

Sounds in Russian may be defined by where they are produced. The various points of articulation not only determine the sounds but provide a convenient way for labeling these sounds, a so-called articulatory definition. Sounds may be characterized in other ways. For example, rather than defining sounds by how they are produced, as we have done here, it is possible to define sounds by how they are heard. Some sounds could be characterized as "harsh" or "smooth," or could be characterized by their sound wave frequency. This method of defining sounds is called "perceptual," or "spectographic." Here we will mainly be interested in articulatory descriptions.

It is important to note that Russian sounds fall into different articulatory groups, because rules of Russian grammar and pronunciation often deal with groups of sounds, not just individual sounds. For example, the consonant mutation which adds an л in the first person sg of 2nd conj verbs involves one group of sounds, namely the labials (п,б,ф,в,м): купи́ть - я купл<u>ю</u>, люби́ть - я люб<u>л</u>ю́, лови́ть - я ловл<u>ю́</u>, корми́ть - я кор<u>м</u>лю́, графи́ть - я граф<u>л</u>ю́. This mutation, the addition (or epenthesis) of an <u>л</u>, occurs only with the labials.

*B 1. What two groups of sounds are involved in the spelling rule which states that <u>и</u> is written in place of <u>ы</u>?

2.   What two groups of sounds is involved in the spelling rule which tells when to write y and a in place of ю and я?

3.   What group of sounds is involved in the spelling rule that tells when unstressed o is written e?

*C Identify the parts of the speech-producing mechanism.

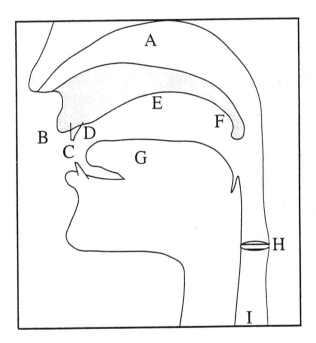

If п and б are both labials, then what is the difference between them? As the air stream passes through the vocal chords, we can tighten the vocal chords to the extent that they begin to vibrate. This vibration of the vocal chords is called voice (го́лос). Sounds that are produced with the vocal chords vibrating are termed voiced (зво́нкий). Sounds produced without the vibration of the vocal chords are voiceless (глухо́й). Russian consonant letters represent either voiced or voiceless sounds:

(1) VOICED   VOICELESS PT. OF ARTICULATION

б	п	labial
в	ф	labial
г	к	velar
д	т	dental
ж	ш	palatal
з	с	dental
й	-	palatal
л	-	dental
м	-	labial
н	-	dental
р	-	dental
-	ч	palatal
-	ц	dental
-	щ	palatal
-	х	velar

Some letters do not have a voiced or voiceless counterpart. This doesn't mean that Russian doesn't have that sound, simply that it doesn't have a special letter in the alphabet to represent it. Thus, we may characterize consonants as to place of articulation (labials, dentals, etc.) and whether they are voiced or voiceless. Voicing or lack of voicing is the only difference between the sounds б and п: the first is voiced, the second voiceless.

The <u>manner</u> of articulation (спо́соб артикуля́ции) is also important in distinguishing between some sounds. The air stream stops completely, albeit briefly, for the sound т but it never comes to a complete stop for the sound с, both of which are voiceless dentals. The former is called a stop (смы́чный), and the latter is called a fricative (щелево́й). These two features allow us to distinguish between sounds that have the same voicing and place of articulation, such as б, a (voiced, labial) stop and в, a (voiced, labial) fricative.

The Russian letters ц and ч represent a combination of stop and fricative. The flow of air is very briefly stopped then allowed to continue, creating a fricative sound. This kind of sound is called an affricate (аффрика́та).

We can now define a sound as to where it is produced (point of articulation), whether or not it is voiced, and how it is produced (means of articulation).

*D Which consonants are being described? Example: voiceless palatal fricative = ш.

1. voiced	labial	stop
2. voiceless	labial	stop
3. voiceless	dental	stop
4. voiceless	dental	fricative
5. voiced	palatal	fricative
6. voiced	velar	stop
7. voiceless	velar	fricative
8. voiceless	velar	stop
9. voiced	dental	stop
10. voiceless	labial	fricative

The sounds represented by the letters м н л р are somewhat different. They are called sonorants (сонóрные). Sometimes they are called "semi-vowels." In some languages they act like vowels, and in Russian, as we will see later, they sometimes act like vowels and sometimes like consonants.

1.3 The Articulation of Vowels

Vowels (глáсные) present only one major obstacle to the air flow, namely the vibrating vocal chords. Even so, vowel sounds can be characterized according to the location of the tongue when each is produced. Russian has the following basic vowel sounds:

а о у э и ы

We will discuss variations of these sounds later. The tongue is able to occupy differing amounts of space in the oral cavity, which acts as a resonating chamber. The air stream, having passed through the vibrating vocal chords, has its timbre or pitch altered according to the location of the tongue. When the tongue is high in the mouth it occupies most of the oral cavity, and the high (высóкие) vowels are formed: и ы and у. When the tongue is relaxed and level it occupies less space, and the mid (срéдние) vowels are produced: <u>э</u> and <u>о</u>. When the tongue is lowered in the mouth it occupies little space in the oral cavity and a low (ни́зкий) vowel is produced: <u>а</u>.

We can differentiate between the two mid vowels by noting that for <u>э</u> the tongue is brought forward slightly, while it is not brought forward for <u>о</u>. The sound <u>э</u> is therefore defined as a "front, mid" vowel. The sound <u>о</u> is a "back, mid" vowel. The three high vowels are also considered to be front (<u>и</u>) or back (<u>ы,у</u>). For the two back high vowels the tongue is very nearly in the same place, but the sound <u>у</u> is characterized by a rounding of the lips. It, like the sound <u>о</u>, is rounded (лабиализо́ванный).

This chart shows the relative position of the tongue for the basic Russian vowel sounds:

(2)

	front	back
high	и	ы у
mid	э	о
low		а

Note: <u>о</u> and <u>у</u> are also rounded.

*A 1. What is the basic difference between vowels and consonants?
 2. What articulatory feature can vowels and consonants share?
 3. Why do you think the sonorants (м, н, л, р) are sometimes called "semi-vowels?" That is, what do these sounds have in common with vowels?

1.4 The Articulation of Hard and Soft Consonants

In addition to being voiced or voiceless, Russian consonants may be hard (твёрдый) or soft (мя́гкий). Soft consonants are those which are pronounced normally but at the same time are "palatalized," which means that soft consonants are formed by raising the body of the tongue toward the hard palate and lowering the tip of the tongue to a position behind the bottom teeth, all while the consonant is being pronounced. In

(1) caught   cut   cute   key

we hear a k̲ sound at the beginning of each word. But as you pronounce
each word notice that the body of the tongue moves forward slightly for
each k̲ sound. In caught, the point of articulation for the sound k̲ (written
c̲) is the back of the mouth: the tongue touches the soft palate. In key,
however, the body of the tongue extends forward to the hard palate. The
k̲ of key is similar to a soft, or palatalized, Russian к̲, as in the word руки́.
The к̲ in this word is soft, or "palatalized." The k̲ sound in caught is similar
to a hard, or velarized, Russian к̲ as in рука́. The к̲ in this word is hard.

Letters of an alphabet represent a sound or sounds of a language. The
Russian alphabet, with letters borrowed from Greek and special Cyrillic
letters such as Ю and Я, does a fairly good job of representing in written
form the sounds of Russian. Like many other alphabets, however, it is not
completely unambiguous. Consider the consonant letter т̲. In one word it
represents a hard consonant (as in мат "check mate"), and in another word
it represents a soft consonant (as in мать "mother"). The soft sign doesn't
represent any sound at all, it only shows that the preceding consonant is
soft. In order to represent Russian sounds unambiguously we will adopt
the system of letters and symbols used in the Russian Academy Grammar.
In addition, whenever we use these symbols, most of which resemble
regular Russian letters, we will enclose them in square brackets [ ], and we
will refer to this as a **phonetic transcription**. For example, in this system
the pronunciation of the word мат is represented [мат], and that of мать
is represented [мат'], where the symbol [т'] represents a soft т̲. The soft
sign is used for an actual sound which we will discuss below. We will use
the symbol ['] to show the softness of any consonant; thus кит "whale"
is phonetically transcribed as [к'ит], the symbol [к'] representing the soft
variation of [к]. Thus, words in square brackets represent how these
sounds are actually pronounced.

In addition to the soft sign, the Russian alphabet has another way of
indicating that a consonant is soft, namely by certain vowel letters. It was
stated above that Russian contains the vowel sounds, а, о, э, у, ы, и.
These six vowel *sounds* are represented by ten vowel *letters* in the
alphabet.

(2) the sound: is represented in writing by:
         [а]   а and я
         [о]   о and ё
         [э]   э and е
         [у]   у and ю
         [ы]   ы
         [и]   и

Two different letters in the alphabet represent each vowel sound, except for [и] and [ы], for which there is only one letter each. There are two letters for each vowel sound because of the need to show whether the preceding consonant is pronounced hard or soft. Vowel letters in the final column above are used to show that consonants preceding these letters are soft. For example, the word в̲ё̲л̲ "he led" is pronounced with an initial soft [в'], followed by the stressed vowel [о], followed by the hard consonant [л]. Thus, the phonetic representation of this word is: [в'ол].

Students sometimes get the impression that the letters in the third column in (2) are "soft vowels." Actually, softness, or palatalization, is a feature associated only with consonants, not vowels. It is therefore incorrect to speak of "soft vowels." If reference must be made to this group of vowel letters, then it is best to refer to them as the (vowel) letters which indicate softening. Instead of using a soft sign everywhere to indicate a soft consonant, Russian uses this ingenious system of paired vowel letters for this purpose.

*A Which Russian words do the following phonetic transcriptions represent?

Example: [м'э́ст] = мест (gen pl of ме́сто)

 1. [п'ат']   7. [т'о́т'у]
 2. [суд'ба́]   8. [т'эн']
 3. [п'ит']   9. [л'ицо́]
 4. [д'э́т'и]   10. [дын']
 5. [п'ис'мо́]   11. [т'у́б'ик]
 6. [труба́]   12. [мыт']

Before [а], [о], and [у], most consonants may be either hard or soft.

Consonants which can be either hard or soft before these vowel sounds are called "paired" consonants. For example, the consonants [п] and [п'] are paired. Either one may occur before these vowels: па [па] as in па́па, пя [п'а] as in пять. The sounds [т] and [т'], for another example, are paired: either may occur before [а], [о], and [у], e.g., [ту] (hard) - [т'о́т'у] (soft). The labials and dentals, except ц, are paired. The palatals (ш, щ, ч, ж), the velars (к, г, х), and й and ц are not paired. The consonants ч, щ, and й are always soft, no matter what sound or vowel letter follows, so they are not paired. And ж, ш and ц are always hard, so they are not paired. The velars are always hard before [а], [о], and [у], and always soft before [э] and [и]. They do not occur before [ы] in the standard language.

When a vowel letter from the final column in (2) occurs in writing after another vowel, at the beginning of a word, or after a soft sign or hard sign, then these letters stand for the vowel sound preceded by a "y" sound, or a yod (transcribed by the symbol [й]):

	written	pronounced
(3) a. <u>after a vowel</u>:		
	мо<u>я</u>	мо[йа́]
	тво<u>ё</u>	тво[йо́]
c. <u>beginning of a word</u>:	<u>ё</u>лка	[йо́]лка
	<u>я</u>лта	[йа́]лта
b. <u>after a soft/hard sign</u>:	пить<u>ё</u>	пи[т'йо́]
	съесть	[сйэ]сть

An exception to this is the vowel letter и. It shows that preceding paired consonants and velars are soft; it is not yodicized at the beginning of words or after vowels but an [й] does precede it after soft/hard signs:

(4) a. <u>after vowels</u>:	мой	мо[й] (not мо[йи])
b. <u>beginning of a word</u>:	изба́	[и]зба́ (not[йи]зба)
c. <u>after soft/hard signs</u>:	чьи	[чйи]

*B Give the following in phonetic transcription.

1. суёт   5. ля́гу
2. лес   6. сел (past masc sg of сесть)
3. сёл (gen pl of село́)   7. клюю́
4. сто́ит   8. име́ть

Ruben Avanesov, a Russian phonetician, described the difference between hard and soft consonants in the following way.

Одной из самых характерных особенностей звуковой системы русского языка является различение твердых и мягких согласных...Чтобы правильно произносить мягкие согласные русского языка, надо знать как они образуются. При образовании мягкого согласного язык занимает положение, близкое к тому, в котором он бывает при произношении [и] или [й], т.е. средняя часть спинки языка высоко поднимается к соответствующей части нёба. Твердые согласные образуются без этой дополнительной "йотовой" артикуляции: средняя часть спинки языка при произношении твердых согласных бывает опущена. (pp. 100-101)

*C According to Avanesov, how does the position of the tongue differ when pronouncing a soft consonant from that of its hard variant?

Since the tongue is placed in a position similar to that for the pronunciation of [и], a front vowel, the point of articulation for soft consonants is closer to the front of the mouth than it is for their hard counterparts. Thus, the body of the tongue is closer to the front of the mouth for те [т'э́] than for the consonant in та [та́].

1.5 The Distribution of Hard and Soft Consonants

We have seen that certain vowel letters indicate that a preceding consonant is pronounced soft, and other vowel letters indicate that a preceding consonant is pronounced hard. Some consonants can be either hard or soft (paired), others are either always hard or always soft, and still others are soft only before the front vowels [и] and [э] (unpaired). Certain patterns can be noted.

(1) The vowel letter ы, a back vowel, is always preceded by a hard consonant: ты, мыть, дым (phonetically: [ты], [мыт'] [дым]). Recall that for soft consonants the body of the tongue is raised high in the mouth and moved towards the front of the mouth. While it is physically possible to pronounce a soft consonant followed by [ы], this combination does not occur in Russian. This fact of pronunciation is reflected in spelling: when a prefix ending in a hard consonant is added to a word beginning with the sound [и], the prefix continues to be "hard," but the vowel и shifts to ы. When we add the perfectivizing prefix с to играть (с + играть) we get сыграть. Other examples are: искать - взыскать, идущий - предыдущий, интересный - безынтересный.

(2) Certain consonants are always hard, namely ж, ш, and ц. It is quite natural for these consonants to be hard--the pronunciation of the first two requires that the body of the tongue be retracted from the front part of the mouth. That is not to say that it is impossible to produce a soft ж, ш or ц, but Russians do not in normal circumstances.

These consonants are hard even if a soft sign is written after them: читáешь, рожь (the soft sign is never written after ц). Instead of indicating pronunciation in these words, the soft sign plays a grammatical role. In the first word the шь is an indicator of the 2nd person sg verbal ending, and in рожь the soft sign indicates that the word is a fem noun, as are all nouns ending in a palatal (ш, ж, ц, ч) plus soft sign. When the three hard palatal consonants are followed by orthographic и, then the latter is pronounced [ы]: жить [жыт'], шил [шыл] цирк [цырк]. We will discuss later why the writing does not reflect pronunciation in these words. Notice that the pronunciation of these words is similar to the spelling phenomenon we saw with words like безынтерéсный.

(3) Some consonants are always soft, namely ч, щ and й. These consonants are produced with the tongue high and moved slightly forward in the oral cavity. The pronunciation of щ is of interest. Avanesov admits two standard literary pronunciations for this letter. The more standard according to Avanesov is a double soft ш sound [ш'ш'] as in ещё: e[ш'ш']ё. The traditional St. Petersburg pronunciation, also considered standard, has the sound end in a slight, not full, [ч]: e[ш'ᶜ]ё. With the exception of щ which we will transcribe as [ш'ш'], there is no need to transcribe an apostrophe next to [ч] and [й], since they are always soft. Instead of writing [ч'] and [й'], we will simply write [ч] and [й].

Occasionally a soft sign is written after these consonants to show grammatical information, such as for the infinitive ending -чь: мочь.

(4) The velars (also called "gutturals" (к г х), present yet a different pattern. They may be hard or soft but they are always hard before certain vowels and always soft before others. They are always soft before the front vowels [и] [э]. They are always hard before the back vowels [у] [а] [о]: кит кот: [к'ит] [кот]. This distribution makes the velars different from most other consonants which are soft before [и] and [э] (те [т'э]) but may be hard or soft before [у] [а] and [о]; examples: тот and тётя: [то]т, [т'о]тя. Thus т can be hard or soft before о. With only one exception (see the conjugation of ткать), the velars are never soft before о.

*A Write the following in normal Russian orthography.

1. [к'инó]	9. [кл'óн]
2. [п'эч']	10. [жывóй]
3. [чйш'ш'у] (Moscow norm)	11. [нóг'и]
4. [рук'й]	12. [рук'ó]
5. [шол]	13. [цэн]
6. [читáйут]	14. [п'ат']
7. [жон]	15. [йáсный]
8. [ид'óт]	16. [гул'áйу]

*B Give the following in phonetic transcription. Be sure to include stress in polysyllabic words.

1. чúстый	6. меч
2. глушь	7. мышь
3. живóт	8. цикл
4. лю́льки	9. лы́жи
5. щи	10. дéньги

1.6 Dialectal Features: Deviations or the Real Thing?

No one speaks Contemporary Standard Russian (CSR), with the possible exception of news reporters on radio and television, and when they leave the studio they most likely lapse into their own way of speaking. One's own way of speaking is called an idiolect. Idiolects differ from the standard language in an infinite number of ways. The standard language, normally taught in college and university classes, is a generalized description of features found in *most* idiolects. If you learn these features most Russians will understand you, and with time, you will understand most Russians. Several idiolects that share many features are grouped together into a <u>dialect</u>. For example, many people raised in and around Baltimore, Maryland, speak in a dialect, as suggested by their pronunciation of the name of the city: Balmer City. While this dialect also has many features found in Standard Literary American, it is also characterized by features not shared by most American speakers. For example, the phrase:

(1) Ah ran out of ahl doin the naht..

might be somewhat confusing to many Americans, who would say this phrase differently: I ran out of oil during the night. In Baltimore, the word is "paramore," outside of Baltimore it is pronounced "power mower." Sometimes a native speaker of a given language cannot understand what another native speaker is saying because of strong dialect differences.

The situation in Russia is similar, and dialect differences there are sometimes as strong as in English. There are three main dialect groups: North, Central (or Moscow), and South. The standard literary language is based on the Moscow dialect. But even in this dialect there are many variations, and when you go to Moscow it is easy to hear them if you are listening for them. Linguists are interested in dialectal variations hoping they will give hints to the composition of the language past and present.

A pronunciation feature characteristic of northern dialects is so-called *cokan'e* (цо́канье). In dialects with cokan'e, the sound [ц] or [ц'] (the latter sound does not occur at all in the Standard Language) is pronounced in place of CSR [ч]:

(2) цай (= CSR чай)   ца́шка (ча́шка)
     цистый (чи́стый)   пец (печь)
     цад (чад)   цужой (чужой)

The following story was related in 1941 by a villager from the Vologda (see map below) region:

(3) Пожар большой был. Как вздунуло (= CSR вздувало "blew up"), подняло крышу и сразу цад пошел. Цаду-то, цаду-то было. Все поселяне приехали, так все в белой пене. Цужых много, лишь хоркают (кричат), ницего не выносят. Я сошла на цердак да цурики-то плохие стала скидывать. Семь рам кинула. Я-то без цувств была. Пришел зять, нашел молотки, все хорошо и сделал. За поломку ницего не дали...

(From Гринкова and Чагишева, pp. 39-40.)

*A Translate the excerpt given in (3). The word "ра́мо" here means "armful."

*B Why do you think [ц] or [ц'] might be exchanged for [ч], instead of, say, [м]?

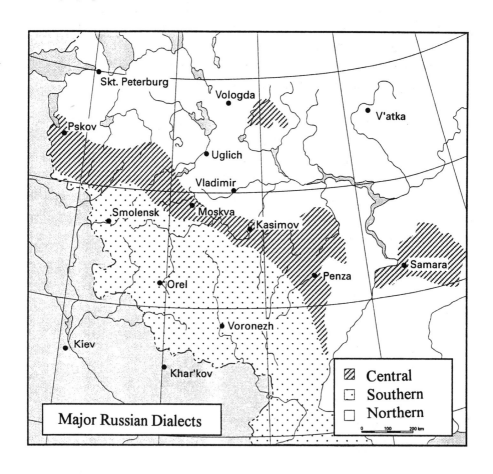

Major Russian Dialects

☑ Central
⊡ Southern
☐ Northern

1.7 Review

As is the case in many scientific endeavors, linguists want to know what the fundamental units, or building blocks, are of their discipline. One set of building blocks is the group of sounds found in any given language. In addition, some unambiguous way of representing these sounds on paper must be agreed upon. In this chapter we have discussed a standard method of representing Russian sounds, a phonetic alphabet. We have seen that normal Russian letters are the basis of this phonetic system. Instead of using the soft sign or hard sign to indicate whether a consonant is soft or hard, the phonetic system uses an apostrophe to show softness and no apostrophe to show a consonant is hard, e.g., [т'] -[т]. Exceptions to this are ч, щ, and й, which are always soft. The symbols ь and ъ are reserved for actual sounds which we will discuss later.

The major advantage to using a phonetic transcription is that it indicates unambiguously how a word is pronounced.

Russian sounds may be classified according to how they are produced in the speech organ. Thus, sounds fall into naturally defined groups. These groups are important because some permutations of sounds often affect not just individual sounds but an entire group of sounds. If our descriptions of these permutations are to be adequate, they will refer to these groups, rather than to individual sounds. For example, to say that т mutates to ч and that д and з mutate to ж and that с mutates to ш would be correct but would miss the wider generalization that all dentals mutate to palatals (hushers) under certain circumstances. It is not simply coincidental that д and з shift to ж; they are part of the set of dentals which always undergo palatalization in a given environment.

*A Give phonetic transcriptions.

1. ся́ду	6. изю́м
2. ступлю́	7. съел
3. сту́пишь	8. я́рус
4. лет	9. щит
5. зима́	10. ю́ный

*B Characterize the following from an articulatory point of view. For consonants use the following features: voiced, voiceless, dental, labial, palatal, velar, stop, fricative. For vowels use:high, mid, low, front, back.

1. т	6. ж
2. б	7. и
3. к	8. х
4. ф	9. о
5. ш	10. з

CHAPTER 2. Describing Sound Changes: Phonology

2.1. Making Hard Consonants Soft: Palatalization

The following table summarizes the distribution of hard and soft consonants:

(1)

	[к] [г] [х]	[ш] [ж] [ц]	[ч] [ш'ш'] [й]	all others
before [и], [э]	soft	--	soft	soft
before [о], [у], [а]	hard	hard	soft	soft or hard
before [ы]	--	hard	--	hard

Note that the information in (1) is based on pronunciation, not on writing, which does not allow the letter ы to follow the hushers (ш, ж, ч, щ). In speech, the sound [ы] does follow the hard hushers [ш] and [ж].

Except for [ш], [ж], and [ц], all consonants are soft before the front vowels, [и] and [э]. This is a natural tendency since "soft" consonants are simply "fronted" varieties of their hard, or non-palatalized counterparts. Consonants before front vowels assimilate (приобретают) the fronted nature of these vowels. It's as if the speaker knows that a front vowel is coming up so while pronouncing the consonant the tongue is fronted in anticipation of the front vowel. Simply stated: consonants (except ж, ш, ц) are soft before front vowels. This generalization helps to explain why stems may vary depending on the case ending. For example the word рука́ is pronounced [рука́], i.e., with a hard [к]. The prep sg form, however, is pronounced with a soft [к']: [рук'э́]. If we remove the endings from these words we discover that there are two different forms [рук-] [рук'-], yet clearly there is only one word here--just two different variants of the same word. In this word, we can say that the sound [к] alternates with the sound [к']. The following is a shorthand way of expressing the same thing: [к] ~ [к'], where the symbol ~ means "alternates with" (чередýется с). The study of phonology is in large part a study of sound alternations, as indicated by phonetics, and accounting for these alternations in a structured way, by means of rules, for example.

We want to say that there is only one root, or base form (основнáя фóрма), for рука́ and руке́, and that the alternate form is predictable by rule. For a start we suggest that the base form in these two words is #рук-#, where the dash represents that part of the base form to which endings are attached and the pound symbol (#) represents a word boundary. If **#рук-#** is the root, then we can determine what the base, or underlying form is for any case form of this word. For example, the underlying form of the nom sg of this word is obtained simply by adding the nom sg fem ending <u>+a</u>, which is stressed in this word: **#рук+á#**, where the plus sign represents an ending boundary. Thus, **#рук+á#** is the underlying form of <u>рукá</u>. As we determine the "surface" form, or the word we actually hear, no changes are made to these sound units; only the word and ending boundaries are deleted since they are not pronounced.

(2) #рук+á# → [рукá]

In (2), the arrow is a symbol for "becomes" or "is pronounced as." Thus, [рукá] is the surface form or phonetic realization of the phonological representation #рук+á#.

The same basic root must be chosen for all declensional variations of any given word. For example, the prep sg of <u>рукá</u> requires the prep sg fem ending <u>+э</u> be part of the underlying form, and that it be attached to the same basic stem as for the nom sg: **#рук+э́#**. We know that consonants are soft before front vowels. The following rule reflects this generalization:

(3) C → C' / ___ и, э

where C = any consonant except <u>ш</u>, <u>ж</u>, or <u>ц</u>.

The rule in (3) states that consonants are pronounced soft before the front vowels. The slash symbol "/" represents "in the following environment" and the line "___" indicates that the stated change occurs <u>before</u> the given sounds, not after. The rule in (3) reflects the process of consonant softening, called "palatalization" (палатализáция). It can be read, "Consonants (except <u>ш</u>, <u>ж</u>, and <u>ц</u>) are soft before the front vowels."

If we apply the rule in (3) to the base form **#рук+э́#** then the combination <u>к+э</u> will shift to <u>к'+э</u>, i.e., the consonant will be pronounced soft according to the rule in (3). This process is illustrated in (4).

(4) #рук+э́# → rule (3) → #рук'+э# → [рук'э́]

We thus account for the intuitive notion that рука́ and руке́ are variants of one word--they have the same underlying form, namely #рук-#. But there is a price for having just one stem per word, namely, we must add a rule to the grammar of Russian. The rule given in (3) is a phonological rule, which expresses an observable fact about the pronunciation of Russian words and which is useful in determining the underlying or base forms of certain words. Phonetics provides observable data about sound alternations, such as the fact that consonants are soft before front vowels in Russian. Phonology provides a structured procedure to account for these data.

There are other ways of accounting for the alternation illustrated above. For example, we might suggest that the base form for рука́ is #рук'-#. The prep sg form then is derived quite easily by simply adding the prep sg ending -э. In order to derive the nom sg form, a rule like that given in (5) would be necessary:

(5) C' → C / ___ a

The rule in (5) states that soft consonants are pronounced hard before the vowel [a]. This rule, however, makes all sorts of false predictions. There are many words that have soft consonants followed by а: мяч [м'ач], пять [п'ат'], дядю [д'ад'у] (acc of дядя), to name just three. Since the rule in (5) is wrong, the underlying form #рук'-# must also be wrong.

*A Write out the phonetic representations of the underlying forms given on the top of the next page. Which words require the operation of rule (3)? One word requires the operation of rule (3) more than once. Which one?

1. #пис'м+о́#
2. #пис'м+э́# (prep sg)
3. #структу́р+а#
4. #бро́в+и# (nom pl)
5. #мо́ст+э# (prep sg)
6. #йзб+ы# (nom pl)
7. #уро́к#
8. #уро́к+и# (nom pl)
9. #кн'а́з'+у# (dat sg)
10. #л'у́д+и# (nom pl)

*B Write the one underlying form (basic stem) that each of the following word pairs share:

1. кни́га - кни́ге   4. зонт - о зонте́
2. бу́лка - бу́лки   5. во́здух - о во́здухе
3. звук - о зву́ке   6. ра́дуга - ра́дуги

*C Avanesov points out:

> Перед буквой и, а также обычно перед е все согласные (кроме ж, ш, ц) произносятся мягко...Эта норма редко нарушается в речи русских. Однако ее нарушение типично для русской речи украинцев, которые произносят перед [и] и [э] твердые согласные. Произношение твердых согласных перед [и] и [э] часто встречается в русской речи представителей многих других народов. Поэтому на произношение согласных перед [и] и [э] надо обратить специальное внимание. («Русское литературное произношение», стр. 104-5)

1. According to Avanesov, how often do Russians pronounce hard consonants before [и] and   [э]?

2. If you do not pronounce soft consonants before the sounds [и] [э], you may be mistaken   for someone from what part of Eastern Europe?

So far we have discussed three kinds of linguistic representations. First, every word has a basic or underlying root, such as #суд-# for суд "court." Underlying or base forms of complete words are built upon such roots. For example, we can add the dat sg ending +y to masc nouns: #суд+у́#. A phonological rule which expresses palatalization or softening of consonants does not apply in this word since it contains no front vowel. Second, the surface form or phonetic representation is determined through the application or nonapplication of phonological rules, and by deleting boundaries: [суду́]. The prep sg case form of this word, however, has a soft д: суде́ [суд'э́]. The notion of underlying form allows us to reduce the number of roots present in the language. Instead of saying that Russian has both #суд-# and #суд'-#, and that by some wild coincidence they mean the same thing, we say there is one root, namely #суд-#. Variants with a soft д (or any other alternation) are explained by phonological rule.

The third kind of linguistic representation is the normal alphabet, which we will refer to as the normal orthographic representation. In this system, the softness in the word суде́ and other words is represented in different ways--by a series of vowel letters (ю, е, и, я, ё) and by the soft sign. This method for explaining sound differences observed within a single root or stem, therefore, requires three separate representations:

(1) underlying representation: #суд+э́#   (prep sg)

   phonological rules (we have
   discussed one so far):   #суд'+э́#

(2) phonetic representation: [суд'э́]

(3) orthographic representation: суде́

2.2 Akan'e

The location of stress in a word greatly affects its pronunciation. In то́т, пылесо́с, and мо́ст the stressed vowel has the sound [o]. When the о is not stressed, however, it does not have this sound, rather it sounds more like a reduced [a]: окно́, одно́, вода́, вдова́. The sound of these unstressed o's is like [a], but the tongue is not quite as low as in [a] and the lips are not spread apart as wide as in a stressed [a]. In the words in (1) the unstressed о is pronounced similarly to but not exactly as the stressed [a].

(1)   гроза́   сосна́   поля́
        мольба́   борьба́   сова́

We will transcribe this unstressed о sound as [ʌ]. Thus the six words in (1) can be transcribed:

(2)   [грʌза́]   [сʌсна́]   [пʌл'а́]
        [мʌл'ба́]   [бʌр'ба́]   [сʌва́]

Unstressed о sometimes represents a sound even more reduced than [ʌ]. It is the sound of о in the word polite, a very short "uh" sound. This sound is transcribed [ъ]. Thus, [ъ] represents a reduced vowel sound in the phonetic level. In the orthographic level, of course, the letter ъ is not pronounced.

*A Examine the data below and determine in what position in the word unstressed o is pronounced as [ʌ] and in what position unstressed o is pronounced [ъ].

молокó [мълʌкó]   гóлову [гóлъву]
молокосóс [мълъкʌсóс]   скóвороды [скóвъръды]
сковородá [скъвърʌдá]   гóродом [гóръдъм]
головá [гълʌвá]   я́блоко [йáблъкъ]
одногó [ʌднʌвó]   ти́хо [т'и́хъ]
островá [ʌстрʌвá]   нóвой [нóвъй]

*B Unstressed a reduces to the same sounds as unstressed o. Determine from the following where unstressed a occurs as [ʌ] and [ъ].

вагóн [вʌгóн]   обжóра [ʌбжóръ]
магази́н [мъгʌз'и́н]   нéдра [н'э́дръ]
рабóта [рʌбóтъ]   зáпах [зáпъх]
агронóм [ʌгрʌнóм]   брáтья [брáт'йъ]
альманáх [ʌл'мʌнáх]   бáбушка [бáбушкъ]

Consider what Avanesov wrote regarding the distribution of [ʌ] and [ъ] in regard to unstressed vowels:

Наместе o и a после твердых согласных в первом предударном слоге произносится звук [ʌ]: в[ʌ]дá, в[ʌ]рóта, пр[ʌ]шý...

Качество звука [ʌ] 1-го предударного слога в литературном языке не одинаково, но в общем он произносится при менее широком растворе рта, чем звук [a] ударного слога.

На месте o и a после твердых согласных в остальных безударных слогах (т.е. во всех безударных слогах, кроме 1-го предударного) произносится также один и тот же звук--очень краткийгласный. Этот звук обозначается буквой [ъ]. Примеры:

в предударных слогах -- г[ъ]родо́к, х[ъ]рошо́, г[ъ]лова́, ст[ъ]рика́ в заударных слогах -- го́л[ъ]ву, бо́р[ъ]ду, ста́р[ъ]м, вы́р[ъ]б[ъ]т[ъ]ть.

На месте букв о̲ и а̲ в начале слова в предударных слогах произносится [Λ]: [Λ]пте́ка, [Λ]ди́н, [Λ]горо́д.

The process of reducing unstressed o̲ and a̲ is called "akan'e" (а́канье), which literally means "saying ah."

*C Write in phonetic transcription:

1. коро́ва	6. старика́
2. ча́сто	7. ско́вороды
3. друго́го	8. кладово́й
4. городо́к	9. сто́рону
5. адмира́л	10. огурцы́

2.3 Rules of Akan'e

We can express akan'e by the following three rules:

(1) a, o → Λ / C₁ ___ (C) v̇   (where v̇ = any stressed vowel and C₁ = any hard consonant)

(2) a, o → Λ / # ___
     [-stress]

(3) a, o → ъ / ___ elsewhere
     [-stress]

Rule (1) states that a̲ and o̲ , when following a hard consonant are pronounced as [Λ] before zero or more consonants "(C)" and right before the stress. Rule (2) states that a̲ and o̲ are pronounced as [Λ] when not stressed ([-stress]) and occurring at the beginning of a word (i.e., when on the right of a word boundary). Rule (3) states that unstressed a̲ and o̲ are realized as [ъ] in all positions except those mentioned in rules (1) and (2).

In order for these rules to derive the correct phonetic or surface forms from base forms, rules (1) and (2) must be ordered in relation to rule (3). In other words, rules (1) and (2) must apply before rule (3) since the environment for rule (3) is simply all environments not covered by rules (1) and (2).

Since rules (1) and (2) must be ordered before rule (3) and since they both effect the same change, we can collapse rules (1) and (2) into one elegant rule:

$$(1) \ a, o \rightarrow \wedge \ / \begin{cases} C_1 \underline{\quad} (C) \overset{\lor}{v} \\ \# \underline{\quad} \end{cases}$$

2.4 Accent on Stress

In discussing akan'e it is useful to refer to the stressed syllable, the syllable right before the stressed syllable, the syllables following the stressed syllable, and the first sound of the word. We will use traditional nomenclature:

stressed syllable: **tonic** or **ultima** (уда́рный слог)

syllable right before the stress: **1st pretonic** or **penultimate** (пе́рвый предуда́рный)

other syllables before the stress: **2nd pretonic**, **3rd pretonic**, etc. or **antepenultimate** (второ́й предуда́рный, и т.д.)

word initial vowel: **word initial** (в нача́ле сло́ва)

after the stress: **post-tonic** (зауда́рный)

2.5 Ikan'e

Another phonological alternation readily heard in Russian involves unstressed e̱ and unstressed я̱. In this process, known as "ikan'e" (и́канье), unstressed e̱ and я̱ are pronounced similar to [и], although the tongue is not quite as high as normal [и]. The shift of e̱ and я̱ to [и] occurs in the first pretonic position only, since at word initial position e̱ and я̱ are always preceded by an i-kratkoe phonetically: ему̱ [йиму́]. In this example the combination [йи] is due to falling in first pretonic position. Note that ikan'e does not affect unstressed и, which is always pronounced [и] after soft consonants. In (1) "word initial" refers to the presence at the beginning of the word of the letters е or я. In addition to being word initial, they are all pretonic.

(1)

Under Stress	1st Pretonic	"Word Initial"
де́ло [д'э́лъ]	дела́ [д'ила́]	Еле́на [йил'э́нъ]
лес [л'э́с]	леса́ [л'иса́]	еда́ [йида́]
ме́сто [м'э́стъ]	места́ [м'иста́]	едва́ [йидва́]
пять [п'а́т']	пяти́ [п'ит'и́]	язы́к [йизы́к]
синя́к [с'ин'а́к]	синяка́ [с'ин'ика́]	Баба Яга́ [йига́]
горя́чий [гʌр'а́чий]	горячо́ [гър'ичо́]	янта́рь [йинта́р']

Note: The vowel sounds of е and я never occur at word initial position, since they will always be preceded by й.

Ikan'e also occurs in other unstressed syllables, as in pretonic syllables that are neither first pretonic nor word initial and it occurs in post-tonic syllables. In these environments unstressed е and я are pronounced somewhat like the vowel sound in the English word "bit," when pronounced quickly. This very reduced sound will be transcribed here as [ь]. Note that this is not the soft sign letter, but a sound heard in normal speech, as illustrated in (2).

In (2) word initial again refers to the presence of е or я at the beginning of the word, but here they are not first pretonic.

(2)

Pretonic/Word Initial	**Post-tonic**
черепа́ха [чьр'ипа́хъ]	вы́несу [вы́н'ьсу]
перенесу́ [п'ьр'ьн'ису́]	де́рево [д'э́р'ьвъ]
рядово́й [р'ьдʌво́й]	вы́тяни [вы́т'ьн'и]
языка́ [йьзыка́]	ка́федра [ка́ф'ьдръ]
егоза́ [йьгʌза́]	за́яц [за́йьц]
мятежа́ [м'ьт'ижа́]	се́мьдесят [с'э́м'д'ьс'ьт]

Note, however, that the shift of post-tonic е and я to [ь] **does not occur** in most grammatical endings. Endings such as the nom sg fem -я (неде́ля, тётя, ку́хня, etc.) and the gen sg masc and neut -я (учи́теля, пла́тья, музе́я, etc.), for example, are pronounced with the reduced vowel [ъ]: [т'о́т'ъ] [муз'э́йъ]. The prep sg and dat sg fem ending -е, however, is normally pronounced as [ь]: в го́роде [в го́ръд'ь].

*A Write a set of rules that expresses ikan'e in Russian. Your rules should have the format:

$$X \rightarrow Y \: / \: Z \underline{\hspace{1cm}} Z$$

where X, Y, and Z are phonological symbols, including the symbol "elsewhere."

*B Write the following in normal orthography. Be careful with your choice of orthographic е or я. If you are unsure, try to think of a word or find a word in the dictionary where the е or я is stressed. For example, [хм'ил'но́й] "drunk" could represent orthographic хмельно́й, хмильно́й, or хмяльно́й, but compare with хмель "drunkeness."

1. [ур'изáт']   6. [ум'ин'шáт']
2. [св'ьтΛвóй]   7. [св'изнóй]
3. [тр'изв'э́т']   8. [пр'имóй]
4. [йид'úный]   9. [р'идьí]
5. [св'итóй]   10. [н'имóй]

*C Write the following in phonetic transcription:

1. чепухá   6. серебрó
2. телефóн   7. óчереди
3. береговóй   8. геройзм
4. веснá   9. в клýбе
5. январь   10. дерéвня

In the story "Витя Малеев," Vitja is helping his friend Shishkin with his Russian spelling:

> Я заставил его снова прочитать правило, в котором говорится о том, что безударные гласные проверяются ударением, и сказал:
> --Вот ты написал «тижёлый». Почему ты так написал?
> --Наверно, «тежёлый» надо писать?
> --А ты не гадай. Знаешь правило--пользуйся правилом. Измени слово, так, чтоб на первом слоге было ударение.
> Шишкин стал изменять слово «тяжёлый» и нашел слово «тяжесть».
> --А!--обрадовался он. --Значит, надо писать не «тижёлый» и не «тежёлый», а «тяжёлый».
> --Верно,-- говорю я.

2.6 Assimilation of Voice

We have seen that alphabetic letters do not always unambiguously represent pronunciation. Sometimes a letter stands for one sound, sometimes it stands for another, as in the English pl ending -s. Consider the pronunciation of the pl ending -s in the following:

(1) a. coats [s]   caps [s]
        racks [s]   rats [s]
    b. codes [z]   cabs [z]
        rags   [z]   rams [z]

Recall that one of the fundamental sound characteristics of a consonant is whether or not it is voiced (see 1.1). Thus, the only difference between, for example, д and т is that the former is voiced and the latter is voiceless. They differ in only one feature of articulation--that of voicing. We characterize voiceless consonants as [-voice] and voiced consonants as [+voice]. Although we write -s as the pl ending for all the words in (1), we pronounce this ending differently, depending on the kind of consonant that precedes. In (1a) the s preceded by voiceless consonants is pronounced [s]. In (1b), the plural suffix preceded by voiced consonants is pronounced [z].

Now consider alternations seen in the stem final consonant of the following pairs of words given in (2).

(2)

gen sg	nom sg	alternation
плодá [плʌдá]	плод [плóт]	д ~ т
глáза [глáзъ]	глаз [глáс]	з ~ с
зýба [зýбъ]	зуб [зýп]	б ~ п
ножá [нʌжá]	нож [нóш]	ж ~ ш
дрýга [дрýгъ]	друг [дрýк]	г ~ к

In the gen sg forms the final consonant is voiced. In the nom sg form the final consonant, although written orthographically as a voiced consonant, is pronounced unvoiced. These word pairs illustrate a fundamental aspect of Russian pronunciation: word final consonants are pronounced voiceless (оглушáются). This generalization can be written in phonological rule form:

(3) C → [-voice] / ___ #

The rule in (3) states that consonants at the end of a word (i.e., located before a word boundary) are voiceless. This rule has no effect on word final consonants that are already voiceless: рыба́к, коммуни́ст, печь.

There are some consonants that do not have voiceless counterparts: й, л, м, н, р. These consonants are said to become "semivoiceless" at word final position. This means they become only partly devoiced. In this text we will consider "semivoiceless" (полуглухи́е) as semivoiced, and we will treat this as voiced. In fact р and л are not pronounced as clearly at word final position as elsewhere, but they often do retain some voicing. The sounds й, м, and н usually retain full voice at word final position. The Academy Grammar sets these sounds apart as "sonorants" (соно́рные), voiced consonants which, when they are produced, have relatively little obstruction to the air stream. These sounds are also sometimes called "semivowels." The symbol "C" in rule (3) must be understood not to include the sonorants. We could rewrite the rule as given in (4).

(4)   C → [-voice] / ___ #
       [-son]

The rule in (4) states that nonsonorant consonants are voiceless at the end of a word. This rule applies when the word in question is followed by a pause or by a word beginning with a vowel, a sonorant, or a voiceless consonant. In rapid speech the rule does not apply if the following word begins with a voiced consonant. As we will see later, rules that are normal for literary or careful speech may not apply in rapid, colloquial speech.

*A Consider the following word pairs and the phonological alternations that they exhibit. Note that devoicing of final consonants occurs as expected throughout. There are other alternations as well. Write out the alternations that you observe and indicate where they occur.

genitive singular	nominative singular
мо́зга [мо́згъ]	мозг [моск]
вождя́ [вʌжд'а́]	вождь [вошт']
по́езда [по́йьздъ]	по́езд [по́йьст]

nominative singular	**genitive plural**
борозда́ [бърΛзда́]	боро́зд [бΛро́ст]
слу́жба [слу́жбъ]	служб [слушп]
изба́ [изба́]	изб [исп]
укори́зна [укΛр'и́знъ]	укори́зн [укΛр'и́зн]

*B Write a phonological rule that would express the alternations observed in exercise *A.

*C Write the following in phonetic transcription.

1. муж	4. хле́ба	7. визг
2. бе́рег	5. хлеб	8. день
3. любо́вь	6. наде́жд	9. пиро́г

In 2.1 the term "assimilate" was used to explain why certain consonants preceding the front vowels [и] and [э] are pronounced "soft." In the process of devoicing we see another case of assimilation (ассимиля́ция). At word final position consonants assimilate the voicelessness of the next segment, which is a word boundary. The data in exercise *A above suggest that assimilation can occur from one consonant to the next, or to be precise: from the final consonant to the one right before it. These data show that when the second of two voiced consonants stands at the end of a word and thus is pronounced voiceless, preceding consonants will also be pronounced voiceless. Schematically:

(5)   #в и з г#
         →rule in (4)→   #в и з к#
         →assimilation→   #в и с к#

This assimilation is expressed formally in (6).

(6)   C → [-voice] / ___ C
        [-son]   [-voi]

The rule in (6) states that nonsonorant consonants are pronounced voiceless before other voiceless consonants. This rule also expresses the assimilation of voicelessness in environments other than in word final position:

(7) тру́бка [тру́пкъ]   коро́бка [кʌро́пкъ]
    ло́дка [ло́ткъ]   ска́зка [ска́скъ]
    вкус [фкус]   второ́й [фтʌро́й]

The rule in (6) reflects the actual pronunciation of these words. A similar process is at work in the words in (8):

(8) про́сьба [про́з'бъ]   вокза́л [вʌгза́л]
    экза́мен [эгза́м'ьн]   сгоре́л [згʌр'ѕл]

The data in (8) show that voiceness may also be assimilated from contiguous voiced consonants. We make the following generalization about the nature of consonant clusters: consonants in clusters tend to be either all voiced or all voiceless. The final consonant in a cluster determines the voicing quality of the preceding consonant(s). If the final consonant is voiced, then the preceding consonant(s) will be voiced. If the final consonant is voiceless, then the preceding consonants will also be voiceless. The rule given in (6) can be altered to reflect this:

(9)   C → [±voi] / ___ C
    [-son]   [±voi]

The rule in (9) states that contiguous consonants will be either voiced [+voi] or voiceless [-voi] and this feature depends on the final consonant of the cluster. Contiguous consonants assimilate the feature of voice from the final consonant in the series. This occurs at any position in the word.

The sound [в] is an exception to the voicing assimilation rule just discussed. As expected, it becomes voiceless when followed by a voiceless consonant, e.g., второ́й [фтʌро́й]. However, it does not <u>cause</u> preceding consonants to become voiced, even though it itself is a voiced consonant: сва́дьба, сво́лочь [сва́д'бъ] [сво́лъч]. In Chapter 4, we will discuss the historical events that led to this exception in the modern language.

The sonorants [м], [н], [р], and [л] neither become voiceless nor do they trigger voicing assimilation, e.g., слой, смотре́ть, сно́ва, срок are all pronounced with a [с] even though a voiced consonant follows. In this respect these sonorants behave like vowels.

*D Write the following in normal Russian orthography.

1. [в'ис'о́лый]   6. [йа́гът мно́гъ]
2. [зд∧ро́ф]   7. [до́шт' ид'о́т]
3. [нушт]   8. [д'э́н'ьк н'э́т]
4. [вошт']   9. [ф кър'идо́р'ь]
5. [мъл∧д'ба́]   10. [бума́шкъ]

2.7 Assimilation of Softness

Recall that consonants can be grouped according to their point of articulation. Consonants may be characterized as being labial, nasal, dental, palatal, or velar. (See section 1.2.) Just as it is easier to pronounce contiguous consonants as either voiced or voiceless, it should also be easier to make consonants in a cluster either all hard or all soft. In Russian, interestingly enough, only the second kind of assimilation occurs, and only sporadically, at least in the modern language. Soft consonants may be followed by hard consonants: про́сьба, пальто́, дово́льно. But hard consonants may assimilate the feature [+palatalized] ("soft") from following palatalized consonants.

(1) часть   [час'т']
     вперёд   [ф'п'ир'о́т]   or   [фп'ир'о́т]
     дверь   [д'в'эр']   or   [дв'эр']
     вместе   [в'м'э́с'т'ь]   or   [вм'э́с'т'ь]

Whether or not this process of assimilation may occur in a given consonant cluster depends on the subgroup to which each consonant in the cluster belongs.

Generally speaking, if the consonant cluster does not involve a prefix (в-, об-, под-, над-, etc.) then a consonant assimilates softness from soft consonants of the same subgroup: hard labials become soft before soft labials, dentals become soft before soft dentals, etc. Usage, however, is not fixed and the tendency is to retain hard consonants before soft consonants, especially if the first consonant is part of a prefix or a suffix. Thus, in the examples given in (1) only the pronunciation for часть is widespread. The initial consonant in the other three words may be pronounced hard or soft. Palatalization of the first consonant in these words characterizes a more traditional pronunciation, while pronunciation of these words with a hard initial consonant has become more widespread in modern speech.

2.8 How to Determine the Base Form

Base forms account for the unity of a word, even though the word may be pronounced in different ways. The differences observed are simply predictable sound variations that occur throughout the language due usually to natural physiological tendencies. Linguists discover the tendencies which have become widespread through the language and reduce them to rules. Generally speaking it is possible to establish an underlying form, upon which these rules will operate, based simply on the way the word is written. The following guideline for determining the base form has the word мясник as an example.

(1)
1. Place word boundaries: #   #
2. Write in the consonants: # м ...с н ... к #
3. Are the consonants hard or soft?
    If the orthography has я, ё, ю, or ь,
    then the consonant is soft: # м'...с н ... к #
4. Only a, о, у, и, э, and ы are used in base
    forms, according to the correspondences
    given in (2) in section 1.3.   # м' а с н и́ к#

How do we know that the final consonant in мясник is really a к? Is it possible that it is a г simply devoiced at word final position? The orthography suggests it is a к, and when we look at this word in another case form, the gen sg for example, we see that we really are dealing with a к: мясника́ [м'ьс'н'ика́].

The word мясник is pronounced [м'ис'н'и́к]. How do we know that the first vowel in the base form is really an a? After all, it could just as easily be an underlying # и # or an underlying # э # reduced, by ikan'e, to [и]. The orthography suggests that we are dealing with a soft consonant followed by # a #, and this can be verified by finding a related word that has stress on the vowel in question: мясо [м'а́съ]. Since we are certain the root is the same in this word as it is in мясни́к, we can be sure that the underlying vowel in both roots is # a #, since it occurs under stress as such.

In summary, the orthography is fairly reliable for determining underlying forms, if the guidelines given in (1) are followed.

*A Determine the base form for the words in the first column. Forms in the second column are for verification of word final consonants and unstressed vowels.

example: ме́сто [м'э́стъ] → #мэст + о#   места́ [м'иста́]

1. леса́ [л'иса́]   лес [л'эс]
2. снег [с'н'эк]   сне́га [с'н'э́гъ]
3. я́года [йа́гъдъ]   я́год [йа́гът]
4. пять [п'ат']   пяти́ [п'ит'и́]
5. связь [св'ас']   свя́зи [св'а́з'и]
6. трясти́ [т'р'ис'т'и́]   тряс [т'р'ас]

2.9 Summary of Phonological Rules

The following table summarizes the phonological generalizations and rules discussed so far. The rules are given in shorthand format. Numbers in the column labeled "Sec." refer to the chapter and section in which the rules were introduced.

(1)

Rule #	Rule	Description	Sec.
1	C → C' / ___ и, э	consonant softening (C is not ж, ш, ц)	2.1
2	a, о → ∧ / # ___ [-str]	akan'e (part 1)	2.2 2.3
	/ C ___ v̇	C=hard consonant	
3	э → и / ___ v̇ a → и / C' ___ v̇	ikan'e (part 1)	2.5

4	а, о → ъ / ___ [-str]	akan'e (part 2)	2.3
5	(a) э → ь / ___ [-str] (b) ъ → ь / C'___	ikan'e (part 2) (e.g., мясника́)	2.5
6	и → ы / ж, ш, ц ___	no [и] after these sounds	1.5
7	C → [-voi] / ___ #	final devoicing	2.6
8	C → [±voi] / ___ C[±voi]	voicing assimilation	2.6
9	C → C' / ___ C' (limited)	assimilation of softness	2.7

Notes:

(1) Rule 6 also applies to и after hard consonant-final prefixes and prepositions: сыграть, без [ы]нтереса.

(2) Ikan'e (part 2) can be expanded to include the pronunciation of words such as жениха́ [жън'иха́] by adding the rule: (c) ь → ъ / C ___ (where C=a hard consonant).

The rules given in (1) represent something that native speakers of Russian know about their language at some level. Other symbols could be used or a different way of expressing the rules could be invented. We will use rules of the type given above as a convenient device for representing phonological alternations.

The concept of <u>alternation</u> is fundamental in language. Even though a word may not be exactly the same or may change from form to form, we still usually recognize what it is. For example, сковорода́ [скъвър∧да́] "pan" shifts dramatically in the pl to ско́вороды [ско́въръды]. Still we recognize it as the same word. To argue otherwise would be to say that it is simply coincidental that these two words share the same basic meaning and phonological characteristics ([ск-вър-д]). This is clearly not the case.

Instead, we are dealing with one basic word which may be represented in a base or underlying form. When different endings are added, phonological alternations may occur; these alternations are predictable and as such may be described and explained by phonological rules. Explanation takes the form of feature assimilation; for example, two contiguous sounds tend to assimilate features from each other, making pronunciation easier.

In most instances it doesn't matter what order phonological rules apply to base forms, or that some rules don't apply at all. There are some instances, however, where the ordering of rules does seem to be important. For example, the pronunciation of the word визг [в'иск] suggests that rule (7) must apply before rule (8). Before rule (8) can apply to devoice з, rule (7) must first apply to devoice the word final consonant. For most of the rules given above, however, ordering is not critical. Only for some words is the ordering of these rules important: визг shows that (7) must precede (8); снег [с'н'эк] suggests that rule (1) must precede rule (9).

2.10 Phonological Derivations

More than one of the phonological rules listed above may apply to one word. The word жи́дкость, for example, is affected by four of the rules given (a dash indicates the given rule does not apply in this word).

(1) underlying form:	# ж и́ д к о с т' #	
(C → C')	--	(does not apply)
(akan'e)(a)	--	
(ikan'e)(a)	--	
(akan'e)(b)	ж ы д к ъ с т'	
(ikan'e)(b)	--	
(и → ы)	ж ы д к о с т'	
(C→-voi)	--	
(C→±voi)	ж ы т к ъ с т'	
(C → C')	ж ы т к ъ с'т'	
phonetic:	[жы́ткъс'т']	

The transition from underlying form to phonetic representation as illustrated in (1) is a phonological <u>derivation</u> (дерива́ция). The phonetic representation is derived from the underlying form through the application of phonological rules.

*A Derive the phonetic representation from the following underlying forms. Indicate which rules are operative. Write in square brackets the phonetic representation.

1. # о́ с т р о в #
2. # п о д п и с а́ т' #
3. # п э р э ш и́ б #
4. # к о с т' о́ р #
5. # о к о́ в ы в а т' #
6. # ж и з н э л' у́ б #
7. # о п л о ш а́ т' #
8. # п э р э т' а н у́ т' #
9. # г р а н' #
10. # с г о р' а ч а́ #

*B Determine the underlying form for the following and derive the phonetic representation of each.

1. долгожи́тель
2. бескоры́стный
3. разыска́ть
4. прие́зд
5. бето́н
6. я́беда

Since alphabetic letters may be ambiguous in representing pronunciation, it is possible that a given sound may be represented by more than one written letter. For example, word final -д and word final -т will both be pronounced the same way: [...т]. A phonetic representation, however, reflects only pronunciation, not writing. Thus, the phonetic representation [пот] reflects the pronunciation of both под "under" and пот "sweat."

*C What are the possible written variations of the following phonetic transcriptions?

1. [кот]
2. [лук]
3. [бок]
4. [мо́лът]
5. [глас]
6. [прут]
7. [л'эс]
8. [л'от]

2.11 Exceptions to Ikan'e and Akan'e: the Pronunciation of Endings

The pronunciation of grammatical endings with the vowels -e or -я when not under stress requires particular attention. Unstressed endings with the vowel -я undergo akan'e instead of ikan'e, i.e., these endings have the vowel [ъ], as illustrated in (1).

(1) Pronunciation of unstressed -я in declensional endings as [ъ]:

GRAMMATICAL ENDING	ENDING	EXAMPLE	TRANSCRIPTION
NOM SG FEM	-я	неде́ля	[н'ид'э́л'ъ]
NOM SG FEM	-ия	а́рмия	[а́рм'ийъ]
NOM SG NEUT	-мя	вре́мя	[вр'э́м'ъ]
GEN SG MASC/NEUT	-я	контро́ля	[кʌнтро́л'ъ]
NOM PL NEUT	-ия	зда́ния	[зда́н'ийъ]
PREP PL	-ях	зда́ниях	[зда́н'ийъх]
DAT PL	-ям	зда́ниям	[зда́н'ийъм]
INST PL	-ями	зда́ниями	[зда́н'ийъм'и]
NOM SG FEM ADJ	-ая -яя	но́вая си́няя	[но́въйъ] [с'и́нъйъ]
3RD PL 2ND CONJ	-ят	чи́стят	[чи́с'т'ът]
IMPF. VERBAL ADVERB	-я	чита́я	[чита́йъ]
REFLEXIVE PART.	-ся	занима́ться	[зън'има́цъ]

The pronunciation of unstressed endings with the vowel -е is not completely fixed, though the general tendency is toward simple ikan'e, i.e., [ь]. An older, Moscow-type (старомоско́вская но́рма, or Old Moscow Norm: OMN), pronunciation is also acceptable for most of these endings, in which the е is pronounced as [ъ].

(2) Pronunciation of unstressed -e in declensional endings.

GRAMMATICAL ENDING	ENDING	EXAMPLE	TRANSCRIPTION
NOM SG NEUT	-e	мо́ре	[мо́р'ь], OMN [мо́р'ъ]
NOM SG NEUT	-ие	зда́ние	[зда́н'ийь], OMN [зда́н'ийъ]
PREP SG	-e	в кни́ге	[фкн'и́г'ь]
DAT SG FEM	-e	Анне	[а́н'н'ь]
INST SG MASC	-ем	учи́телем	[учи́т'ьл'ьм], OMN [...л'ъм]
INST SG FEM	-ей	ту́чей	[ту́чьй]
NOM PL MASC	-e	армя́не	[Λрм'а́н'ь]
GEN PL	-ей	жи́телей	[жы́т'ьл'ьй]
GEN PL MASC	-ев	геро́ев	[г'иро́йьф], OMN [г'иро́йъф]
GEN SG MASC/NEUT ADJ	-его	вече́рнего	[в'ичэ́рн'ьвъ], OMN [...н'ъвъ]
DAT SG MASC/NEUT ADJ	-ему	вече́рнему	[в'ичэ́рн'ьму], OMN [...н'ъму]
INST SG FEM ADJ	-ей	вече́рней	[в'ичэ́рн'ьй]
SIMPLE COMPARATIVE	-ее	нове́е	[нΛв'э́йь], OMN [нΛв'э́йъ]
PRESENT TENSE 1ST CONJ	-ешь -ет -ем -ете	чита́ет	[чита́йьт], OMN [чита́йът]

The following two endings constitute exceptions to the general rule given above. The -e in these endings is still normally pronounced as [ь].

(3)

NOM SG NEUT ADJ	-ое/-ее	нóвое, сѝнее	[нóвъйъ], [с'ѝн'ьйъ]
NOM PL ADJ	-ые/-ие	нóвые	[нóвыйъ]

2.12 Speaking Without Akan'e

One of the most striking features of CSR is the reduction of unstressed o̲ and a̲ and the shift of unstressed e̲ and я, that is, akan'e and ikan'e. This feature is found most often in the southern and central dialects, and in the large cities in the northern region. However, akan'e and ikan'e are not the only -kan'es found among Russian speakers. The country speech of the north, particularly to the north and east of Novgorod (Нóвгород), is often characterized by so-called "okan'e" (óканье) and "jokan'e" (ёканье). In its fullest form, okan'e is the antithesis of akan'e: all o̲'s are pronounced as [o] and all a̲'s are pronounced as [a], with no reduction or shifts. The following examples of okan'e were transcribed from the speech of villagers from Gosttsi (Гóстцы) east of Novgorod, in 1948.

(1) Spelled in CSR	Gosttsi (Okan'e) Pronunciation	CSR Pronunciation
водá	[водá]	[вʌдá]
одѝн	[од'ѝн]	[ʌд'ѝн]
тóполь	[тóпол']	[тóпъл']
хорошó	[хорошó]	[хърʌшó]
человéк	[чилов'э́к]	[чьлʌв'э́к]
осторóжно	[усторóжно]	[ʌстʌрóжнъ]
какóй	[какóй]	[кʌкóй]
рýба	[ры́ба]	[ры́бъ]

Note that okan'e pronunciation more closely matches spelling. This is because spelling often is more conservative, that is, changes more slowly, than does the speech it represents. The northern dialects are the most conservative of Russian dialects, so it is not surprising that they closely match Russian spelling. In regard to the grammar of these speakers, we may characterize it as simply not containing the akan'e rules discussed earlier in this chapter.

Note the okan'e pronunciation of the word осторо́жно in (1). In some areas where okan'e can be found, word initial о, if not pretonic, is often pronounced as у or as и!

(2) [у]дного́   [и]дного́
     [у]блака́
     [у]горо́д
     [и]гуре́ц

Finally, note that with okan'e pronunciation, in some words pretonic а is pronounced [o] (cf. Bromlei p. 44):

(3) **CSR Spelling**   **Okan'e**
     рабо́та   [робо́та]
     расти́   [рос'т'и́]
     забо́та   [зобо́та]
     стака́н   [стока́н]
     дава́ть   [дова́т']
     сказа́ть   [скоза́т']

In these words the okan'e pronunciation does not appear to follow traditional spelling, and the pronunciation of [o] for written а seems to be an innovation. This is, in fact, true for the last two words on the list. But a comparison of other Slavic languages and Old Russian suggests that in the first five words, an о was pronounced at an earlier time in a wider area:

(4) **CSR** рабо́та: **Ukrainian** робо́та, **Czech and Polish** robota
     CSR расти́: (cf. past tense: рос): **Ukr.** рости, **Pol.** rość
     CSR забо́та: **Old Russian** зобота, **Slovenian** zobati
     CSR стака́н: **Old Russian** достокан "box"

Okan'e equates to the way unstressed о's used to be pronounced in an older, that is, earlier form of Russian, and often equates to standard spelling.

*A Why do you think CSR spells рабо́та with an а, if it was once pronounced as an о?

*B Why do you think words which never had an o̲, e.g., дава́ть, are now pronounced with an [o], e.g. [дова́т'] in the okan'e regions of Russia?

V. V. Ivanov says this about the development of akan'e in Russian:

> ВXV-XVI вв. количество случаев написания буквы а̲ вместо о̲ в безударных слогах быстро возрастает. Вместе с тем появляется написание и о̲ вместо безударного а̲, например: обязон, толант, запода, задовити и т.п., что является косвенным отражением неразличения [о] и [а] в безударном положении... Появление о̲ вместо этимологического а̲ объясняется влиянием акающего произношения: так же как при произношении [вада́], [нага́] писец привыкает писать на месте безударного [а] букву о̲, так он начинает писать такое о̲ и на месте этимологического [а] в словах [дала́], [тала́нт]. Если в памятниках аканье получило отражение в XIV в., то ясно, что оно должно было возникнуть в языке раньше, чтобы к XIV в. получить отражение в письменности.

*C What kind of written evidence would prove that akan'e was operating at some early stage of Russian?

*D According to Ivanov, when did akan'e develop in Russian?

*E Why did scribes write an o̲ in words where they should have written an a̲?

2.13 Review

While phonetics is the description of how sounds are produced, phonology is an attempt to relate what happens to sounds when they are placed next to each other. If sounds were not modified in various environments there would be no phonology and very little reason for these chapters. We have seen how the pronunciation of certain sounds depends on which sounds follow them and on where the stress falls in the word. Phonology is simply a stating of these rules of pronunciation. Beginning students of Russian have difficulty understanding normal speech not only because they have a limited vocabulary but also because they don't know how the pronunciation of words they do know changes in given situations. A student used to seeing дед may well not recognize this word when spoken by natives as [д'эт]; nor will natives not used to dealing with foreigners easily recognize [д'эд].

In addition to changes in sounds that occur within modern Russian, changes in sounds have taken place over time. Historical phonology attempts to uncover these changes, thus revealing reasons for sound alternations in the modern language which do not lend themselves to normal phonologically based operations.

Phonological explanation takes the form of underlying base representations. A set of rules operates on these underlying representations and produces various (often historically relevant) outputs, or phonetic representations. Dialectal differences in pronunciation can often be explained as the presence or absence in the dialect of a particular phonological rule. For example, the speech of the okan'e region does not have the rules which reduce unstressed o and a. In this respect the dialect is simpler than CSR. On the other hand akan'e in CSR and in the southern dialects is a result of articulatory simplification--the reduced sounds [ʌ] and [ъ] are easier to pronounce at least in regards to muscle tenseness than rounded [o]. Which dialect's grammar is simpler, or is any dialect simpler? What are the best ways to define simplicity or complexity in grammar? These questions are important because their answers may help determine how languages are described, taught, and learned.

CHAPTER 3: Two Other Fundamental Alternations

3.1 Phonetic vs. Phonemic

In the previous chapter we discussed several phonological alternations. It was proposed that if the pronunciation of a word differs when different endings are added then this does not imply we are dealing with different words. If the difference in pronunciation can be generalized or predicted and the basic meaning of the word remains unchanged, then we assume that we are dealing with variations of a single word. The generalizations, or phonological rules, are a formal representation of what speakers know about how the pronunciation of a word varies in given contexts. We have seen that the motivating factor for nearly all the phonological rules discussed so far is assimilation. Consonants are pronounced in a manner to prepare for the ensuing front vowels and thereby become palatalized (fronted, or "soft") when followed by front vowels. Voiceless consonants next to voiced consonants assimilate the feature of voicing. Voiced consonants at the end of a word assimilate the voiceless feature of a word boundary. In this chapter we will examine several phonological alternations that are not readily characterized as being due to assimilation.

Just as a single word may be pronounced in various ways, so can a single sound be pronounced in set ways without altering the fact that we are dealing with one sound. For example, the letter o̲ may be pronounced as [o], [ʌ], or [ъ], as illustrated in the following semantically related words (they have a similar meaning):

(1) молодóй   [мъл∧дóй]
     мóлод   [мóлът]
     молóже   [м∧лóжы]

In (1) the first two vowels of each word are pronounced in different ways depending on the location of stress. Even though these vowels are pronounced differently, we still recognize the variations as belonging to one basic vowel sound, namely o̲. A basic vowel sound of this type is called a "phoneme" (фонéма), and an observed variation from the pronunciation of the phoneme is called an "allophone" (аллофóн). Phonemes are usually written in angle brackets: /o/ and are what we have been using as the building blocks for our base forms. Phonemes are the sound units in any language which when altered, may alter the meaning of a word. For example the phonemes /o/ and /a/ differentiate meaning in the

Russian words:

(2) том   там

In Russian, soft consonants are phonemic, that is, they differentiate meaning:

(3) мат "checkmate"   -   мать "mother"
    у́гол "corner"   -   у́голь "coal"

The phoneme and allophone are useful devices for discussing the shifts of a single sound, because they imply that even though a sound is different in certain circumstances, it is still the same basic sound. Thus, a phonological description of an utterance can be seen as being composed of a string of underlying phonemes which may be altered by rule.

3.2 e̲ vs. ë̲

From a physiological point of view it is easy to see why consonants are palatalized before the front vowels и̲ and э̲. But why are some consonants also soft before the back vowel о̲, as in нёс [н'ос] "he was carrying?" Since we do not have a rule that states that consonants become soft before о̲ (such a rule would make false predictions), the soft н̲' in нёс must be considered basic, or present in the base form: # н' о с #. So, we want to explain why a fronted consonant occurs before a back vowel. Consider the following word pairs. A soft consonant followed by о̲ can be seen in the second partner of each pair.

(1) легла́   -   лёг
    темно́   -   тёмный
    звезда́   -   звёзды
    несла́   -   нёс
    село́   -   сёла

The alphabetic letters in (1) suggest that we are dealing with an alternation of e̲ (in the left column) with ë̲ (in the right column). When we write out the word pairs in phonetic transcription, however, we see that the alternation in sounds in these semantically related word pairs is really between /э/, pronounced as [и] or [ь] due to ikan'e and /o/, pronounced [o] under stress:

(2) [л'иглá] - [л'ок]
    [т'имнó] - [т'óмный]
    [н'ислá] - [н'ос], etc.

The basic <u>sounds</u> which alternate in (1) are /э/ or, to be precise, its reduced allophonic variant [и] or [ь] and /o/. This is really exciting, because /э/ is a front vowel, just the thing to account for preceding soft consonants. If we can determine when [o] is produced in place of underlying /э/, then we can suggest that in all the words in (1), the base form of each pair contains an /э/, which in certain circumstances is pronounced [o].

The data in (1) provide a clue to the distribution of these alternating sounds. Notice that the ё in the words on the right always occurs under stress, while the е in the words on the left is not stressed. The following phonological rule expresses this:

(3)   э → o / _____
                    [+stress]

The rule in (3) states that [э] shifts to [o] when under stress. In conjunction with the rule that softens consonants before front vowels, the rule in (3) accounts for the data in (1):

(4)

underlying:	# с э л + ó #	# с э́ л + a #
(C → C' before и, э):	с' э л + ó	с' э́ л + a
(э → o):	(does not apply)	с' ó л + a
akan'e, ikan'e:	с' и л + ó	с' ó л + ъ
phonetic:	[с'илó]	[с'олъ]

*A Why would a rule be incorrect that states that every <u>o</u> shifts to <u>э</u> when not stressed ?

You can think of the two dots over the ё as a stress mark. This sound (soft consonant followed by an [o]) occurs only under stress in Russian. But certainly the rule in (3) cannot be correct either. The careful reader may have already thought of examples where stressed е̲ does not shift to ё̲, such as in руке́, ключе́. Clearly, the rule in (3) must be rewritten so as not to apply at word final position. Since ё̲ also never occurs before a vowel we can specify that the shift indicated in (3) occurs only before a consonant:

(5) э → o /____ C
   [+stress]

Here are some more word pairs that illustrate the shift of [э] to [o].

(6) ель "fir"   -   ёлка "fir"
    Пе́тя "Pete"   -   Пётр "Peter"
    печь "to bake"   -   пёк "he baked"
    день "day"   -   подённо "by day"
    пе́рья "feathers" -   пёрышко "little feather"
    пче́льник "apiary" -   пчёлы "bees"
    зе́лень "greens"   -   зелёный "green"

Words in the left column differ from those in the right by virtue of having stressed vowels before soft consonants.

*B How must the rule in (5) be changed so that it does not incorrectly produce forms such as *ёль, дёнь, and пёчь?

Valerij Vasil'evich Ivanov, wrote:

Изменение [э] в [o] происходило в положении после мягких согласных перед твердыми, причем при таком изменении мягкость предшествующего согласного сохранялась. Таким образом, основным фонетическим положением в котором в русском языке осуществлялось изменение [э] в [o], является положение перед твердым согласным. *В положении перед мягким согласным, как правило, [э] сохраняется.* (Italics added.)

The data in (6) bear out Ivanov's remarks. However, consider the following data:

(7) берéзник "birch forest"   -   берёза "birch"
    лéдник "ice house"   -   лёд "ice"
    передний "forward"   -   перёд "front"
    смéрть "death"   -   мёртвый "dead"
    жéлть "yellow paint"   -   жёлтый "yellow"
    колéсник "wheelwright"   -   колёса "wheels"
    дешéвле "cheaper"   -   дешёвый "cheap"

The words in the left column in (7) may appear at first glance to be counterevidence to Ivanov's statement that [э] shifts to [o] before a hard consonant. In section 2.7 we discussed a process in which the first consonant of a consonant cluster is soft if followed by a soft consonant (e.g., часть is [час'т']). The stressed vowel of the words in the left column in (7) precedes a consonant cluster. The second consonant of each cluster is soft. The pronunciation of e in these words as [э́] instead of as [ó] suggests that the initial consonant of each cluster is also soft, or, at least it was soft at one time, due to the softness of the following palatalized consonant. Ivanov's description remains valid.

*C In the following words stress falls on the underlined vowel. Mark stress on the underlined vowel by using the acute sign ´ or the umlaut sign ¨.

1. сельский   6. искривлéние
2. сéла   7. искривлéнный
3. звéзды (nom pl)   8. истéчь
4. созвéздие   9. истéк
5. шéрсть   10. шéрстка

3.3 Another Problem with э → o and Analogy

Stress is not normally marked in Russian and it is not always possible to predict whether or not a stressed e is é or ё. According to section 3.2 stressed e before a hard consonant becomes ё, and before a soft consonant remains é. This is expressed by (1):

(1) э → о / _____ C
          [+stress]

where C = a hard consonant.

The following data, however, provide strong counterevidence to this rule:

(2) мёд (nom sg)   but   о мёде (prep sg)
    ёлка (nom sg)   but   ёлки (nom pl)
    берёза (nom sg)   but   о берёзе (prep sg)
    живёт (3rd sg)   but   живёте (2nd pl)
    тёмный (lng frm)   but   тёмен (short form)
    полёт (nom sg)   but   о полёте (prep sg)

The data in (2) illustrate another aspect of sound alternations. Sometimes they do not occur where it seems they should. This breaking of phonological rules is called <u>analogy</u> (аналóгия). For example the sg and pl paradigms for the word берёза are given in (3):

(3) nom   берёза   берёзы
    acc   берёзу   берёзы
    gen   берёзы   берёз
    prep   берёзе ←←   берёзах
    dat   берёзе ←←   берёзам
    inst   берёзой   берёзами

In all cases of the sg except the prep and dat sg, and in all cases of the pl the stem of this word ends in a hard consonant. The stem ends in a soft consonant only in the prep/dat sg. By analogy to all the other forms of this word, the prep/dat sg forms of this word also keep the stem vowel ё. Analogy can be seen at work in the other words given in (2). For the purposes of phonology, we will consider analogical forms such as о мёде as trivially exceptional insofar as analogy explains their existence.

    In addition to the analogical forms given in (2), there are words which have stressed é before a hard consonant and which do not exhibit the same analogical relationship as discussed above. Consider, for example, the words in (4).

(4) снег   лес   место
     дело   небо   нет
     рек (gen pl)   лето   монета

If the rule given in (1) is correct, then the stressed vowels in (4) are exceptional. They do not shift to [o] as predicted by the rule in (1). The derivation of one of these words, дело, would proceed as follows:

(5) underlying: # д э́ л + о #
    C → C'   д' э л   о
    э → о   д' о л   о
    akan'e   д' о л   ъ

    phonetic: *[д'о́лъ]

The asterisk before a cited or derived form indicates that it is ungrammatical (i.e., does not occur in the dialect in question).

Compare the derivation in (5) with the one in (6), where the rule [э] → [o] does apply correctly:

(6) underlying: # п э к #
    C → C'   п'э к
    э → о   п'о к

    phonetic: [п'ок]

Why does the stressed [э] shift to [o] in пёк "he baked," but not in дело? It is clear that the type of consonant following the stressed vowel does not play a role here, cf. рек "river" (gen pl) and сёл "villages" (gen pl). We can also rule out analogy here since most of the inflected forms of the words in (4) end in a hard consonant. The vowel in дело seems to be exceptional; it does not allow the operation of the э → о rule. How is this word different from other words where we do see the э ~ о alternation?

In order to understand why the words in (3) do not reflect the /э/ ~ /о/ alternation, it is useful to ask if this has always been the situation in Russian, or if the words given above used to be different. This is a good question to ask because even though new speakers are born every day, languages do not just spring into existence with each new speaker. Instead, languages are the result of numerous phonological shifts, some of which result in the kind of dilemma presented above. Before reviewing the historical shifts which have led to this situation, we will first examine one other complication in the modern language.

3.4 Fleeting Vowels

One of the most striking sound alternations in Russian is the vowel ~ zero alternation. The following word pairs exhibit this alternation.

(1)

nom sg	gen sg	alternation
отéц	отцá	[ə] ~ Ø
рот	рта	[o] ~ Ø
мох	мха	[o] ~ Ø
лёд	льда	[o] ~ Ø
день	дня	[ə] ~ Ø
сон	сна	[o] ~ Ø

The words in the left column in (1) have the vowel [ə] or [o] (written e, o, or ё) which disappears in the gen sg forms of the same words. The vowels which alternate with Ø are often referred to as "fleeting" or "unstable" vowels. There are about 19,335 different words in Russian that have a fleeting vowel in at least one form of the word. Words with fleeting vowels occur in all grammatical categories. The gen pl of fem and neut nouns often has a fleeting vowel, as illustrated in (2) below.

(2)

nom sg	gen pl	alternation
ло́дка	ло́док	Ø ~ [о]
окно́	о́кон	Ø ~ [о]
письмо́	пи́сем	Ø ~ [э]
кре́сло	кре́сел	Ø ~ [э]
тюрьма́	тю́рем	Ø ~ [э]

Fleeting vowels are also seen in verbal forms and short form adjectives.

(3)

infinitive	1st sg	alternation
звать	зову́	Ø ~ [о]
брать	беру́	Ø ~ [э]
fem	**masc**	**alternation**
пришла́	пришёл	Ø ~ [о]
больна́	бо́лен	Ø ~ [э]

The data in (1) - (3) give rise to several questions. When will the fleeting vowel be o̲ and when will it be e̲ or ё̲? Is it possible to predict where fleeting vowels will occur? Why does Russian have fleeting vowels anyway? We will examine each question in turn.

Is it possible to predict when the fleeting vowel will be o̲, e̲, or ё̲? The following distributions should be noted.

3.4.1 Location of fleeting vowels.

Fleeting vowels occur only in certain consonant clusters and if no other vowel follows. Not all consonant clusters are liable to have fleeting vowels.

(1) ten monosyllabic masc nouns:

лоб, ров, лёд, лён, сон, пёс, рот, мох, лев, день

(2) short form masc adjectives with the suffix -к- (not -ск-):

бли́зкий - бли́зок, го́рький - го́рек, ре́дкий - ре́док

(3) short form masc adjectives with the suffix -н- (not soft -н-):

спосо́бный - спосо́бен, кра́сный - кра́сен, у́мный - умён

(4) a few short form masc adjectives whose stems end in -p or -л:

хи́трый- хитёр, о́стрый - остёр, во́стрый - востёр, шу́стрый - шустёр, тёплый - тёпел, ки́слый - ки́сел, све́тлый - све́тел

(5) 3 short form end stress adjectives (in -о́й):

дурно́й, хмельно́й, больно́й (ду́рен, хме́лен, бо́лен)

(6) thousands of masc nouns with the suffix -ец or -ок:

оте́ц - отца́, зубо́к - зубки́

(7) thousands of fem nouns and neut nouns with the suffix -к-:

студе́нтка - студе́нток, око́шко - око́шек

(8) hundreds of disyllabic, nonsuffixed, nouns:

свёкор - свёкра, сестра́ - сестёр, сосна́ - со́сен

(9) in the stems of a handful of verbs:

брать - беру́, звать - зову́, шёл - шла

(10) in some verbal prefixes: отпере́ть - отопру́

The ten locations given above could be part of a very complex formal rule that would predict when a fleeting vowel would occur. Instead of writing such a rule, we will simply assume that fleeting vowels, or to be precise, a place holder for a fleeting vowel is part of the underlying form of words that in one case or another show the fleeting vowel. Thus the word сестра́, which has a fleeting vowel in the gen pl сестёр, will have an underlying form:

(11)   # с э с т / р + а́ #

In the derivation of the gen pl of this word, the slash sign, which stands for "some fleeting vowel" will be replaced by the proper fleeting vowel (see next section).

*A Write out the underlying (base) form of the words in the left column. Words in the right column are given for information regarding the occurance of a fleeting vowel.

1. спи́чка	спи́чек (gen pl)
2. лы́сина	лы́син (gen pl)
3. секрета́рша	секрета́рш (gen pl)
4. ору́дие	ору́дий (gen pl)
5. семья́	семе́й (gen pl)
6. аккура́тный	аккура́тен (masc short form)
7. значо́к	значко́в (gen pl)
8. рыба́к	рыбако́в (gen pl)
9. цини́зм	цини́зма (gen sg)
10. тигр	ти́гров (gen pl)

To understand why fleeting vowels occur in some consonant clusters but not in others, and to understand why fleeting vowels occur in Russian, it will be useful to consider how these words were written and pronounced at an earlier time.

3.4.2 Type of fleeting vowel.

Fleeting vowels appear only within certain consonant clusters (see 3.4.1). The choice of vowel in the underlying form depends on the kind of consonants in the cluster. If either consonant is a velar, then the fleeting vowel is realized as an o in base forms. In all other cases the base form of the fleeting vowel is э:

(1) Fleeting vowel insertion rule:

(a) / → o / K ___ C #
           C ___ K #

(b) / → э / elsewhere

The rule in (1) accounts for the distribution of almost all fleeting vowels, some examples of which are given in (2).

(2)
лёгкий	лёгок	#л ё г / к#	short form masc
кýбок	кýбки	#к ý б / к#	nom pl
чухнá	чýхон	#ч ý х / н#	gen pl
окнó	óкон	#ó к / н#	gen pl
дóлгий	дóлог	#д ó л / г#	short form masc
письмó	пúсем	#п ú с' / м#	gen pl
свáдьба	свáдеб	#с в á д' / б#	gen pl
тюрьмá	тюрем	#т' у р' / м#	gen pl
крéсло	крéсел	#к р э́ с / л#	gen pl
удóбный	удóбен	#у д ó б / н#	short form masc

Words such as gen pl дéвушек, кнúжек, кáрточек also have an underlying o, since a velar is one of the two members of the consonant cluster. In these words, however, a spelling rule applies to shift unstressed #...o.# (as in #кáрточок#) to e: кáрточек. The spelling rule that brings about this change states, "unstressed o is written as e after hushers and ц." We formalize this spelling rule:

(3) *spelling rule*: o → e / Č, ц ___   where Č = any husher
                                    [-str]

The further derivation of the fleeting vowel depends on the quality of the preceding consonant. If it is soft (ч or щ), then ikan'e applies to derive ь as illustrated in (4).

(4)   # к á р т о ч / к # (gen pl)

/ → о,э   к á р т о ч о к
akan'e   к á р т ъ ч ъ к
ikan'e   к á р т ъ ч ь к

phonetic: [кáртъчьк]

If the husher is hard (ш or ж) or the preceding consonant is ц, then simple akan'e applies: дéвушек > #дѕвушок# → [д'ѕвушък].

We see the same spelling shift of unstressed o̲ to e̲ when the consonant preceding the fleeting vowel is *any soft consonant*: сосýлька - gen pl сосýлек < #сосýл'/к#. In fact, it is not possible to write an unstressed o̲ after a soft consonant in Russian: it comes out as a e̲ every time. We therefore expand the rule given in (3) to:

(5) *spelling rule*: o → e / Č, ц, C'___   Č = any husher
                                    [-str]

Rule (5) states that unstressed o̲ is written e̲ after any husher, ц, and after and a̲n̲y̲ soft consonant. We will see later that this is really a simplification of the rule (3) and that this rule applies throughout Russian. For now, we see that it applies to the spelling of underlying # o #:

(6)   # р ѕ́ д' / к #

/ → о,э   р ѕ́ д' о к
C → C'   р'ѕ́ д' о к
akan'e   р'ѕ́ д' ъ к
ikan'e   р'ѕ́ д' ь к

            [р'ѕ́д'ьк] spelled рéдек (gen pl of рéдька "radish")

When the first consonant of the consonant cluster is soft and stress falls on the fleeting vowel, then the underlying o̲ is heard, and Russian writes ё: серьгá, gen pl: серёг [с'ир'óк], хорёк "polecat" [хʌр'óк], cf. gen sg хорькá.

Here is an example of the second part of the rule given in (1). In this word the fleeting vowel is not contiguous to a velar:

(7) underlying: # с й л' / н #   (сильный shows there is
                                                   a fleeting vowel)

    / → о,э   с и л' э н
    C → C'   с'и л' э н
    ikan'e   с'й л' ь н
    [с'йл'ьн]   силен (short form masc)

When the environment of (1) is not met, i.e., a vowel follows the consonant cluster that contains /, then the fleeting vowel is not realized. Compare the derivation in (7) with that of (8).

(8) underlying # с й л' / н ы й #
    / → о,э   does not apply
    C → C'   с'ил' / н ы й
    [с'йл'ный]

The rules in (1) and (5) account for the type fleeting vowel in thousands of words. In words where the fleeting vowel э is stressed before a hard consonant the э → о rule (section 3.3) shifts stressed э to о as expected:

(8) умный   умён   short form masc
    котёл   котла́   gen sg
    лёд   льда   gen sg
    осёл   осла́   gen sg
    котёл   котла́   gen sg
    костёр   костра́   gen sg
    кайма́   каём   gen pl

(9) Derivations of со́сен (fv not stressed), котёл (fv stressed):

underlying	# с о́ с / н #	# к о т /' л #
/ → о,э	с о́ с э н	к о т э́ л
C → C'	с о́ с'э н	к о т'э́ л
э → о	--	к о т'о́ л
other	с о́ с'ь н	к ʌ т'о́ л
	[со́с'ьн]	[кʌт'о́л]

A major exception to the rules given above occurs when the final member
of the consonant cluster is ц. Then the fleeting vowel is always e̲, whether
under stress or not. In effect, the э → o rule does not apply before ц.

(10)   немец   немца   gen sg
       кольцо́   коле́ц   gen pl
       иностра́нец   иностра́нца   gen sg
       бра́тец   бра́тца   gen sg

The following words are exceptional since they take the fleeting vowel -o̲
instead of expected -ё̲: сон, зол (#з/л#), мох, рот, лоб, ров. The
following have the fleeting vowel -e̲, but it does not shift to -o̲ as expected
when under stress and before a hard consonant: лев, тем (gen pl of тьма),
хребе́т. The word шёл (and its relatives, пошёл, пришёл, etc.) is
exceptional in that ё̲ is written rather than o̲ after a palatal. The short form
of the adjective по́лный is exceptional: по́лон. Finally, the fleeting vowel
before an i-kratkoe is e̲, as expected, but only if stressed: семья́, gen pl
семе́й, судья́, gen pl суде́й; if not stressed then the fleeting vowel is и̲:
копьё, gen pl ко́пий!

The following summary may be made regarding the general distribution of
fleeting vowels:

(11)   (a) / → o /   K ___   where K = any velar
                         ___ K   Note: this o̲ is subject to the
                                           (o → e) spelling rule

       (b) / → э /   elsewhere Note: this э̲ is subject to the
                                           (э → o) rule

*A Following are some fem and neut nouns in the nom sg. All take
    a fleeting vowel in the gen pl. What fleeting vowel should occur
    in the gen pl of these nouns according to the rules given above?
    Which are affected by the rule given in (5)?

1. подстилка
2. мышка
3. капля
4. чайка
5. кукла
6. кухня
7. ёлочка
8. туфелька
9. сказка
10. деревня

11. яблочко
12. седло́
13. число́
14. гуля́нье
15. полотно́
16. крыльцо́
17. бревно́
18. судья́
19. кошка
20. масло

*B Which part of rule (11), part (a) or (b), predicts the fleeting vowel in the nom sg forms of the following nom sg - gen sg pairs?

1. лёд - льда́
2. кошелёк - кошелька́
3. прила́вок - прила́вка
4. коне́ц - конца́
5. козёл - козла́

6. ого́нь - огня́
7. кита́ец - кита́йца
8. продаве́ц - продавца́
9. перешеек - перешейка
10. кашель - кашля

In Chapter 4 we will review why stressed э shifts to o before hard consonants and why this change is not reflected in some modern words. We will also examine the source of fleeting vowels.

3.5 Dialect evidence regarding э → o

The distribution of CSR stressed e can be confusing to students of Russian. Sometimes it is pronounced [э], as in ме́сто and sometimes it is pronounced [o], as in мёд. Some Russian dialects have still other pronunciations for stressed e. In some northern dialects stressed e is pronounced similarly to [и]. This sound, transcribed as [ê], is called a "closed e." Before a soft consonant this sound often becomes an [и]:

(1) **CSR Written**   **Northern Dialect**
лес   л[ê]с
ле́то   л[ê]то
ве́ра   в[ê]ра

CSR Written	Northern Dialect
свѐт	св[ê]т
сѐльский	с[и́]льский
вмѐсте	вм[и́]сте
бѐрег	б[и́]рег

The dialects that have this pronunciation also have stressed [э] and stressed [o] (ё), as found in CSR: ц[э́]рковь (not ц[ê]рковь), уткнёт [уткн'от] "bury."

Other northern dialects have a diphthong [иэ] where CSR has [э́] and where other dialects have [ê]: л[иэ]с, л[иэ]то, с[иэ]но, св[иэ]т. (See Bromlei, Avanesov, and particularly Mel'nichenko for citations.)

It is curious that these dialectal variations of e occur exactly in those words where the shift of [э] to [o] does not work in CSR.

*A The following was related in 1978 by an inhabitant of the village of Pezhma just east of lake Onega. It describes some of the folk traditions which prefaced the marriage ceremony (венѐц). It is given in phonetic transcription. Write the story into normal CSR spelling and point out which words exhibit northern dialectal features. In this transcription (see Mel'nichenko) the slash "/" indicates a pause.

[рáн'шэ хóц'эш н'э хóц'эш / а зáмуш нáдо бы́ло ит'т'и / анна п'итракóс'ка говор'и́ла / м'ин'á оболокáйут в мáт'ир'ину пáру / дóлг'ийэ шырóк'ийэ йýпки до сáмово пóлу / штобы нок н'и в'идно было / а йа р'ивл'у да н'э дайý в рукавá совáт']

[к в'ин'цý врóзно в'изýт / н'ив'э́сту на свойи́х лошад'ах и жон'их на свойи́х / а от в'ин'ц'а вм'и́с'т'э / на гóлову н'ив'э́с'т'э-то ц'в'иты́ наклáдывайут восковы́йэ / б'и́лым'и ц'в'итóц'кам'и]

Gloss: оболокáть = to cover
мáтерина = mother's
пáра = suit of clothes
реви́ть = to roar, bellow (cf. CSR ревѐть)
врóзно = separately (cf. CSR врозь)

3.6   Review

Russian contains several thorny sound alternations which are not obviously explainable by assimilation, namely the shift of stressed e̱ to ë (несла̱ - нёс) and fugitive vowels (оте́ц -- отца̱). It is possible to delineate where these alternations occur by means of rules; the rule for the e̱ to ë shift not applying everywhere, for example, снег does not become *снёг, and the rules for the fleeting vowels are somewhat awkward and intricate. Neither set of rules explains why Russian has fleeting vowels or the bothersome ë. Furthermore we found in dialects the pronunciation of closed [ê] and [иэ] for CSR e̱ in exactly those words that do not undergo the e̱ to ë rule. In order to answer questions regarding these and other apparent irregularities in Russian, we must direct our attention to antecedent layers of the language.

CHAPTER 4: HISTORICAL PHONOLOGY

4.1 Why Study the History of Russian

Languages change over time. While we are normally able to speak with parents, grandparents, and when they are available, great-grandparents, the language of distant ancestors such as speakers from the Old English period, judging by the way it was written, is not readily understandable to us. It is sometimes difficult for speakers of American English to understand speakers of British English although both languages derive from a common ancestor. Dialects of a single language can become so distinct in time that speakers of the same "language" may not understand each other, as might be the case with speakers of standard American English and speakers from the southern mid-atlantic Appalachian region.

In previous chapters, we found that some rules involving Russian pronunciation have exceptions. For example, contrary to rule, stressed e̱ sometimes does not shift to ë̱ in words where it should. We have reviewed other sound changes such as those illustrated in the spelling rules and in disappearing vowels, and have wondered why such transformations occur. An examination of the history of the language will help us answer questions regarding modern evident irregularities and explain why observed alternations currently exist. Once the reasons behind these idiosyncracies are understood, it is often easier to remember them and to know where to expect them.

Evidence of language change can come from written records, from comparing related languages, and from data obtained by comparing a language against itself, including dialectal data. Eastern Slavic people, the ancestors of the Russians, have been writing for over nine hundred years. What hints regarding the make up of modern Russian can be derived from earlier written records?

4.2 The Alphabet of Bygone Years

If you look at a book or newspaper printed in Russia before 1917 you will immediately notice that there are certain differences in the way Russian was written then. Consider, for example, the following selection entitled "Наши Предки." This page is from a history book for children published in 1912 in St. Petersburg. A speaker from the early twentieth century reading this text would sound much like a modern Russian speaker. In other words, the text is not a phonetic representation of how the words were spoken.

НАШИ ПРЕДКИ.

ДАВНО, давно въ странѣ, гдѣ мы теперь живемъ, не было ни богатыхъ городовъ, ни каменныхъ домовъ, ни большихъ селъ. Были одни только поля, да густые темные лѣса, въ которыхъ жили дикіе звѣри.

По берегамъ рѣкъ, далеко другъ отъ друга стояли бѣдныя избушки. Въ избушкахъ жили наши предки—славяне, такъ назывался тогда русскій народъ.

Славяне были храбрымъ народомъ. Они много воевали со своими сосѣдями и часто ходили на охоту, чтобы убивать дикихъ звѣрей, которые выбѣгали изъ лѣсовъ и нападали на людей.

We know this from descriptions of the pronunciation of Russian published at that time and from the speech of Russians who were alive at the beginning of the 20th century. It is not surprising that spelling and speech do not always match. Writing often tends to be representative of how a language was spoken at an earlier time, which, having become fixed in print, changes very slowly. Thus the English ni<u>gh</u>t and <u>kn</u>ow are not pronounced the way they are spelled. The spelling of these words represents a much older pronunciation which has been lost today. In Russian, it took a major social revolution to change its standardized spelling.

Following the 1917 revolution orthographic changes were made so that written Russian matched its pronunciaton more closely. In particular, several letters were either dropped from the language or replaced.

*A The writing in "Наши предки," although easily recognizable and readable, is somewhat different from what we are used to today. The differences can be classified into two types: (1) letters that are no longer used in Russian, and (2) letters that are still used but used differently. Read through "Наши предки" and determine which letters belong to each group.

*B 1. What modern Russian letters correspond to ѣ and і?
   2. What is the distribution of ъ in Наши предки (where in words is this letter normally seen)?
   3. What is the distribution of ъ in Modern Russian?
   4. What kind of words in Наши предки has the letter і?

4.2.1   <u>e</u> vs. ѣ

In modern Russian, there are really two kinds of <u>e</u>. One alternates with the sound [o] (orthographic ё) when under stress. The other remains <u>e</u> when under stress. This distribution is illustated in (1).

(1)

	e1	e2
Written as:	e	e
becomes under stress:	[o]	[э]
as in:	нес [н'ос]	снег [с'н'эк]

The writing in Наши предки gives us a hint about why these two e's are pronounced in the way indicated in (1).

*A. Read the first three lines of Наши предки out loud. Which letter in the text equates to e1 in (1)? That is, which letter equates to modern ё?

We conclude that an older stage of Russian contained the vowels e and ѣ. The letter ѣ is called yat' (ятъ). It became e (é) in modern Russian. It did not become ё. Russian dictionaries published before the twentieth century give, for example, снѣгъ. On the other hand, original e when under stress and before a hard consonant corresponds perfectly with modern Russian ё; cf. in Наши предки: живемъ, селъ, темные. The e in words like теперь does not correspond to modern Russian ё because it is not under stress, or if it is under stress it does not fall before a hard consonant (cf. also берегамъ, людей). Note that the word предки is borrowed from South Slavic, the Russian root being ПЕРЕД-.

*B How would the following words have been written before 1917?

1. нет (remember final -ъ)
2. место
3. мёд
4. берёза
5. река (gen pl рек)
6. нести (past masc: нёс)
7. стена (nom pl стены)
8. сесть (он сел)
9. жена (nom pl жёны)
10. смех

4.2.2 The Pronunciation of ѣ

Recall that Old Russian -e̲ under stress and before a hard consonant yielded modern Russian -ё: берéза → берёза. Old Russian yat' (ѣ) yielded modern Russian -e̲: снѣгъ → снег. How did the pronunciation of ѣ differ from e̲ in Old Russian? Since all instances of ѣ have shifted to e̲, we must consult closely related languages, namely other Slavic languages, which may have had--or perhaps still have--a sound corresponding to ѣ. By comparing words that have this letter in older Russian with similar words in other Slavic languages we try to get an approximation of what sound this letter represented.

Consider the words in (1). They all have the stem vowel ё in the Russian forms, i.e., they go back to Old Russian words that had the stem vowel e̲.

(1) **Russian**	**Ukrainian**	**Polish**	**SCr**	**Bulg**
мёд	мíд	miód	мед	мед
лёд	лíд	lód	лед	лед
свёкор	свекор	świekier	свекар	свекър
жёлудь	жолудь	żołądź	желуд	желъд
лёгкий	легкий	lekki	лак	лек

First, compare Russian with Ukrainian. The data suggest that the shift of e̲ to o̲ was not as widespread in Ukrainian as in Russian. Other Ukrainian data show that in this language the shift of e̲ to o̲ can be seen only after hushers, though not necessarily only under stress! The shift did occur in Polish but only before hard dentals, and not always then (cf. Russ орёл - Pols orzeł). In Serbo-Croatian and Bulgarian (both South Slavic languages) the shift did not occur at all. So words borrowed into Russian through the church language (also South Slavic based) have e̲ where ё might be expected: крест, небо (cf. pre-1917 крестъ, небо). The vowels in these words do not go back to ѣ. The overwhelming majority of stem vowels in those languages where the shift did not occur or occurred only sporadically is e̲. It is likely, then, that Old Russian e̲ represented a sound much like that found in the modern language: [э]. This is supported by the pronunciation of the stem vowel in the first four words in Serbo-Croatian, all the words in Bulgarian and two of the words in Ukrainian.

Now consider the pronunciation of the words in (2). The Russian forms all have the stressed stem vowel e̲, that is, they go back to words that had the stem vowel ѣ. (Note the j in Serbo- Croatian is pronounced much like [й].)

(2)

Russian	**Ukrainian**	**Polish**	**SCr**	**Bulg**
лес	ліс	las	лиjес	лес
снег	сніг	śnieg	сниjег	сняг
мéсто	мíсто	miasto	мjесто	мя́сто
бéлый	бíлий	biały	биjела	бял

A comparison of Russian and Ukrainian consistently shows two different modern pronunciations for Old Russian ѣ: e̲ and i̲. Polish shows a diphthong (ie or ia) in three of its forms and diphthongs are prominent in the Serbo-Croatian forms, while Bulgarian consistently gives я̲. Thus:

(3)

	ѣ
Russian	e
Ukrainian	i
Polish	ia, ie, a
SCr	иje, je
Bulgarian	я, e

The comparative method provides a variety of sounds to choose from as representing the pronunciation of ѣ. But certain tendencies surface. Judging from the data given above, ѣ must have been a front vowel. We know that it was not [ə], since this pronunciation attends another letter, e̲, and since [ə] shifts to [o], whereas ѣ does not. Another possibility is that ѣ was pronounced as the front vowel [и], but [и] does not shift to [ə], cf. Old Russian говоритъ - Modern Russian говори́т. Besides, another letter represented [и] in Old Russian, namely ___ . Other comparative data suggest either a diphthong [ia] or [ie] or, according to Bulgarian a front vowel like [ä], as in English ca̲t.

The fact that Russian words with yat' were borrowed into Finnish usually with a long [ä] or a diphthong supports the proposition that Old Russian ѣ was pronounced as [ä] or as a diphthong. Examples from Finnish: määrä < мѣра, läävä < хлѣвъ "cattle shed", pätsi < пѣчь. (See

Shevelov for a good discussion of the pronunciation of yat'.)

*A It has been suggested that the pronunciation of ѣ in Old Russian was [иэ], rather than [ä], which corresponds more closely with t h e pronunciation of ѣ in the South Slavic languages. The [иэ]in Old Russian was then simplified to [э]. Review the dialectal data given in 3.5. Given the conservative nature of these northern dialects, do these data support or contradict the suggestion that Old Russian yat' was pronounced as [иэ]. Why?

4.2.3 Front and Back Jers

Another plain difference that can be seen in Наши предки is the presence of a "hard sign" (ъ) at the end of many words, as in богатыхъ, where in modern Russian there is no hard sign. Thus all words in the text Наши предки end in a vowel, й, ь, or ъ. The preponderance of vowels at word final position suggests that at some earlier time in Russian, when the hard sign and soft sign were pronounced, they also represented vowel sounds. A quick check of Bulgarian, where ъ is still pronounced, confirms this suggestion: compare Bulg. сън, църква - Russ. сон, це́рковь. In Old Russian, the hard sign is called a "back jer" (ер) and the soft sign is called a "front jer" (ерь). Back jers are found in words whose modern counterparts do not contain hard signs. Compare words from Наши предки:

(1) **Older Russian**   **Modern Russian**

въ	в
городовъ	городо́в
селъ	сёл
рѣкъ	рек
народомъ	наро́дом

The letter ъ has not survived at the end of words in modern Russian. The front jer, however, continues in basically the same position it occupied in older Russian texts: тепе́рь, for example. Neither ъ nor ь is pronounced today. At the end words ъ has been lost altogether. However, the sign ь has been ingeniously retained to <u>show</u> that the consonant preceding it is pronounced soft. For this reason we can propose that this jer must have been a front vowel capable of causing palatalization of consonants, like the other front vowels и and э. Soft consonants do not occur when followed by back jers (ъ), so we may be safe in assuming that ъ was a back vowel, and thus not capable of causing palatalization. Here is how V. V. Ivanov (p. 70) characterizes the pronunciation of jers in Old Russian:

В древнерусском языке были две гласные фонемы неполного образования, так называемые редуцированные или глухие. Это были ослабленные гласные, произносившиеся, вероятно, неполнымголосом. Условно эти гласные обозначаются [ъ] (ер) и [ь] (ерь).

Гласная фонема [ъ] характеризовалась признаками непереднего ряда среднего подъема, а [ь] -- переднего ряда среднего подъема.

Ivanov characterizes both jers as reduced vowels, and characterizes ъ as a nonfront mid vowel and ь as a front mid vowel. The letter ъ at one time was pronounced as a reduced "uh" sound as the o in the word "polite," and the letter ь was pronounced as a reduced "ih" sound as the i in the word "massive." Try reading aloud the words in the left column in (3), giving proper pronunciation to the jers.

As indicated above, the actual pronunciation of jers at word final position have been lost in modern Russian. Traces of front jers remain in the softness of consonants that previously preceded front jers:

(2) Old Russ.: тепе[р'ь] → final jer lost → Modern Russian тепе[р']

A trace of the front jer is present in the palatalized quality of the final consonant. The writing in "Наши предки" shows that an earlier stage of Russian had an enriched vowel system, containing at least three more vowel sounds (ъ, ь and ѣ) than are found in the modern language. The presence of these vowels helps to explain why consonants are soft before soft signs: they used to be front vowels. In addition, it provides clues to the question of why the e in снег does not shift to ё (earlier it was not a e, but a ѣ (снѣгъ).

We will return later to the jers and we will discuss more fully the shift of e to ё and the shift of ѣ to e. First we will review the relationship between the various Slavic and Indo-European languages.

4.3 Linguistic Relatives

In the preceding sections Russian, or an older variant of Russian was compared to other Slavic languages in order to arrive at an approximation of how ѣ may have been pronounced. We did not try to find commonalities with non-Slavic languages, such as Mandarin Chinese or Hopi, an American Indian language, because research has shown that these languages have very little in common with Russian. It has been shown, however, that many languages spoken in Central and Eastern Europe share many features, particularly in word roots and grammar. Russian, Ukrainian, and Belorussian are particularly close and compose a language group, the East Slavic languages. They are close because they largely derive from a single source. Kondrashov writes,

> Послерасспадения праславянского языка самая многочисленная группа славянских племен, занявшая обширные территории Восточной Европы, переживает процесс консолидации и кладет начало древнерусской, или восточнославянской, народности, носителю древнерусского языка.
>
> Все [эти] племена говорили на близкородственных восточнославянских диалектах. Нарастание диалектных особенностей в области звукового и грамматического строя, а также словарного состава древнерусского языка было обусловлено именно указанным обособлением в XIII-XIV вв., усилившимся после захвата польско-литовскими феодалами южных и западных земель. Конечным результатом этого процесса явилось образование трех восточнославянских народностей--русской, украинской и белорусской, и соответственно трех самостоятельных языков.

Russian derives from Early Russian or Old Russian (OR), which was an eastern dialect of late Common Slavic (общеславянский), an ancient language which died out (=evolved out) about one thousand years ago. It is the basis of three language groups that form today's Slavic languages. Proto-Slavic (праславянский) was the earliest Slavic dialect of Indo-European. Listed in (1) are the principal modern West, South, and East

Slavic languages. There are no written records of either Common Slavic or Proto Slavic, but by means of internal reconstruction and the comparative method, they have been reconstructed to a large degree. The table in (1) indicates main genetic relationships only and does not necessarily indicate relative chronology for the formation of the languages involved.

Old Russian writing was based on the writing of Church documents known as Old Church Slavic (OCS). The language expressed in these documents has strong affinities to the South Slavic languages, see (1).

(1)

	Modern Languages	Ancient Languages	Preshistoric Languages
East Slavic	ру́сский / украи́нский / белору́сский	древнеру́сский	
South Slavic	болга́рский / македо́нский / сербо-хорва́тский / слове́нский	общею́жные диале́кты	общеславя́нский
West Slavic	че́шский / по́льский	общеза́падные диале́кты	

Horace Lunt has shown that there are also clear affinities between OCS and the Old Russian spoken language. This leads to the suggestion that OR and OCS are simply two variants of late Common Slavic. In any event, it is not surprising that a southern Slavic variant of writing should be adopted in Old Rus' since the Greek church spread its influence, including writing, via the South Slavic lands.

The Common Slavic language family is a daughter language of Indo-European, one dialect of which was Proto-Slavic. Sister languages to Common Slavic include Germanic (a source of English), Celtic, Hindi, Armenian, Greek, the Romance group (French, Italian, etc.), Albanian, Persian, and the Baltic group (Lithuanian, Latvian, Old Prussian).

The Slavic languages, while dissimilar enough to be separate languages, have similar words and grammar. One interesting aspect of Russian is the presence of numerous words with the combination оло, оро, and ере in the root: хо́лод, го́род, бе́рег, for example. Yet these roots appear in an abbreviated form in other words хладнокро́вный "cool, composed," градостро́итель "town planner," безбре́жный "boundless." The roots of these words (ХЛАД-, ГРАД-, and БРЕГ-) are semantically related to хо́лод, го́род, and бе́рег. We suspect that they may be historically related as well, that is, each pair (i.e., город- and град-) goes back to one word. It is difficult to determine from Russian alone which variant is historically derived from the other: the one filled out with vowels, such as го́род, or the one with only one vowel, град. Or perhaps they both go back to some form now not present in the modern language. Historical documents could certainly help resolve this problem, if only we had documents written in Common Slavic, but we may also resolve this question by means of the comparative method: similar words in closely related languages can be compared. Then a decision can be made regarding an earlier stage of the words, when the compared languages were one. The decision must take into account as much information as is available. Consider, for example, the pairs of words given in (2).

(2)

Russian	Bulgarian	S-Croat	Polish	Czech	OCS
голос	глас	глас	głos	hlas	гласъ
город	град	град	gród	hrad	градъ
голова	глава	глава	głowa	hlava	глава
волос	власи*	влас	włos	vlas	власъ
берег	брег	бриjег	brzeg	břeh	брѣгъ
береза	бреза	бреза	brzoza	bříza	not cited
борода	брада	брада	broda	brada	брада
дерево	дърво	дриjево	drzewo	dřevo	дрѣво
золото	злато	злато	złoto	zlato	злато
молоко	мляко	млиjеко	mleko	mleko	млѣко

*tresses, locks

Words with the sequence illustrated in (2) are usually called TORT forms in Slavic, where T=any consonant, O=the vowel o or e, and R=one of the sonorants p or л. As shown in (2) TORT forms in Russian are generally fully voiced, that is, they are TOROT forms. In Russian this is called полногласие "full voicing."

*A Judging by the data in (2), which sequence is represented most in the Slavic languages: TORT, TOROT, or TROT?

*B Of the languages which have TROT, which consistently have the vowel a and which have the vowel o?

*C What form, TORT, TOROT, or TROT appears to have been used in the Common Slavic?

In spite of the numerical preponderance of TROT forms in the modern languages it is generally believed that these words in Common Slavic had the form TORT and that the shift to TROT and TOROT took place in a late stage of Common Slavic, when the latter was breaking up. This view is supported by evidence of obsolete words from various Slavic languages: Russ за́портак "dried out egg" cf. Russ за́пороток; Medieval Bulg балтина "swamp", малдичие "youth", залтарин "gold smith", Polabian storna "side", morz "frost", korvo "cow". Old Records from northern Polish have karw "bullock" and place names such as Wyszegard. See Shevelov for these and additional examples. Around the middle of the 9th C Common Slavic TORT forms began shifting into the forms we see today. A Byzantine text written previous to 860 AD has the name Valdimer, and the earliest loan words into Finnish do not show the shift: Finnish palttina "linen", talkkuna "oatmeal", taltta "chisel", and värttinä "spindle"; cf. Russian полотно, толокно, долото, веретено. These data provide evidence for the belief that these words in Common Slavic had the form TORT.

A non-Slavic language which has many correspondences with Slavic is Lithuanian, an Indo-European language spoken in the Baltic region, neighboring the Slavic area. In (3) we compare the TOROT forms given above with their Lithuanian counterparts. We are particularly interested in the shape of the stem in Lithuanian: will it be TORT, TOROT, or TROT? (Note: the nom sg ending for masc nouns in Lithuanian is -as or -us.) There is no clear Lithuanian counterpart for бе́рег.

(3)
1. го́лос - balsas "voice"
2. го́род - gardas "fold, pen"
3. молоко́ - malkas "draught"
4. во́лос - vilna "wool"
5. зо́лото - geltonas "yellow"

6. голова́ - galva "head"
7. бе́рег - Ø
8. берёза - beržas "birch"
9. борода́ - barzda "beard"
10. де́рево - derva "resin, pitch"

Note that the Lithuanian words have the sequence TORT. Lithuanian has seen relatively few changes since the breakup of the Indo-European mother language. The Lithuanian forms suggest that these words were originally TORT forms. In this regard it is interesting to note the English correspondences to these words (none for голова́).

(4)

1. го́лос - call
2. го́род - yard
3. молоко́ - milk
4. во́лос - wool
5. зо́лото - gold

6. голова́ - Ø
7. бе́рег - park/burg
8. берёза - birch
9. борода́ - beard
10. де́рево - tree

We may make the following summations. The Slavic languages present different root sequences for roots with the sonorants р and л, also known as liquids (пла́вные): TOROT (East Slavic), TROT and TRAT (West and South Slavic). Other Indo-European languages (notably Lithuanian and Germanic) present the sequence: TORT. For this reason TORT is considered the older form, TOROT and TROT are innovations in Slavic.

If TOROT forms are normal for Russian, why do TROT or TRAT variants also occur in Russian? Speakers of Old Russian were likely influenced by the language used in religious settings, Church Slavic. Church Slavic derives from Old Church Slavic, a South Slavic language identified as старославя́нский by Russian writers. Church Slavic, like other Slavic languages did not undergo full voicing, and is the source of the second form in pairs such as го́род and -град, хо́лод and -хлад in Russian. These forms are borrowings into Russian. They are not considered unusual by modern speakers of Russian, just as most speakers of modern English don't think about the historical source of words such as beef, mirror, or cemetery (all from French), even though in most dialects "English" words co-occur with these: cow, looking glass, graveyard.

The comparison of words with the sequence TOROT in Russian with corresponding words in other languages provides information about the sequence of sounds in earlier variants of these words, and explains why Russian has dual forms such as го́род and -град. This comparison shows there is a consistent relationship between Russian and other Indo-European languages and, most importantly, as we shall see in Chapter 8 "Stress," it provides the background upon which other facts regarding the modern language may be elucidated.

4.4 Other ancient letters

Two variations of Slavic were spoken in the area of present-day European Russia and Ukraine at the end of the first millenium A.D.

The commonly used language was Old Russian (древнеру́сский язы́к), written in the Cyrillic alphabet. It was descended from a language spoken even earlier, Common Slavic (общеславя́нский язы́к). The second variation in use was employed in services in the Orthodox Church. This language, which had many resemblances to Old Russian, was Church Slavic (церко̀внославя́нский), also a descendent from Common Slavic. Clerics have left a fairly sizable corpus of manuscripts written in Church Slavic. Fewer writings from this early period remain from nonreligious sources. The following selection was written in Church Slavic (Russian recension, i.e., East Slavic dialect of Church Slavic) during the eleventh century A.D. It is from the so-called Turov Gospel.

(1) Въ врѣмѧ оно въниде ісъ въ каперънаоумъ въ градъ галилейскъ и бѣ оучѧ въ сѫботы и оужасахѫ сѧ оученициего ꙗко съ властиѭ бѣ слово его. (Лукъ IV,31-32)

In this selection the word ісоусъ "Jesus" is abbreviated to ісъ. Some words are recognizable (Въ, оно, градъ, и, слово, etc.), even if they are encumbered with jers. Other words look familiar (врѣмѧ, его). And other words in this selection are unfamiliar to most educated speakers of Russian (оужасахѫ, for example).

*A What letters in this text are not used in modern Russian? What letters does modern Russian use in their place?

*B What is the modern equivalent for the following? Use context to help determine grammatical category, or look it up in a Russian Bible.

1. врѣмѧ	6. оужасахѫ сѧ
2. въниде	7. оученици
3. градъ	8. его
4. бѣ оучѧ	9. ꙗко
5. сѫботы	10. бѣ

The selection given above is harder to understand than later texts, such as Наши предки, because it differs more radically from modern Russian. In addition to different letters such as оу and ѫ, both of which are replaced by modern у, we are faced with a different set of grammatical endings and a few completely different words. Still, the text provides some important clues to our questions regarding sound alternations in modern Russian. Recall that some consonants are soft before back vowels [y], [o], and [a]. Why? Russian also has a mutation of the type [г] ~ [з] as in друг - друзья́. Why? A spelling rule in Russian contradicts the idea of assimilation; it states that ы, a back vowel, is never written or pronounced after the back consonants к, г, х; instead we write the front vowel и. Why? Older writings such as the Turov Gospel provide clues to these questions.

4.4.1 Ancient Vowels

Recall that paired consonants in the modern language may be hard or soft before the back vowels o and a or y. This makes little sense physiologically because only front vowels are candidates for the kind of assimilation that brings about consonant softening (see section 2.1). For instances of soft consonants before o, we have already seen that this o has its source in the front vowel e which shifts to o under stress and before a hard consonant (мёд [м'от] < Old Russian мэдъ).

The excerpt from the Turov Gospel given in section 4.4 helps us see a similar origin for soft consonants before a. Consider the second word from that selection. It equates to the modern Russian вре́мя. This word is interesting because in the modern language it has a soft consonant followed by a back vowel, namely мя, phonetically: [вр'эм'ъ]. Note the letter in the Old Russian manuscript is not я, but some other letter. The letter that usually represents я in Old Russian is ꙗ as in the word ꙗко "because." We conjecture that the letter ѧ represents a different sound, perhaps a front vowel of some kind, since soft consonants precede it. It appears that ѧ was a type of front vowel capable of causing palatalization which later shifted to a. A glance at the modern Russian inflectional paradigm of this word gives us a clue to how ѧ was pronounced.

(2)   Nom   вре́мя
           Gen   вре́мени
           Prep   вре́мени
           Dat   вре́мени
           Inst   вре́менем
           etc.

A suffix (-ен-) is present in all the case forms of this word, except the nom sg. We can say that the "ending" of the nom sg -я alternates with the suffix -ен- throughout the rest of the paradigm. What is particularly interesting about this suffix is that it contains a front vowel. It turns out that ѧ is an [э] with a nasal sound attached to it, like the [ę] in modern French and Polish. We will transcribe this sound as [э̨], a nasalized front vowel. We can be sure we are dealing with a front vowel since consonants directly preceding it were and are soft. Ultimately nasal vowels were lost in Russian and [э̨] shifted to [a]. These changes are given in chronological order in (3). The postulated Common Slavic is a reconstructed form, based on information about the word present in the modern language. Compare this form with the way it was written in Old and Modern Russian.

(2)

Common Slavic (postulated):	в р э м э н
Consonants became soft before front vowels:	в р'э м'э н
Vowels became nasalized before a nasal cons:	в р'э м'э̨н
Nasal consonants were lost after nasal vowels:	в р'э м'э̨
Old Russian (attested):	врэмѧ
Nasal vowels became oral vowels:	в р'э м'a
Unstressed vowels are reduced (akan'e):	в р'э м'ъ
Modern Russian (attested):	время

The sequence of sounds -эн in the Common Slavic form was not just made up to account for the soft quality of the preceding consonant. It can be seen elsewhere in the paradigm of this word, for example, gen sg времени. This "internal reconstruction" of Russian, that is, reconstructing what an earlier stage of Russian might have been like by comparing modern word alternations also suggests that an earlier form of the nom sg of врéмя was времен.

The presence of ѣ in врѣ́мѧ corresponds to modern e̲ as expected. The letter ѣ also occurs in (1) in the word бѣ "was." This is one of the letters with which words end in this excerpt. Other letters are: о̲, ъ̲, є̲ (=modern e̲), и̲, ы̲, ѧ̲ (all vowels). Another letter which falls at the end of several words is ж̲. This letter also occurs in the word сж̲боты "Sabbath," modern Russian суббóта. Church Slavic ж̲ was a back nasal vowel which ultimately became у̲ in modern Russian. Compare, for example, the following words in Church Slavic and in Modern Russian.

(3)	**Church Slavic**	**Modern Russian**
	грж̲бъ	груб
	дж̲бъ	дуб
	живж̲тъ	живу́т
	властиж̲	влáстью

We can be sure that the vowel ж̲, however, was a back vowel, since there is no evidence of consonant softening before it. It is transcribed as [ǫ]. The reason some consonants are soft before the back vowel [у], (i.e., богиню [бʌг'и́н'у]), lies elsewhere.

4.5 Velar palatalizations

The excerpt we have been studying points to a shift in velars, one that probably occurred very early in the Common Slavic period. Consider the following clause from the excerpt given above:

(1) и оужасахж сѧ оученици кего
    "and his disciples were astonished"

This clause differs greatly from Modern Russian (MR). The conjugated verb, оужасахж, contains a recognizable root: оужас (cf. MR у́жас), and the following vowel resembles the MR verbal suffix seen in verbs like читáть, but the ending -хж- does not resemble any modern Russian ending. This verb is the precursor of MR ужасáться "to be horrified, terrified." It seems likely that this was not the meaning of this verb in Church Slavic. Instead the word meant something like "to be astonished, amazed." The ways and direction of shifts in meanings (semantic shifts) constitute an entire discipline in linguistics: semasiology (семасиология). We will limit ourselves here to noticing that this is one important and as yet poorly understood way in which languages change over time.

The third word in (1) is the reflexive particle, where we see the letter ѧ for MR я, i.e., сѧ = ся. The fourth word has the letter ц in the nom pl form. The nom sg is оученикъ. This presents us with the phonological alternation к - ц, one that also can be seen in modern Russian in some word pairs. Modern Russian has ученик - ученики; there is no change of к to ц before the ending -и. But consider the following word pairs:

(2) кабáк tavern   кабáцкий coarse, vulgar
    казáк Cossack   казáцкий Cossack (adj.)
    восклúкнуть exclaim   восклицáть exclaim (imperf.)
    óблик face, appearance   лицó face

(3) княгúня princess   князь prince
    друг friend   друзья́ friends

These and other words like those illustrated in (2) and (3) suggest that earlier there existed the phonological alternations: к ~ ц, г ~ з. The shift of к and г to ц and з, respectively, occurred twice in the development of Russian. The first instance, usually called "the progressive velar palatalization," took place during the early Common Slavic period. Up to now we have only seen regressive phonological shifts, where the second of two adjacent sounds affects the first. In the progressive velar palatalization, a preceding front high full vowel (и) affected a following velar (к or г), if the back vowel a, o, or y immediately followed. This shift occurred even if a sonorant intervened between the front vowel and the velar. Thus from kuningas "king" and atikas "dad" developed Old Russian кънязь and отьць. The final front jers suggest that the з and ц were soft.

This progressive velar palatalization was followed by the first regressive velar palatalization (discussion below), which in turn was followed by the second regressive velar palatalization. The results of the second regressive velar palatalization are similar to those of the progressive palatalization, that is к → ц and г → з. In addition, in this sound change х

→ <u>c</u>. This shift occurred before front vowels, including ѣ, thus отрокъ "boy" is <u>отроцѣ</u> in the loc sg and ржка "arm" is <u>ржцѣ</u> loc sg. The attested form <u>оучѐници</u> is due to the second regressive velar palatalization.

In the modern language these alternations do not occur in paradigms (except in друг-друзья́). Scholars understandably have suggested that the shift of, for instance, <u>ц</u> back to <u>к</u> in MR was due to analogical pressures (see section 3.3): the final stem consonant found in most cases in the paradigm, including the nom, has been generalized throughout: now учени́к - об ученике́, ученики́. A few traces remain of the old system: друг - друзья́, for instance. However, recent investigations suggest that the shift of <u>к</u> → <u>ц</u> never took place in northern Russia and that words that do exhibit this alternation were borrowed from southern and southwest (Church Slavic) sources. Varied influences have produced a mosaic in the modern language, where these kinds of mutations occur sporadically. It is important, however, to see that <u>ц</u> has its origins in <u>к</u>, and thus occasionally appears to alternate with <u>ч</u>, even when no <u>к</u> is found in related words: оте́ц - оте́ческий.

The first regressive velar palatalization is responsible for the <u>ч</u> in оте́ческий. Also a very early shift, this sound change may be expressed:

(4) к, г, х → ч', ж', ш' / _____ v̈

The rule in (4) states that velars became palatalized before a front vowel. Another way of saying this is that velars became fronted before front vowels. The final result of becoming fronted was that they mutated to hushers. Note that the loc sg and nom pl endings at this time in the history of Russian were <u>-ай</u> and <u>-ы</u>, respectively. Later these endings shifted to ѣ and <u>и</u> subsequently resulting in the second regressive velar palatalization.

It is not simply by chance that the sounds involved in this rule are all velars. Instead we observe a general tendency for back (hard) consonants to be fronted before front vowels.

We can collapse the rule in (4) into a more general rule which states that velars became palatals before front vowels:

(5) K → Č' / _____ v̈

where K = a velar, Č' = a husher, according to the distribution given in (4)

It is natural that these palatals were originally pronounced soft since they resulted from a fronting process. We know that subsequently ш, ж, and ц underwent velarization or hardening (отвердéние). Janovich presents evidence for when this took place in Russian.

Шипящие [ш], [ж], [ч], [ц] были в древнерусском языкеисконно мягкими, так как они возникли в результате палатализации заднеязычных еще в праславянскую эпоху. В дальнейшем в истории языка происходит их отвердение (за исключением[ч'], которое, однако, развивалось не дновременно и не одинаково в восточнославянских диалектах).

Наиболее достоверные свидетельства отвердения шипящих-- написание [ы] вместо [и] после шипящих. Такие написания отмечаютсяс XIV в.: слышышь (1300г.) жывите, держыть (до 1389 г.). Следы отвердения [ц'] появляются позднее, с конца XV в.: улыцы (1499 г.), концы (XVI в.). О позднем отвердении [ц'] свидетельствует и тот факт, что перед этим согласным звук [э] не изменился в [о]. (p. 108)

*A In what way does the pronunciation of modern hushers and ц differ from the way they were pronounced a thousand years ago?

Since all hushers were soft it would have been redundant to write ю and я after them, since these letters show that preceding paired consonants are soft. For that reason we find y and a written after hushers. After the hushers became hard any possible reason for writing ю and я after them disappeared.

One of the front vowels which triggered the first regressive palatalization of velars was ѣ. We saw earlier that in most instances this sound shifted to e: OR снѣгъ → MR снег. However, when following a husher (brought about by the first regressive palatalization) ѣ shifted to a: Proto-Slavic крикѣти → кричѣти → MR кричáть. This shift partially accounts for the distribution of MR a following hushers (слýшать, отличáть, звучáть, etc.) when there is no evidence of earlier front vowel plus nasal, as in начáть / начнý, which implies начати.

The hushers ч and щ still retain their palatalized characteristics in MR but the other hushers have hardened; when they are pronounced, the body of the tongue is raised toward the roof of the mouth, rather than toward the ridge in the front of the mouth. V. V. Ivanov places the hardening of [ш] and [ж] at the end of the fourteenth century and the hardening of [ц] during the sixteenth century. Ivanov (p. 223) points out, however:

> Известно, что [ц'] сохранился больше, чем [ш'] и [ж'] и в современных говорах: мягкие [ш] и [ж] известны теперь островкамив Кировской, Ивановской и других областях, а [ц'] есть в значительной части северновеликорусских диалектов.

We represent the hardening of the hushers and ц in the literary language by the rules given in (6).

(6)   Č' → Č / _____   where Č' = [ш'] [ж']
        ц' → ц / _____

In the modern language ы is not written after hushers because all hushers were once soft and followed by и. After ш and ж became hard, any и following these consonants assimilated the hard (nonfront) feature from the hushers, i.e., began to be pronounced [ы], but the spelling did not change. The spelling *has* changed, however, after ц: у́лицы.

The sound changes illustrated by the rules in (5) and (6) account for the distribution of stem final hushers in 2nd conj verbs. Verbs with the suffix -и (ть) do not have roots that end in a velar, instead they end in a husher. In other words, there are no verbs in Russian that end: -гить, -кить, or -хить. Instead they end in -жить, -чить, and -шить. Compare the related words in (7):

(7) легко́   but   облегчи́ть   to facilitate
    су́хо   осуши́ть   to dry
    дру́г   дружи́ть   to be friends

This is not to say that velars do not occur before front vowels. Due to analogy they occur before front vowels that are endings: кни́ги, о подру́ге, руки́, пеки́. Due to a sound change that was occurring in the twelfth century (see section 4.5.1), the sound [ы] was no longer possible after the velars; it was replaced by the sound [и]: хи́трый, Ки́ев, ги́бкий. Thus, velars may also occur before [и] in roots. With the exception of endings discussed above, the combination of <u>velar</u> + <u>e</u>: <u>ге</u>, <u>ке</u>, <u>хе</u> occurs only in borrowed words. Finally, many words have been borrowed into Russian since the rules in (3) ceased being active. These borrowings do not reflect the palatalization of velars: гимн, кит, хи́мия.

4.5.1 A Spelling Rule Problem

We may now ask why Modern Russian does not allow the spelling of <u>ы</u> after velars, requiring <u>и</u> instead: столы́ but пироги́, руки́.

In Old Russian just the opposite distribution can be observed in regard to the velars: only <u>кы</u>, <u>гы</u>, and <u>хы</u> were written (and presumably so pronounced). In the twelfth century, however, documents begin to show that the velars were undergoing some change; they are palatalized and followed by <u>и</u>. A. A. Shakhmatov suggests that at one time <u>к,г,х</u> were rounded consonants: the lips were rounded when they were pronounced (as is <u>o</u> in Modern Russian). According to Shakhmatov, when this rounding was lost the velars began to be pronounced closer to the front of the mouth. He suggests the following sequence of events (where K° = any rounded velar, and K' = any soft velar):

(1)   K°ы   →   K'ы   →   K'и

Janovich adduces the following dialectal evidence in support of Shakhmatov's explanation. Some dialects have soft velars followed by back vowels similar to the second stage in (1): dialectal чайкю, Ольгя. Janovich also points to some dialects where the "fronting" process was extreme, where velars became dentals! Compare:

(2) рути, ноди, Овдотья (cf. Russian руки́, ноги́, Евдоки́я)

Shakhmatov proposed that these consonants became soft when followed by <u>ы</u> to compensate for the loss of roundness. The soft consonants in turn provided an environment for the <u>ы</u> to shift to <u>и</u>. Evidence for this course of events is based on dialects which have palatalized velars followed by back vowels. Here is some more dialectal evidence of the same sort. Final soft velars occur in the Archangel subdialect:

(3) [л'эк'] (imperative of лечь, compare with CSR ляг [л'ак])
[поп'ир'э́к'] = CSR поперёк

In addition, some northern dialects still have the original sequence:

(4) [кы]слый, мо[гы]ла, кня[гы]ня, [хы]трый

Finally, there are some dialects which have soft velars before back vowels:

(5) пекёшь, текёшь, Нинкя, надолгё, четвергя, сверхю

These forms show that softening of velars occurs in dialects in environments where softening does not occur in CSR. Thus, there are traces of soft velars before back vowels. This provides some support to Shakhmatov's claim that velars may at one time have been soft and followed by back vowels. There is no evidence, however, of rounded velars in any of the dialects.

The shift of [ы] to [и] after velars may also been explained on the basis of analogy. In the eleventh century Russian did not have the sequence sound к'и, though other consonants freely combined with и: т'и, н'и, etc. Instead, it had ц'и according to the second regressive palatalization of velars. It may be suggested that when the analogical shift of ц to к took place paradigms (ученици → ученики) the palatalized quality of the affricate may have been retained in connection with the stop (ц' → к'). The presence of [к'и] in paradigms may then have served as an analogical basis for the shift of all instances of кы to ки.

*A The shift of [к°ы] to [к'ы] to [к'и] contradicts assimilation. Given historically original [кы] as expressed in manuscripts, another sequence of events might be proposed for the development of modern [к'и], namely:

[кы] → [ки] → [к'и]

This sequence illustrates dissimilation, the process of making contiguous sounds dissimilar in order to pronounce them clearer. Is this sequence any less reasonable than the one proposed by Shakhmatov? Does the dialectal data given above support or challenge this sequence?

*B Why do soft consonants occur before the vowels и and э in Modern Russian? Data: место [м'э́стъ], миг [м'ик]

*C Why do soft "paired" consonants occur before back vowels о and а in MR? Data: пёк [п'ок], пять [п'ат']

*D Why does Russian have the spelling rule that states к, г, х are never followed by ы, only by и? Data: но́ги [но́г'и], за́сухи [за́сух'и]

4.6 The Loc2, Gen2 and Infinitive Endings

Leftovers from an earlier grammatical system sometimes turn up in the modern language as exceptional forms. For example, students of Russian must generally memorize the monosyllabic masc nouns that take the so-called locative- or prep-2 ending -у́ (в снегу́, в лесу́, etc.). In older texts we see these endings with this group of nouns in cases other than the prep.

In the Novgorod region Old Russian was written on birch bark and many of these writings were preserved and have been excavated. The following birch bark text was written toward the end of the twelfth century in Novgorod.

(1) отъ гостаты къ васильви • ѥже ми отьць даалъ
и роди съдаали а то за нимь а нынѣ вода
новоую женоу а мънѣ не въдастъ ничьто
же избивъ роукы поустилъ же ма а иноую
поалъ доеди добрѣ сътвора •

It may be translated

(2) From Gost'ata to Vasilii. That which father gave me and
relatives gave is now his. But taking a new wife he will
give me nothing. Having divorced me, he has driven
me out and another (wife) he has taken. Please come.

While this text contains much that is distinct from modern Russian, it is closer to modern Russian than the text in the Turov gospel in several ways. It contains only one nasal vowel letter (ѧ, which corresponds to modern Russian я), and it is "misspelled" in all words here except поѧлъ, which did have a nasal vowel (cf. взял - возьму). The nasal vowel letter ѫ of Common Slavic has already become the back vowel [y], written оу: compare Church Slavic рѫка with Old Russian роука. This letter contains the same set of jers seen in the earlier two texts. The birch bark writing also contains verbal forms which are similar to the modern language: past tense съдаали "(they have) given," past verbal adverb: избивъ "having broken." The noun endings are also familiar, with the exception of the dat ending after the preposition къ: васильви. Modern Russian has the dat ending for this word -ю: к Василию. The ending -ови, which we see in (1) in its soft variant -ьви, comes from another set of endings, which for the most part do not exist in the modern language. This set of endings occurred with the so-called "u-stem nouns," predominantly monosyllabic masc nouns. These nouns are referred to as u-stem nouns, because the set of endings they took featured the vowel sound u in one form or another, including ъ, оу, ъви, ове, овъ.

It is possible to make two kinds of [в] sounds. In the first, the upper teeth touch the lower lips to create a point of articulation resulting in the fricative [ф] and [в]. The other pronunciation of [в] is called bilabial. In it, both lips barely touch each other so that a fricative is created. The bilabial variant was the one used at a very early stage in the development of Russian. Having been derived from Indo-European [u] or [w], it is considered a sonorant, and like other sonorants does not trigger voicing assimilation. The close connection between Indo-European [u] and Slavic [в] can also be seen in a set of endings that occurred in Common Slavic. Traces of these noun endings are still evident in the modern language.

Recall that ъ was a very reduced "uh" sound. Here is a full Old Russian paradigm of a u-stem noun, сынъ "son".

(3)

	sg	dual	pl
nom	сынъ	сыны	сынове
acc	сынъ	сыны	сыны
gen	сыноу	сыновоу	сыновъ
loc	сыноу	сыновоу	сынъхъ
dat	сынови	сынъма	сынъмъ
ins	сынъмъ	сынъма	сынъми
voc	сыноу	сыны	сынове

As indicated in (3), Old Russian had in addition to sg and pl another number, namely dual, used when discussing two of a certain item. There was also another case, the vocative (voc) case, used when addressing a person or thing. Nearly all the endings associated with u-stem nouns in Old Russian have been lost in Modern Russian. The word мёд "honey," an old u-stem noun, is now declined like стол. Some of the u-stem endings, however, have survived, and one has become the normal gen pl ending for masc nouns ending in a hard consonant: -ов. Other survivors of the u-stem paradigm can still be found in certain masc nouns in the prep sg and in the gen sg cases. Consider, for example, the forms in (4) and (5):

(4) о мёде "about honey"   в меду́ "in the honey"
    о снéге "about snow"   в снегу́ "in the snow"
    о лéсе "about the forest"   в лесу́ "in the forest"
    о бéреге "about the shore"   на берегу́ "on the shore"

While the spelling is slightly different (Old Russian -оу, modern Russian -у), the endings seen in the right-hand column of (4), the so-called locative-2 ending, is a leftover from the older u-stem paradigm.

(5) без дóма "without a house"   и́з дому "from the house"
    без лéса "without a forest" и́з лесу "from the forest"
    без гóлода "without hunger" с гóлоду "from hunger"

The gen-2 endings on the words in the right column in (5) also show traces of the old u-stem paradigm. This ending has become generalized to form a separate partitive ending for some masc nouns: cáхару, чáю, шоколáду "some sugar, some tea, some chocolate," etc. The dat sg ending -ови, or as it appears in the text in (1) -ьви is no longer used in the modern language. It has been replaced by the normal masc declensional dative ending -у.

Older written texts provide direct evidence of language change. While they may not be perfect representations of how a language was spoken they do provide many clues to earlier stages of a given language and are useful in explaining variations in the modern language.

*A Consider the following data from Modern Russian. If the loc-2 forms represent a remnant of another case, what can we conclude about the endings of that case? Compare also with the loc-2 in masc nouns.

Nom	Prep	Locative-2
связь	о свя́зи	в связи́
глубь	о глу́би	в глуби́
даль	о да́ли	в дали́
кровь	о кро́ви	в крови́
пыль	о пы́ли	в пыли́

*B There are three infinitive endings in Russian: -ть, -чь, -ти. The following illustrates these three forms. What do the words in each column have in common that distinguishes them from the words in each of the other two columns? If you are stumped, consider the conjugation of the words in each column.

(1) читáть	(2) печь	(3) нести́
говори́ть	течь	вести́
гуля́ть	мочь	идти́
смотре́ть	бере́чь	ползти́
лезть	сечь	спасти́

*C Here are several infinitives from Ukrainian, a close relative of Russian: читати, гуляти, лізти, пекти, текти, могти, берегти, сікти, нести, вести.

1. The data in *C suggest that at an earlier time Russian may have had only one infinitive ending, namely _____.

2. What sound events must have occurred in Russian to arrive at the other infinitive endings found in Modern Russian?

3. Referring to your answer in 1, write out the Common Slavic form of the following three infinitives: говори́ть, мочь, нести́. Show the step-by- step sound developments for each. Refer to your answer in 2 and to the chart given in (2) in 4.4.1 for the word вре́мя.

4.7 Why э → о?

In section 3.2 we discussed the phonological alternation of [э] to [о], as found in word pairs such as сме́рть ~ мёртвый. There it was suggested that [э] shifts to [о] when under stress and before a hard consonant. In section 3.3 it was pointed out that there exist many exceptions to this rule, such as снег, нет, ме́сто. Section 4.2.1 explains why these exceptions exist, namely that historically these words contained the so-called yat' (ѣ) which shifted to [э] after the change of [э] to [о] was complete. Having made a lengthy excursus into other past phenomena we are now ready to examine in detail *why* [э] shifted to [о].

Recall that vowels can be charted according to where they are produced in the mouth (see section 1.3). Thus [и] is a high front vowel (the tongue is raised and approaches the front ridge of the mouth) and can be charted so with the other vowels:

(1)

	front	**back**
high	и	ы у
mid	э	о
low		а

By using binary markings (+ and - for each articulatory feature) we can define each sound in terms of all its features, as shown in (2).

(2)

	[и]
high	+
low	-
front	+
rounded	-

The feature "rounded" refers to whether or not the lips are rounded in pronunciation of the vowel. It is needed to distinguish between [ы] and [y]. We don't need to make reference to the feature "mid" because any sound that is [+high] is automatically [-mid] and any sound that is [+low] is automatically [-mid]. Mid vowels, namely [э] and [о] are characterized as being neither high nor low, i.e., [-high, -low]. Similarly, we don't need to use the term "back" because a sound that is [+front] is by default [-back] and one that is [-front] is automatically [+back].

We can now assign binary markings to all the vowels in (1):

(3)

	и	э	y	ы	o	a
high	+	-	+	+	-	-
low	-	-	-	-	-	+
front	+	+	-	-	-	-
rounded	-	-	+	-	+	-

Notice that all vowels are characterized differently. The only difference between [ы] and [y] is that the former is marked [-rounded]. The feature [+rounded] is generally only used to distinguish between these two sounds. It is redundant for [о], since no other vowel is characterized [-high, -low, -front].

*A What vowel(s) is/are:

1. [+high, +front]
2. [-high, -low]
3. [+front, +low]

4. [-high, +front]
5. [-high, -front]
6. [+rounded]

We can define the sound [и] by means of all the features given above, but notice that some features are redundant. There is only one vowel that is [+high, +front], namely [и]. The other features ([-low] [-rounded]) are redundant for [и].

*B Without using the feature [rounded], what are the nonredundant (defining) features for:

    1. [ə]   2. [o]

*C In which feature do [ə] and [o] differ?

By using binary features phonological rules may be written that express actual changes in articulation, rather than just rewriting letters. For example, if we wanted to say that the sound [ə] shifts to [o] in some environment, we could write

    (4) ə → o / ___ X   (where X = some environment)

But what is really happening in this sound change is a change in articulation, namely:

    (5) [-high, +front] → [-front] / _____ X

The rule in (5) states that any vowel that is [-high, +front] (there is only one, namely [ə]) shifts to a vowel that is [-high, -front] in the environment of X. That is to say, the only change is the feature [+front] shifts to [-front]. Any sound that is [-high] and [+front] becomes [-front]. Schematically, with salient features in italics:

(6)	[ə]	→	[o]	
	-high		*-high*	(no change)
	-low		-low	(no change)
	+front		*-front*	(changed by rule)
	-round		+round	(automatic)

Remember that the feature [+rounded] is redundant (automatic) for [o], so it need not be specified in the rule. So the actual shift of e̱ to o̱ really involves just one change, namely the shift of [+front] to [-front]. Why should such a shift occur?

In modern standard Russian [o] occurs after a soft consonant only when under stress. This sound is written ё. Example: мёд "honey." The sound [o], written as o occurs only after hard consonants. Example: мод "styles" (gen pl). We know that at an earlier time words with modern ё had е. Then a sound change occurred, namely [ə] shifted to [o]. Why did it? We have also see that in okan'e dialects the shift of e to o also occurs when not under stress. Why weren't Old Russians satisfied with saying [ə] when it was under stress before a hard consonant? Why did they start pronouncing it as [o]?

Usually when a language changes, it does so to become simpler. It rarely changes to become more complex, although complications in one part of the language may arise due to a simplification in another part. Change often first shows up in nonliterary usage, in dialects or in colloquial or rapid speech. One kind of simplification is assimilation. This means that one sound takes on a feature of a contiguous sound. This makes the two sounds easier to pronounce together. At the time of the shift of [ə] to [o] weak jers had already been lost and strong jers had already become fully voiced. Here is the inventory of vowel sounds in Russian at the time of the change of [ə] to [o].

(7)

	front	back
high	и	ы у
mid	ѣ	
	э	о
low		а

When a sound change occurs it often involves the shift of only one feature, such as mid to low (as in modern Russian [o] to reduced [a] (akan'e) in unstressed position).

*D What feature shift occurred when [ə] shifted to [o]?

*E Why should this shift occur? (Hint: Recall that in the pronunciation of hard consonants, the body of the tongue is [-high, -front] in comparison to soft counterparts.)

4.8 The Origin of Fleeting Vowels

Why does Russian have fleeting vowels? In section 4.2.2 we discussed the loss of reduced vowels (jers) at the end of a word during an earlier period. In the text given in 4.2 jers can be found written only at word final position. In the text in 4.4, jers also occur within words. The fate of the jers in Russian has been called one of the most significant events in the history of the language.

As stated earlier, Old Russian contained two reduced vowels, the front jer, a front reduced vowel (ерь) and a back jer, a back reduced vowel (ер). The jers were found in endings (nom sg masc -ъ, gen pl fem -ъ, for example). However, in addition to occurring at word final position, jers were also found within words and in prefixes. Compare the words in the left column of (1), taken from a dictionary of Old Russian, with their modern equivalents.

(1)	**Old Russian**	**Modern Russian**
	отьць	оте́ц
	чьто	что
	лодъка	ло́дка
	лодъкъ	ло́док (gen pl)
	мъхъ	мох
	пришьлъ	пришёл
	дьнь	день
	вьсь	весь
	съмыслъ	смысл
	съмьртъ	смерть
	жьньць	жнец

As expected, the MR equivalents have lost the final jer. (In the case of весь, день and смерть, a trace of the jer remains--the softness of the word final consonant.) Note, however, that many of the other jers have become full vowels in modern Russian: ъ has become о and ь has become е. In addition, these vowels appear to be unstable, that is, these vowels are fleeting vowels in these words, as illustrated by the nom sg лóдка, gen pl лóд̲о̲к.

Fleeting vowels originated as jers. Some jers developed into full vowels, others were dropped.

*A From the data in (1) identify the environment in which jers became full vowels and the environment in which they were lost.

Jers in Old Russian can be categorized into two major groups: jers in strong position or jers in weak position. Strong jers were those followed by a weak jer in the <u>next</u> syllable. Jers in weak position, or weak jers, came at the end of the word or were followed by a strong jer or a regular vowel in the <u>next</u> syllable. Examples (w=weak, s=strong):

(2) р ъ т ъ   с ъ м ь р т ь   с ъ м ы с л ъ

    s w   w s w   w   w

    2 1   3 2 1   1   1

In (2) jers have been numbered starting at the end of the word and working backward. Odd numbered jers are weak and subsequently disappear from the word. Even numbered jers are strong and become full vowels. Notice that if a full vowel intervenes (e.g., ы̲ in съмыслъ) the counting starts over.

The gen pl form of fem and neut nouns often contains a fleeting vowel because one of the gen pl fem and neut endings was -ъ. If the stem ended in a syllable with a jer, then this gen pl ending caused the stem jer to become strong:

(3) **Nom Sg**   **Gen Pl**

поговóрка (= O.R. поговóръка)   поговóрок (= O.R. поговóр̲ъ̲к̲ъ̲)

                        w   s w

окнó (= O.R. окънó)   óкон (= O.R. óк̲ъ̲н̲ъ̲)

              w   s w

The ending -ъ was also used for nom sg masc nouns, the masc sg ending for the so-called "l participle" (modern Russian past tense), and for masc sg short form adjectives:

(4) **nom sg masc**: сон (= O.R. съ̱нъ̱)
    gen sg: сна (= O.R. съна)

    l-part. masc: пришёл (=O.R. пришьлъ̱)
    l-part. fem: пришла́ (= O.R. пришьла)

    short form masc: бо́лен (= O.R. больнъ̱)
    short form fem: больна́ (= O.R. больна)

The words in (4) show how a jer could be weak in one case form of the word (when followed by a full vowel) and could be strong in another case form of the word (when followed by a jer).

*B Write how you think the Old Russian form may have been written for the following words. Note that each but the last has a "fleeting vowel."

1. ло́дка (gen pl ло́док)   5. оте́ц (gen sg. отца́)
2. де́вушка (gen pl де́вушек) 6. окно́ (gen pl. о́кон)
3. совсе́м   7. дово́лен (fem. дово́льна)
4. сон (gen sg сна)   8. лес (gen sg. леса)

4.9 Dialectal Pronunciation of Velars and Hushers

The pronunciation of г̲ is one of the most telling dialectal features of spoken Russian. In the northern and central regions, г̲ is pronounced [г] in all positions except word final position where devoicing occurs. In southern regions г̲ is pronounced as a voiced [x] (transcribed [γ]) which devoices to [x] at word final position. Examples:

(1) Northern/Central   **Southern**

    [г]о́род   [γ]о́род
    бе́[г]ает   бе́[γ]ает
    доро́[г]а   доро́[γ]а
    мно́[г]о   мно́[γ]о
    [г]од   [γ]од
    тво́ро́[к]   творо́[x]

In CSR the gen sg adj ending -ого and the pronoun его are pronounced with a [в]: ста́рого [ста́ръвъ], сего́дня [с'иво́д'н'ъ], его́ [йиво́]. In Old Russian these were pronounced with a [г], and this pronunciation can still be heard in the speech of some very elderly Russians in the far north: никого́ [н'икого́] (with okan'e).

When Russians speaking the southern dialect moved into the central region in the thirteenth to fourteenth centuries they brought with them their pronunciation of г as [γ]. For unknown reasons this pronunciation was adopted by central Russian speakers--but it has been retained only in the gen sg and the pronoun "его́." Since the voiced fricative [γ] was not a sound in the speech of central Russians they substituted the sound that seemed closest, namely the voiced fricative [в]. This pronunciation in these words and in ecclesiastical words, which also reflect a southern influence, such as [γ]о́споди, бо[х] have become standard pronunciation in CSR.

V. V. Ivanov relates the following regarding Anna, Queen of France and daughter of Jaroslav the Wise:

Предполагают также, что о фрикативном образовании [г] на юге древней Руси XI в. свидетельствует подпись французской королевы Анны Ярославны. Дочь Ярослава Мудрого--Анна, вдова Генриха I, выросшая в Киеве, оставила свою подпись, сделанную кириллическими буквами, на одной из латинских грамот1063 г. Эта подпись состоит из двух слов: **ана ръина**, т.е. Anna regina--«Анна королева». В слове regina пропущена буква g, что, возможно, связано с чуждостью для Анны взрывного образования[g] латинского языка. Именно на этом основании и предполагают, что в XI в. в Киеве уже был [γ]. Однако это основание не может считаться достаточно веским, так как в написании **ръина** может отражаться старофранцузское произношение данного слова reine «королева».

The progressive palatalization of velars, the shift of к to ц, had an intermediate step of к → ц', still seen in a few northern dialects. These dialects also exhibit "soft" cokan'e

(1)	[ц']арь	ку́ри[ц']а	оте́[ц']
	до́[ц']ка	[ц']ай	пе[ц']

In some southern dialects one can find the pronunciation of ч and ц without their iniital stop, i.e. pronounced [ш'] and [c].

(2)   [c]арь   кури[c]а   оте[c]
         до[ш']ка   [ш']ай   пе[ш']

In the map below areas in white indicate the standard pronunciation of ч̲ (soft) and ц̲ (hard). It also indicates <u>cokan'e</u> (both ц̲ and ч̲ are pronounced as ц̲), and <u>chokan'e</u> ([ч'] for ц̲ and ч̲) and other pronunciations of ч and ц.

(3)

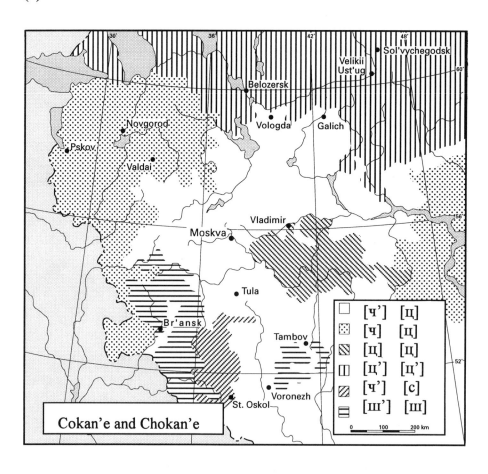

*A Given the distribution of sounds in (4), how might you expect to hear the words девица, цепь, час, меч, and учитель pronounced in the areas of the following towns:

1) Москва́, 2) Ста́рый Оско́л, 3) Брянск, 4) Валда́й, 5) Псков, 6) Вели́кий Устюг

As you can see from the map in (4), cokan'e is a fairly widespread phenomenon in Russia. What would cause ч to shift to ц in just these areas? Janovich writes:

А. А. Шахматов связывал это явление с воздействием польских говоров, которым свойственно неразличение свистящих и шипящих. Однако эта гипотеза обнаруживает несостоятельность в связи с тем, что цоканье проявляется и в территориально удаленных от западнославянских языков говорах.

Современныеисследователи поддерживают мнение о том, что цоканье обусловлено иноязычным влиянием со стороны финских племен. Дело в том, что в ряде финских языков или вообще отсутствуют переднеязычные глухие аффрикаты (как ц), или известна только одна аффриката.

*B How do linguists referred to by Janovich explain cokan'e?

Another explanation for cokan'e is that Russian had no pairs of words that were distinguished soley by ч and ц (i.e., no word pairs such as час and *цас). It therefore simplifies the grammar to have just one affricate, either ч or ц, as found in these dialects.

4.10 Review

In order to understand why certain phenomena occur in modern Russian we have resorted to a brief excursus into its history. We found that many irregularities in the modern language resulted from historical sound changes (for instance, врэмэн → врема → вре́мя). Spelling rules find their origin in historical sound shifts (for instance, и is written after ш and ж because the latter were once soft. We can see that the shift of stresssed e̲ to o̲ before hard consonants was a simple case of assimilation, with e̲ assimilating the [-front] feature of hard consonants. Through comparison with other related languages and dialects we learn how certain Russian letters, which are no longer written, might have been pronounced. The historical development of reduced vowels, the jers, is the basis for modern fleeting vowels. The sound changes discussed in this chapter are outlined in (1).

(1)

Sound Change	Description	Sect
K → Ц' / v̈ __ a,y,o	progressive velar palatalization	4.5
K → Ч' / __ v̈	1st regressive velar palat.	4.5
C → C' / __ v̈	consonant softening	2.1
v̈N → A / __ #, C	nasalization of vowels	4.4.1
A → a /everywhere	loss of nasal vowels	4.4.1
K → Ц' / __ и, ѣ	2nd regressive velar palat.	4.5
TORT → TOROT	full vocalization	4.3
Č' → Č /everywhere	hardening of ж, ш, ц	4.5
ъ, ь → o, э / strong	vocalization of jers	4.8
ъ, ь → Ø / weak	loss of weak jers	4.8
э́ → ó / __ C (hard)	velarization of э́	4.7
ѣ → a / Č __	loss of diphthong/long vowel	4.5
ѣ → э / elsewhere	loss of dipthtong/long vowel	4.2.1

Understanding the reasons behind irregularities in the modern language may help students remember them more easily. But an understanding of the principles of sound change can also help uncover simplicity and order in the declensional and conjugational systems, the topics of Chapters Five and Six.

*A Here are a few words as they might have been pronounced in Proto-Slavic. How is each pronounced today? What sound changes can you recognize in the historical development of these words?

1. рътъ	6. къто
2. лодъка	7. лѣсъ
3. нэсъ	8. дьнь
4. накьнти	9. пришьла
5. улика	10. пришьлъ

SECTION 2: MORPHOLOGY AND STRESS

CHAPTER 5. The Inflectional Morphology of Nouns and Adjectives

5.1 Introduction

In the first three chapters of this text we discussed the sounds and sound alternations of Russian. Chapter 4 presented historical information to explain why certain sound alternations occur. Having carefully listed all the sounds that can be heard in Russian we may ask how these sounds are put together to make words. It appears that this is done in a consistent way because, as in other languages, a given object or action is normally named by the same series of sounds. For example, the object that grows out of the ground, has branches and leaves or needles is named repeatedly by the same sequence of sounds, namely [д'э́р'ьвъ], or as Russians write it: де́рево. Whenever Russians want to refer to this object they consistently use this sequence of sounds. This suggests that the method for associating one set of sounds with the object which they represent remains constant. The sounds used may be arbitrary, but *the same sounds are used repeatedly to express the same item.*

Upon closer examination, however, we find that the one sequence of sounds that expresses the concept "tree" isn't always precisely the same. There are many slight variations, often involving the final sound of the word. For example in some instances the word is pronounced [д'э́р'ьвъ], in others it is pronounced [д'э́р'ьв'ь] or [д'э́р'ьвъм]. In still others there is a slight change in the first two vowels of the word in addition to a change in the final sounds: [д'ир'э́в'йъм'и]. Non-natives find that whenever we use any of these sequences of sounds for "tree" we are more or less understood, although sometimes, judging by the looks we get, we may not have used exactly the right variation. Some of the changes in the sequences of sounds are always the same. For example, when stress falls on an [э] sound it always sounds the same: [э]. When stress falls elsewhere in the word, then this sound becomes either [ь] or [и]. Since Russians do this consistently and rarely make a mistake, it may be assumed that they know something, or have made a generalization, about these sounds. "Generalization" is another word for "rule." They know a rule. What other rules do they know? Particularly for our purposes, what rules do they know about how words change? Russians seem to have little difficulty in forming the gen pl while to many non-natives the gen pl of nouns seems to be one chaotic hodgepodge of endings. Who can remember, for example, that the gen pl of ружьё is ру́жей? Why does the soft sign drop out? Where does the i-kratkoe come from?

As non-natives learning Russian we are taught endings which fasten onto words. These endings are important because they indicate the subject of the sentence, direct or indirect object, etc. As each week goes by more and more endings are added to the list. There get to be so many endings that some students actually begin to be confused. Teachers pass out lists to help students memorize endings. These lists are invariably based on how the word looks when written--not simply on how it is pronounced. In addition to the numerous endings for nouns, there is a whole slate of endings for adjectives and verbs.

One learns, for example, that there are two ways to write the sound [o] in Russian: o̲ and ё̲. It is rarely mentioned that the difference between the two is that the former occurs after a hard consonant and the latter after a soft consonant, a vowel or ъ/ь. One also learns that there are four nom sg neut endings (not counting the irregular -мя nouns!): o̲, ё̲, e̲, and и̲е, and how these endings change for each of the twelve possible cases (sg and pl). Good students (or, good memorizers) are able to commit these endings to memory and are able to place them correctly on tests. Some can add them correctly to words when speaking. Until the endings are an automatic part of a student's speech, however, the question of which ending to use continues to be a thorny one, hindering confidence and communicative ability.

"Inflectional morphology" (морфоло́гия or more specifically словоизмене́ние) refers to the processes of adding endings to word stems. "Inflectional" means "having to do with endings." "Morphology" means "putting together." Inflectional morphology shows the underlying order and simplicity (as far as these exist) in the system of endings used in Russian, and is therefore a valuable topic of study for students of Russian. The main goal, however, of inflectional morphology has little to do with the manifold language-learning problems associated with Russian. Instead, it is an attempt at understanding the generalizations associated with sequences of sounds and the grammatical information attached to them. It's a little like the early physicians who opened up the first bodies in the Middle Ages just to find out the composition of the body. Through inflectional morphology we open up words to discover their composition. It is not obvious where this knowledge will lead. Showing students that a simpler system underlies the one they have memorized is a start. Most

Russians are not conscious that the four nom sg neut endings discussed above are actually variations of just one ending, but they know it intuitively. In short, we are leaving the language-learning arena now and moving into a strictly scientific endeavor. What are the basic endings in Russian?

5.2 The spelling rule o → e

An important spelling rule of Russian pertains to the hushers, or palatal consonants: ш, ч, щ, ж and to the sound ц. The spelling rule involving these letters is often expressed:

(1) Unstressed o is written e after hushers and ц.

We may represent this spelling rule:

(2) Spelling Rule: o → e / $\begin{cases} \text{Č} \_\_\_ \\ \text{ц} \_\_\_ \end{cases}$

The instr sg masc noun endings provide good examples of the operation of this spelling rule:

(3) журна́лом   карандашо́м   отцо́м
    but   ду́шем   ме́сяцем

Beginning students of Russian often forget this rule or confuse it with other rules. This is understandable; the rule seems totally capricious.

The historical antecedents of this rule go back to ProtoSlavic, a dialect of Indo-European spoken around the fifth century A.D. According to Shevelov and Meillet original o lost its labial qualities after j and other palatalized consonants, resulting in o - e variations seen, e.g., in Common Slavic instr sg рабомъ - мжжемъ. The shift of o to e after palatalized consonants may have been a result of assimilation, or simply the loss of labialization of o after a nonlabial (palatalized) consonant, resulting in the fronting of o. If this shift was due to progressive assimilation then it must have occurred at a time when the hushers were still soft. Khaburgaev (p. 114) remarks,

В ряде слов и форм славянский [е] (short e) = є появился на
местеиндоевропейского *о (short o) в положении после мягких
согласных. Так, например, в им. п. ед. ч. ср. р. в соответствии
с [о] после твердых согласных в положении после мягких
согласныхнаходим [е]: сєло, окъно, ново и т.д. (ср. русск. село,
окно, новое), но после мягких согласных: полє, морє, синє и
т.д. (ср. русск. поле, море, синее и т.д.)

This suggests that the spelling rule mentioned above is incomplete. As
discussed in section 3.4.2 the spelling rule should read:

(3) Unstressed o is written as e after hushers, ц, and after any
    soft consonant.

The rule in (3), together with akan'e and ikan'e, reveal much about the
seemingly exceptional inflectional forms in Russian.

5.3 Masc nouns

You know the basic facts about Russian nouns--gender, case, and
number. In addition, you have learned spelling rules that account for
differences in some endings, eg., inst sg masc столóм but мéсяцем. We
have seen that this rule really is just the tip of a much more general rule,
one whose operation will uncover much of the orderliness of the
inflectional system.

In a sense, this rule allows us to limit the number of endings that occur
in the noun system. Thus, instead of saying there are two inst sg masc
endings -ом and -ем, we can say there is only one, namely -ом, and that
-ем occurs orthographically because of the generalization given in (3).
Phonologically the ending -ем represents both [ъм] and [ьм]; see table 2
in section 2.11.

The masc sg endings are given in (1). In this chart there are three sets
of endings. Each set corresponds to the three traditional nom sg masc
endings: # (consonant), ь (soft sign), and й.

(1) nom	#	ь	й
acc	↕	↕	↕
gen	а	я	я
prep	е	е	е
dat	у	ю	ю
inst	ом	ем	ем

The chart in (1) has eighteen endings. Inflectional morphology lets us see in these endings five <u>basic</u> endings. The other 13 endings are simply variants of the five basic endings.

The alphabet is what makes us think there are 18 endings in (1). First we can eliminate the acc endings as being identical to the nom and gen endings.

*A 1. When are the acc sg masc endings identical to the nom sg masc endings?

   2. When are the acc sg masc endings identical to the gen sg masc endings?

Phonetic transcriptions of words illustrating the three nom sg endings are given in (2).

(2) стол [стол]   кисéль [к'ис'э́л']   музéй [муз'э́й]

While each of these words ends in a different sound, the sounds are all consonants. We can say that there are not three nom sg masc endings, but one, namely the "zero ending," or lack of an overt ending. In morphological transcription "zero ending" is transcribed as a ∅. The term ± ∅ implies that there is no vocalic ending. In Russian the absence of an overt vocalic ending, however, counts as a case marker. The words in (2) may be written in morphological transcription (enclosed in curly brackets with endings following the plus sign (+)):

(3) {стол + ∅}   {кис'э́л' + ∅}   {муз'э́й + ∅}

*B How does the ending for the masc nom sg differ from all other case endings for masc nouns given in (1)?

Note the following differences between types of transcription.

Phonetic: Uses square brackets and shows exactly how a word is pronounced. One letter equals one sound. No word or suffix boundaries are employed: [к'ис'э́л'].

Phonological: Uses pound signs for word boundaries and shows the underlying form of a word upon which phonological rules operate to produce the phonetic transcription: #кисэ́л'#.

Morphological: Uses curly brackets. This is like a phonological representation except that morpheme boundaries are used to separate the word stem from endings {...+...} and from prefixes {..=...}: {кисэл' + ∅}.

In (3) the phonological transcription of the nom sg forms <u>стол</u> and <u>музе́й</u> are readily derived from the morphological transcription. The soft sign written at the end of <u>кисе́ль</u> is represented in the morphological transcription as a soft <u>л'</u> followed by a zero ending.

The vowel in morphological combinations of <u>й + VOWEL</u> and <u>SOFT CONSONANT + VOWEL</u> is written by a single letter in normal Russian orthography according to the following chart (where т' stands for any soft consonant other than й):

(4)

Й + VOWEL		SOFT CONSONANT + VOWEL	
morphological	orth.	morphological	orth.
й + а́ →	я	т' + а́ →	тя
й + о́ →	ё	т' + о́ →	тё
й + у́ →	ю	т' + у́ →	тю
й + э́ →	е	т' + э́ →	те
й + и́ →	и	т' + и́ →	ти
й + ы́ →	и	т' + ы́ →	ти

The table in (4) is for stressed vowels. Unstressed vowels show the same results, except for unstressed o̲, as illustrated in (5). In this table т̲' stands for any soft consonant and̲ for hushers and ц̲ (all were once soft).

(5)

| й + о → | е | т' + о → | те |

The orthographic device illustrated in (4) accounts for the "differences" in the gen sg masc endings, where there is only one ending, namely -a̲. Examples are in morphological transcription:

(6) morphological: {стол + á}   {кисэл' + á}   {музэ́й+ а}

orthographic: столá   киселя́   музе́я

*C Which vowel letters are used in the <u>morphological</u> transcription of endings? Which vowel letters are never used in the <u>morphological</u> transcription of endings?

*D What are the prep, dat, and inst masc sg endings in morphological transcription? Give an example of each case and ending as well as the orthographic representation of each as in (6) above.

*E Write out the following in morphological transcription:

1. бе́рег   3. мудрецо́м   5. зу́бе
2. ле́бедь   4. ле́бедю   6. му́жем

5.4 Declension vs. Gender

A traditional designation for the endings given in (1) in 5.3 is "sg masc." Another designation is "1st declension (decl) class" (пе́рвое склоне́ние). Reference to declension class (the set of endings given above) is more precise than "masc" because there are masc nouns that take different endings, such as де́душка and доми́шко. These latter belong to the 2nd and 4th decl classes respectively. Thus 2nd decl nouns end in the vowel {+a} in the nom sg (see below), 3rd decl nouns are fem nouns ending in zero in the nom sg, for example, ночь, and neut nouns in -мя. Finally, 4th decl nouns take the vowel {+o} in the nom sg.

Two other endings not discussed above are the so-called "loc-2" and "gen-2" endings. The loc-2 ending {-ý} is used only in certain monosyllabic 1st decl nouns after the prepositions в or на: в лесу́, на мосту́. The gen-2 ending is {-y}, normally used with certain 1st decl nouns indicating a partitive notion: ча́ю, шокола́ду, са́хару; "some tea," etc. See section 4.6 for the historical background of these endings.

5.5 Second Declension

Fem sg noun endings (or better, 2nd decl sg endings--not all nouns taking these endings are fem) are listed in their orthographic form in (1).

(1) nom   а   я   ия
    acc   у   ю   ию
    gen   ы   и   ии
    prep   е   е   ии
    dat   е   е   ии
    inst   ой   ей   ией

Examples for the nom case are given in (2):

(2) газе́та   неде́ля   аллерги́я

*A 1. Using the generalizations in 5.3 regarding the morphological source of я, tell what the <u>one</u> 2nd decl nom sg ending is.
   2. Write out the three words in (2) in morphological transcription.
   3. Write out the basic ending for the acc, the basic ending for the gen, and the basic ending for the inst case.
   4. Which two cases in 2nd decl have identical endings?

Note that the prep and dat case ending appears to have two forms: -<u>е</u> and -<u>и</u> (as in в а́рмии). This is a case of ikan'e actually being reflected in the orthography, since the historical -<u>е</u> ending is not normally stressed in words ending in -<u>ия</u>, the spelling reflects ikan'e: -<u>ии</u> (from {ий+э}). We will consider this ending the same as that for the gen {ии} and dat {ии} in the modern language, since the two words that do have stressed -ия́ in the nom have prep sg -ий.

Second decl nouns whose stems end in a velar (к, г, х) or a husher (ч, ш, щ, ж) are subject to the spelling rule which states that ы is never written after velars or hushers; rather write и. (See section 4.5 and 4.5.1 for the historical reasons for this rule.) The morphological transcription of the gen sg ко́шки is: {ко́ш/к + ы}.

The inst sg of неде́ля (неде́лей) is morphologically transcribed: {нэдэ́л' + ой}. The spelling rule regarding the writing of о after soft consonants (see section 5.2) reflects akan'e and ikan'e of the unstressed о. Schematically:

(3) morphological	{нэдэ́л' + ой}	Ending is -ой
phonological	#нэдэ́л'ой#	
C → C'	н'эд'э́л'ой	
akan'e	н'эд'э́л'ъй	
ikan'e	н'ид'э́л'ьй	
phonetic	[н'ид'э́л'ьй]	spelled: неде́лей

When stress falls on the ending of a 2nd decl noun whose stem ends in a soft consonant, then akan'e and ikan'e do not apply and neither does the spelling rule. In these forms the о of the instr ending {+ ой} can be heard:

(4) morphological	{з'эмл' + о́й}
orthographic	землёй

In землёй, the letter ё is used in place of о to show the preceding consonant is soft.

*B Write in normal orthography the following words given in morphological transcription and tell which case ending is being used.

1. {дол'и́н + а}	4. {ба́шн' + а}	7. {стат'й + а́}
2. {дол'и́н + ой}	5. {ба́шн' + ой}	8. {стат'й + о́й}
3. {дол'и́н + ы}	6. {ба́шн' + ы}	9. {стат'й + ы́}

*C Write the following words in morphological transcription.

1. ли́ния (nom sg)	7. пе́сня (nom sg)
2. ли́нии (gen sg)	8. пе́сни (gen sg)
3. кни́ги (gen sg)	9. пе́сней (inst sg)
4. семью́ (acc sg)	10. пе́сню (acc sg)
5. ступнёй (inst sg)	11. ку́хне (dat sg)
6. ли́нией (inst sg)	12. ли́нию (acc sg)

5.6 Third and Fourth Declensions

The 3rd decl class is composed mostly of fem nouns that end in a soft sign (stems end in a soft consonant followed by the zero ending), e.g., дверь, ло́шадь, ночь. Also belonging to this class is the single masc noun путь "path" and the ten neut nouns ending -мя (время, имя, etc.). Here are the endings in both orthographic and morphological representation, as illustrated by the paradigm of ло́шадь.

(1) nom	ло́шадь	{+ Ø}
acc	ло́шадь	{+ Ø}
gen	ло́шади	{+ и}
prp	ло́шади	{+ и}
dat	ло́шади	{+ и}
inst	ло́шадью	{+ йу}

Since all stems in the 3rd decl end in a soft consonant it is possible to posit the basic ending for the gen sg as {+ ы}, which would duly change to -и by orthographic spelling rule. We have chosen basic {+ и}, however, because this is the historically correct ending (see section 4.6) and it shows the syncretism (identity) of endings in this declension (gen=prp=dat).

In Russian the combination {C + й} (consonant plus i-kratkoe) is always followed by a vowel. This combination is represented in the orthography as a consonant followed by a hard sign or soft sign, followed by a vowel. Thus, while a soft sign at the end of a word shows the softness of the preceding consonant, when it is followed by a vowel letter, then it implies the presence of i-kratkoe. In the paradigm in (1), the soft sign disappears in the gen, prep, dat. In these cases the vowel letter и shows preceding softness. The soft sign reappears in the instr both to indicate preceding softness and to indicate the presence of an i-kratkoe.

The 4th decl is made up primarily of neut nouns. Here are the endings as they occur orthographically.

(2) nom	о	е	ие
acc	о	е	ие
gen	а	я	ия
prp	е	е	ии
dat	у	ю	ию
ins	ом	ем	ием

Examples of words that take these endings are: ме́сто, по́ле, and зда́ние. It is clear that except for the nom/acc endings and prp ending for nouns in -ие, the basic endings of the 4th decl are identical to those of the 1st decl: gen {-а}, prep {-е}, dat {-у}, inst {-ом}, and 2nd decl (prp {-и} following ий). Let us look more closely at the nom/acc endings.

The orthography makes it appear that we are dealing with three endings: -о, -е, and -ие. But if we appeal to akan'e, ikan'e and the о → е spelling rule we can see that there is only one nom sg neut ending, namely {+ о}. When not stressed and following a soft consonant or a husher, this ending shifts to -е:

(3)

morphological	{мэ́ст + о}	{по́л' + о}	{зда́ний+о}
phonological	#мэ́сто#	#по́л'о#	#зда́нийо#
C → C'	м'э́сто	--	зда́н'ийо
akan'e	м'э́стъ	по́л'ъ	зда́н'ийъ
ikan'e	--	по́л'ь	зда́н'ийь
orthographic	ме́сто	по́ле	зда́ние

We can confirm the assertion that {-о} is the basic ending for the neut nom with stems ending in a soft consonant by finding a word with final stress, such as питьё. In this word we hear the [o] sound of the ending.

*A Write the following words in morphological transcription.

1. питьё
2. дочь
3. пло́щади
4. свинья́
5. ко́мнаты
6. дверь

7. любо́вь
8. питья́
9. ло́шадью
10. го́ре
11. учи́телю
12. две́рью

*B Words whose nom sg form ends in a soft sign followed by -я̲, е̲, or -ё̲ (eg., судья́, статья́, сва́тья, бельё, чиха́нье) have an {й} in the stem: {суд'й + а́}, for example. Why doesn't the soft sign drop off in any case of the sg?

*C Why does the soft sign disappear in all but the nom and inst sg of 3rd decl nouns? Why does the soft sign suddenly reappear in the inst sg of 3rd decl nouns (ло́шадью)?

*D Nouns ending in -и̲е -и̲я in the nom conceal an {-й} as in чте́ние {чте́ний + о}. In what case in the pl of these nouns does the {-й} become visible in the normal orthography?

5.7 Plural Endings

Differences between declension classes in the pl occur only in the nom and gen cases. In the pl, the acc is the same as the nom for inanimate nouns for all declensions. For animate nouns, the acc pl matches the gen pl for all declensions. The prep case ending is {+ax} for all declensions, dat has {+ам} and inst takes {+ами} for all declensions. Differences between declensions occur partly in the nom pl and to the greatest degree in the gen pl. We will discuss the nom pl first.

As indicated in (1), 1st, 2nd, and 3rd decl nom pl ending is either ы or и. For 1st and 2nd decl, we can say that the basic morphological ending is {ы}, and that the spelling rule which specifies that -ы is written -и after hushers, velars, and soft consonants is responsible for the orthographic alternations seen in these two declensions.

(1)

	1st Decl	2nd Decl	3rd Decl	4th Decl
nom sg:	Ø ь й	а я ия	ь	о е ие
nom pl	ы и и	ы и ии	и	а я ия
acc pl	↑	↑	↑	↑
gen pl	ов ей ев	Ø ь ий	ей	Ø ей ий
prep pl	ах ях ях	ах ях иях	ях	ах ях иях
dat pl	ам ям ям	ам ям иям	ям	ам ям иям
inst pl	ами ями ями	ами ями иями	ями	ами ями иями

For 3rd decl we could similarly posit morphological {+ы} and refer to the same spelling rule to render orthogrpahic -и for nom pl. However this declension has the ending -и throughout the sg, and since the historical nom pl ending -и for this declension never alternates with -ы, we choose the former as the morphological ending.

The one basic nom pl ending for 4th decl nouns is {+a}.

(2)

1st Decl	{завóд + ы}	{мучи́тэл' +ы⌐	{гэрóй + ы}
orthographic	завóды	мучи́тели	герóи
2nd Decl	{кáрт + ы}	{нэдэ́л' + ы}	{áрмий + ы}
orthographic	кáрты	недéли	áрмии
3rd Decl	{тэтрáд' + ы}		
orthographic	тетрáди		

*A Write in morphological transcription the following nom pl 4th decl nouns:

1. существá   2. моря́   3. здáния

We now turn to the gen pl. According to the chart in (1) there are ten regular gen pl orthographic endings, with three being repeated (∅, ей, and ий). How many basic endings do these ten orthographic endings represent? In the 1st decl we may combine the endings -ов and -ев into one ending, -ов, since by the о → е spelling rule the latter can be derived from the former as in: {музэ́й + ов}. The combination of й and unstressed о yields orthographic е: музе́ев. That means first decl takes only two gen pl endings, {+ов} and {+эй}.

The gen pl 2nd decl ending -∅, -ь, and the gen pl 4th decl ending -∅ are clearly the same ending, namely {+∅}, as in:

(3) {р'эк + ∅}   {нэдэ́л' + ∅}   {мэ́ст + ∅}

Words ending in -ия and -ие in the nom sg (2nd and 4th decls) have identical gen pl endings, namely, -ий. We saw earlier that nouns with these endings in the nom sg all have a stem final й. This stem final й can be seen in the gen pl. Thus, the gen pl ending for these words is also zero.

(4) **nom sg**   а́рмия {а́рмий + а}   зда́ние {зда́ний + о}
     gen pl   а́рмий {а́рмий + ∅}   зда́ний {зда́ний + ∅}

We have identified three basic gen pl endings: {+ов}, {+эй}, and {+∅}. There are no others. All orthographic gen pl endings are derived from these three.

The gen pl ending {эй} occurs in three types of nouns. First, it normally occurs in nouns that both take the zero ending in the nom sg <u>and</u> end in a soft consonant:

(5) <u>1st decl</u>   <u>3rd decl</u>
    nom sg учи́тель {учи́тэл' + ∅}   ло́шадь {ло́шад' + ∅}
    gen pl учителе́й {учитэл' + э́й} лошаде́й {лошад' + э́й}

Thus if the nom sg ends in a soft consonant orthographically, the gen pl ending will be -ей.

The gen pl ending -эй also occurs in 1st decl nouns whose stems end in a husher. This is understandable from a historical perspective; all hushers were once soft consonants. Although ж and ш have become hard consonants in modern Russian, 1st decl nouns ending in these sounds as well as other hushers (щ ч) continue to take the gen pl ending {-эй}:

(6) **nom sg** врач {врач + ∅}   това́рищ {това́риш'ш' + ∅}
   gen pl враче́й {врач + эй́}   това́рищей {това́риш'ш' + эй}

Notice that this ending is normal for stems that end in a husher <u>only among</u> <u>1st and 3rd decl nouns</u>. Among 2nd and 4th decl nouns whose stem ends in a husher, the vowel of the nom sg is usually replaced by the zero ending: 2nd decl: ту́ча - туч, ро́ща - рощ, 4th decl: чудо́вище - чудо́вищ.

Finally, the gen pl ending {-эй} also occurs in two 4th decl nouns whose stems end in a soft consonant but that also take a vocalic ending in the nom sg: мо́ре - море́й, по́ле - поле́й, eg., {мор' + эй́}. (Note that there are no 4th decl nouns that take the zero ending in the nom sg.)

A rule of thumb is that if the nom sg ends in a soft consonant or husher, the gen pl ending is -<u>ей</u>. First decl nouns whose stems end in a hard consonant or -<u>й</u> take {+ов}, and all others take {+∅} for the gen pl. Note that words such as статья́ - gen pl стате́й do not take the ending -<u>ей</u>, instead, they take the zero ending in the gen pl, as do nearly all nouns that take a vocalic ending in the nom sg (with the exception of мо́ре and по́ле, which take gen pl -ей):

(7) кни́га   →   gen pl   книг
   неде́ля   →   gen pl   неде́ль
   а́рмия   →   gen pl   а́рмий
   ме́сто   →   gen pl   мест

This is also true for nouns ending in -<u>ья</u> and -<u>ье</u> in the nom sg; the <u>е</u> seen in the gen pl sequence -<u>ей</u> is a fleeting vowel:

(8) статья́   {стат'/й + а́}   →   стате́й   {стат'эй́ +∅}
   семья́   {сэм'/й + а́}   →   семе́й   {сэм'эй́+∅}
   ружьё   {руж/й + о́}   →   ру́жей   {ру́жэй+∅}

The following chart summarizes the rules for the gen pl endings. They assume the operation of the phonological rules, including the rule о → е. These rules define the notion "regular" for gen pl. Deviations from these rules, and there are several, are "irregular."

(9)

GENITIVE PLURAL MORPHOLOGICAL ENDINGS BY DECLENSION CLASS			
STEM FINAL CONS	1st Decl	2nd & 4th Decl	3rd Decl
hard or й →	-ов	-∅	
husher →	-эй	-∅	-эй
soft →	-эй	-∅/-эй	-эй

In (9) the gen pl ending is {-∅} for 2nd decl nouns and {-эй} for по́ле and мо́ре (4th decl).

The information in (9) can be simply stated in the following set of ordered rules:

(10)   a. The nom sg ends in a vowel → the gen pl is {+∅} (except по́ле, мо́ре)

         b. The nom sg ends in a hard consonant or <u>й</u> → the gen pl is {+ов}

         c. The nom sg ends in a soft consonant → the gen pl is {+эй}

*B Is the gen pl form in the following regular or irregular?

1. стол - столо́в
2. паде́ж - падеже́й
3. край - краёв
4. сапо́г - сапо́г
5. ёж - еже́й
6. боги́ня - боги́нь
7. мело́дия - мело́дий
8. змея́ - зме́й
9. свеча́ - свече́й
10. жили́ще - жили́щ
11. не́мец - не́мцев
12. армяни́н - армя́н
13. во́лос - воло́с
14. солда́т - солда́т
15. ку́хня - ку́хонь
16. страна́ - стран
17. семья́ - семе́й
18. ханжа́ - ханже́й
19. ноздря́ - ноздре́й
20. донесе́ние - донесе́ний

*C Why is the first cell under "3rd Decl" in (9) empty?

*D What is the gen pl of the following words?

1. коро́ва	11. крите́рий	21. у́лица
2. звук	12. душ	22. ту́ча
3. ры́нок	13. ситуа́ция	23. боло́то
4. стиль	14. слова́рь	24. ружьё
5. слу́чай	15. бога́ч	25. вещество́
6. гроза́	16. ста́туя	26. музе́й
7. ли́чность	17. ава́рия	27. очеви́дец
8. достиже́ние	18. я́мочка	28. лы́жа
9. деви́ца	19. войско́	29. свинья́
10. иде́я	20. о́вощ	30. ключ

*E Write the gen pl forms of the following in morphological transcription.

1. заво́д	3. мора́ль	5. душа́
2. геро́й	4. да́ча	6. кре́сло

5.7 Adjectival endings

Short form adjectives decline for gender only in the sg and these three endings oppose one pl ending:

(1) sg: бога́т бога́та бога́то   pl: бога́ты

The orthographic endings are identical to those of the 1st (for masc), 2nd (for fem), and 4th decl (for neut) nom sg noun endings ({+ Ø} {+ a} {+o}) and to the pl ending {+ ы} (for pl). Agreement (согласова́ние) between short form adjective and noun takes place on the basis of the identity of endings: Окаса́на была́ бога́та. The nom of long form adjectives also shows this correspondence:

(2)	**masc**	**fem**	**neut**	**pl**
hard	ый (о́й)	ая	ое	ые
soft	ий	яя	ее	ие

All these endings have one sound in common: [й]. It is the final sound in the masc endings, and occurs in the middle of the fem, neut and pl endings. The endings in (2) have the following morphological form:

(3)　　masc:　{+ ы + й + Ø}
　　　　　　　{+ ó + й + Ø}
　　　　fem:　{+ а + й + а}
　　　　neut:　{+ о + й + о}
　　　　pl:　　{+ ы + й + э}

The i-kratkoe seen in the endings in (3) is a remnant of an Indo-European pronoun which had the meaning "the one which." In Russian it is used to form long form adjectives, which differ from the short form in that the former impart a notion of a permanent quality to the noun. By adding the pronoun -й̆- to the short form ending and then adding the short form ending again at the end of the sequence, the long form ending is obtained in the nom sg (all genders--see (2)), and acc sg fem. This can be seen most clearly in the fem and neut forms, where {+ а + й + а} = -ая, and where {+ о + й + о} = -ое. The masc form historically had jers: {+ ъ + i + ь} (where the i-kratkoe was written as i). The combination ъ + i + ь yields modern о + й which was retained under stress but by akan'e shifted to [ъй] ("jer-i" is the name of the letter ы), represented and now pronounced -ый, though the pronunciation [ъй] is still widespread.

The initial segment of the nom pl ending -ые is the short form pl ending, the second segment is the pronoun, and the final segment is the pronoun ending, as seen in forms such as те, and все., and in dialects: онé (= они). The acc sg fem adjectival ending also betrays the presence of the pronoun й: {+ у + й + у} = -ую. With the exception of the vowel in the inst sg masc/neut where the adjective has the vowel ы, rather than е (тем), and in the pl forms which show the result of analogy of the short form pl ending, the rest of the long form paradigm copies the pronominal paradigm:

(4)	**masc/neut**	**fem**	**pl**
gen	ого	ой	ых
prp	ом	ой	ых
dat	ому	ой	ым
ins	ым	ой	ыми

Soft variations (nom sg masc -ий, fem -яя, neut -ее, etc.) are due to the spelling conventions discussed in 5.3. In these adjectives the stem ends in a palatalized consonant: {с'ин' + ы + й + Ø} → синий.

5.8 Comparative endings

The simple or synthetic comparative is normally formed by adding the ending {+эйэ} to the adjectival stem: новее {нов + эйэ}. Historically this suffix was much more complex, and the following variants were also used: {+эй}, {+йэ}, {+э}.

Adjectives ending in a velar (к, г, х) take the variant -э, with concomitant mutation of the velar: дорогой comparative: {дорог + э} → дороже, яркий {ярк + э} → ярче. In colloquial speech the last element of the suffix {+эйэ} is often dropped and the variant {+эй} is used: новей. For <u>some</u> adjectives whose stem ends in a dental or labial, however, just the first element of the suffix is lost and the variant {+йэ} is used. This results in a dental or labial consonant followed by -й, which yields mutation. Examples:

(1)   молодой   {молод + йэ}   →   моложе
       низкий   {низ + йэ}   →   ниже
       короткий {корот + йэ}   →   короче
       дешёвый   {дэшэв + йэ}   →   дешевле

The comparatives in (1) illustrate an important feature of Russian morphology, namely that when a dental or labial is followed by an i-kratkoe, the two sounds mutate into a husher or add an л, according to the following table.

(2)   тй   →   ч   as in   крутой / круче
       дй   →   ж   "   твёрдый / твёрже
       зй   →   ж   "   близкий / ближе
       сй   →   ш   "   высокий / выше
       стй   →   щ   "   чистый / чище
       вй   →   вл   as in   дешёвый / дешевле
       пй   →   пл   (does not occur in adjectives)
       бй   →   бл   (does not occur in adjectives)
       фй   →   фл   (does not occur in adjectives)

As the examples above show, the adjectival suffix {к} or {ок} is often dropped with the abbreviated comparative suffix. There are instances when it is retained, however: чёткий / чётче. In the following the {к} is truncated in the comparative, e.g., у́зкий → у́же.

(3) га́дкий   далёкий (да́льше)   глубо́кий (глу́бже)
    гла́дкий   бли́зкий   широ́кий (ши́ре)
    сла́дкий (сла́ще)   ни́зкий   высо́кий   (вы́ше)
    ре́дкий   у́зкий
    жи́дкий   то́нкий (то́ньше)

In other -кий adjectives the {к} is mutated to [ч]. Note most -кий adjectives form no comparative: ру́сский, у́мненький.

Only a few adjectives form the comparative by means of a variation of the suffix {-эйэ}. Only adjectives ending in a velar invariably form the comparative with the abbreviated suffix {-э}. And only for adjectives ending in a dental is {-йэ} widespread. By far the most productive comparative suffix is the full one, even for adjectives ending in labials: сла́бый - слабе́е, глу́пый - глупе́е.

5.9. Simplification of Endings in Dialects

5.9.1 Prep = Dat (= Gen?)

You may have noticed a similarity between many case endings. For example the acc sg 1st decl ending of inanimate nouns is the same as for the nom sg. The acc pl of animate nouns is the same as the gen pl. Endings which are exactly the same but fill different case, number, or declension slots are said to be syncretic (синкрети́ческие). Consider the prep and dat sg endings for 1st, 2nd, and 4th decl nouns given in (1).

(1)

	1st	2nd	4th
Prep	е	е	е
Dat	у	е	у

It is clear that the <u>same</u> ending is used for certain case slots, namely the dat ending for 1st and 4th decl and the prep ending for 1st, 2nd, and 4th decl which is also syncretic with the dat ending for 2nd decl nouns.

In some Russian dialects the gen sg ending for 2nd decl nouns is also -<u>e</u>, instead of -<u>ы</u>, particularly when preceded by the preposition <u>у</u>:

(2) у сестрé   у женé

Some researchers have suggested that the preposition <u>у</u> in these dialects takes the prep case ending instead of the gen. Data in dialects where the gen sg ending -<u>e</u> is found after prepositions such as от, óколо, and из imply that the gen sg 2nd decl ending is falling together, or is becoming syncretic, with the prep and dat sg ending (as already occurs in the adjectival forms):

(5) óколо   э́т<u>ой</u>   водé
    до   э́т<u>ой</u>   водé
    от   э́т<u>ой</u>   женé

This can also be seen in the Alaskan Old Believer dialect:

(6) у мáме, из Хóмерской больни́це

Avanesov and Orlova cite "у женé", "от сестрé", and even "нет сестрé" in a southern Russian dialect, whose isogloss extends nearly as far north as Moscow. The occurrence of this feature among the Alaskan Old Believers is puzzling because nearly all features in their dialect have affinities to <u>northern</u> Russian dialects.

*A In what other set of endings for nouns are the endings for gen, prep, and dat syncretic? What gender are these nouns?

5.9.2 Other inflectional curiosities

In the southeastern dialects the shift of the nom pl masc ending to -á is much wider than in CSR and in some areas has completely taken over:

(5)   шоферá, стаканá, месяцá, корня́

Many more individual dialectal variations occur involving inflectional endings in nouns, such as the generalization of the gen pl ending -<u>ов</u> for all genders: мест́ов, дел́ов, бол́отов, ́ягодов, ́банев. Another shift involves the loss of the instr pl ending -<u>ами</u> in favor of the dat pl ending -<u>ам</u>. The following map shows this and other case ending variations for instr pl throughout European Russia.

*A According to the map in (6), how might you hear "with books" in Novgorod, Voronezh, Sol'vychegodsk, and Vologda?

(6)

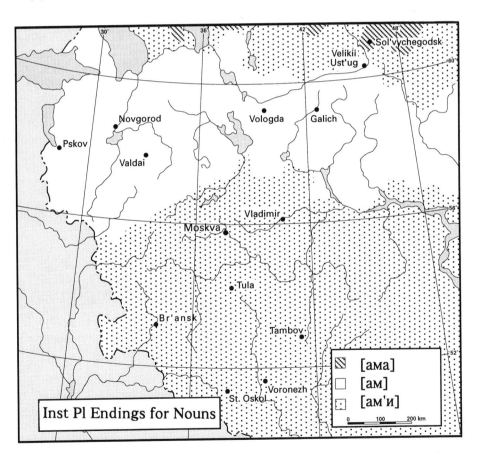

Inst Pl Endings for Nouns

⧄ [ама]
☐ [ам]
⊡ [ам'и]

5.10 Review

The four noun declensional paradigms (the 1st and 4th being nearly identical) represent a set of endings which are used to allow nouns to function differently in sentences, without respect to position in the sentence. These four declensional paradigms were inherited from Common Slavic and Indo-European which had additional declensional classes. Syncretic endings and principles of morphological transcription permit us to see single endings where the orthography leads us to believe there are several endings (e.g., nom sg 2nd decl: -а̲, -я̲, -и̲я̲ ⊢ {+a}).

Adjective declension is based on a system of agreement with noun endings, which in some cases, actually have the same vowel repeated in both adjectival ending and noun ending. Mutations in the comparative of adjectives occur when velars are followed by a front vowel or when dentals are followed by i-kratkoe and are thus due to assimilation.

In Chapter 6 we will see how the principles of morphology reveal the order in the sometimes confusing system of verbal conjugation.

Chapter 6: The Inflectional Morphology of Verbs

6.1 Present/Future Tense Endings

Unlike nouns which have four different sets of inflectional endings (1st and 4th declension being quite similar), verbal inflection is limited to two conjugations (conj) with only four irregular verbs that do not belong wholly to either conjugation. Much of the regularity of conjugation can be seen even on the orthographic level, which we will review in this section. Conjugation (спряжёние) refers to the set of endings a verb takes in the present tense. In this chapter "present tense" refers to conjugation in the present tense or simple (perfective) future. There are three variants of the 1st conj, illustrated as (a), (b) and (c) in (1):

(1) FIRST CONJUGATION ENDINGS

	(a)	(b)	(c)
я	читá + ю	ид + ý	стáн + у
ты	читá + ешь	ид + ёшь	стáн + ешь
он/а/о	читá + ет	ид + ёт	стáн + ет
мы	читá + ем	ид + ём	стáн + ем
вы	читá + ете	ид + ёте	стáн + ете
они	читá + ют	ид + ýт	стáн + ут

While the endings are similar in the three paradigms given above, certain variations are evident. Is one of the three sets of endings basic for 1st conj verbs and if so, what information is needed to predict the other two sets?

The paradigms in (1) exhibit three differences in inflection. The first sg ending of the verb in (a) differs from those in (b) and (c). In the former the ending is -ю, in the latter the ending is -у. It is clear that stress does not play a role in the choice of endings here, because the ending -ю may occur under stress (даю́) and the ending -у may occur without stress (стáну). For 1st conj verbs, the ending -у is used in the first sg when the verbal stem ends in a consonant, -ю when the stem ends in a vowel. The second variation evident in the endings in (1) can be seen in the endings for the ты, он/а/о, мы, and вы forms. In the verbs in (a) and (c) these endings have the vowel -е-, while this vowel becomes -ё- in (b). The presence of -ё- can be predicted on the basis of stress. When stress falls on these endings, then the vowel will be -ё-. When stress falls on the stem, then the vowel in the ending is -е-. These differences are all predictable on the basis of information that is part of the verb itself--the location of stress and the type of sound found at the end of the verbal stem.

*A The third difference in the endings in (1) is in the third person pl forms.
1. What are the differences?
2. How can you predict the differences?

So far we have seen that the differences in endings observed in 1st conj verbs are predictable. We have not yet provided reasons for considering one variation the basic or morphological form, from which we derive the other endings. Before doing so, we must consider several apparent exceptions to the principles regarding the distribution of the endings -ю/у and -ют/ут. There is a set of 1st conj verbs that do not have a vocalic stem in the present tense, that is, their stems do not have a vowel. They all end in -ить in the infinitive: бить, пить, лить, etc. Consider the я form for these verbs: я бью, я пью, я лью. These stems all end in a consonant: бь-, пь-, ль-. According to the generalization given above, the ending -у should follow a stem ending in a consonant. We can complicate matters by changing the generalization given above regarding these endings: the ending -ю occurs after vowels or after soft signs. This is not too bad, since we know that the soft sign historically was a vowel. We will see below that inflectional morphology allows us to eliminate this exception, but it is valid when dealing strictly on the orthographic level.

Another apparent exception to the generalization regarding the endings -ю/у and -ют/ут are verbs that have the form -ороть or -олоть in the infinitive. For example: боро́ться - я борю́сь. This is a clear violation to the statement that the ending after consonants is -у. Neither of these exceptional classes of verbs (1st conj verbs in -ить and -ороть/олоть verbs) will be exceptional when we look in more detail at the morphological structure of 1st conj verbs.

Second conj verbs have only two variations in the endings they use. They occur only in the я and они́ forms, as illustrated in (2).

(2) SECOND CONJUGATION ENDINGS

	(a)	(b)
я	говор + ю́	спеш + у́
ты	говор + и́шь	спеш + и́шь
он/а/о	говор + и́т	спеш + и́т
мы	говор + и́м	спеш + и́м
вы	говор + и́те	спеш + и́те
они	говор + я́т	спеш + а́т

The spelling rule which states that ю and я are written as y and a is sufficient to account for these variations on the orthographic level. (See section 4.8.7 for the historical antecedents of this spelling rule.)

6.2 First Conjugation: "Regular" vs. "Unusual"

The main structural difference between 1st and 2nd conj verbs is in the "theme" vowel of the ending. In 1st conj verbs, that vowel is either е or ё depending on stress. Second conj has и. Another difference is in the ending of the они́ form. 1st conj has -ют/-ут while 2nd conj has -ят/-ат. Except for these differences, however, both conjugations are quite similar. These similarities are given in (1):

(1)

я	vowel (written -y or -ю)
ты	vowel + шь
он/а/о	vowel + т
мы	vowel + м
вы	vowel + те
они	vowel + т

The consonant endings in (1) are person/number endings. They are the same for both conjugations. Furthermore, the vowel ending may be broken down into basic segments. Recall that orthographic -ю results from the morphological combination of soft consonant (including й) + y. With this in mind we can break down the я form of 1st conj verbs to determine its morphological components.

(2) читáю < {чит -а -й + у}
                    1   2   3   4

1 = root   3 = present tense marker
2 = verb-forming suffix   4 = ending

The same structure is present in the rest of the 1st conj verbal paradigm
with the addition, for most 1st conj verbs, of a "theme" vowel--a vowel
which separates the two consonants. In (3), the theme vowel is underlined.

(3) читáю   < {чит -á -й + у}[1]
     читáешь   < {чит -á -й -о + шь}
     читáет   < {чит -á -й -о + т}
     читáем   < {чит -á -й -о + м}
     читáете   < {чит -á -й -о + те}
     читáют   < {чит -á -й + ут}[2]

1. no theme vowel; у is not a consonant
2. no theme vowel; ут does not begin with a consonant

Note that the theme vowel in the morphological representation is {o},
and that this comes out as е in the orthography. This is in accordance with
the spelling rule o → e (following soft consonants). One may wonder if the
vowel is not {э} which shifts to [o] when under stress and before a hard
consonant. However, we have seen that the latter sound shift is no longer
operative in the modern language, cf., снег, нет, and therefore we cannot
propose that the theme vowel is {э}. We can be certain that the theme
vowel is an {o}, even though it appears written as е, because an [o] is
pronounced when stress falls on this segment: даёшь.

In modern Russian the first sg and third pl forms (e.g., читáю and
читáют) have no theme vowel. Its slot is filled by a zero marker: {чит +
á + й + Ø + у}. For the shift of Indo-European ом and онт to Common
Slavic ж and жт, ultimately to Russian у and ут, see section 4.3.1. These
endings go back to Indo-European -om and -o + nt (cf., я даМ, я еМ),
where o was the theme vowel.

The distribution of the theme vowel and endings in (3) defines 1st conj.
There are many 1st conj verbs which appear to be "irregular," but we will
see that in fact they are simply a little different, and not irregular at all.
Their idiosyncracies are predictable from the infinitive form.

Some 1st conj verbs are famous for shifting the verb-forming suffix in the present tense. Verbs in -овать are a good example:

(4) a. {совэ́т -ова + т'}   (совéтовать)
    b. {совэ́т -у -й -∅ + у}   (совéтую)
    c. {совэ́т -у -й -о + ш}   (совéтуешь)

(Note that the present tense marker {+й} is not present in the infinitive or past tense, and neither is the theme vowel which occurs only after a consonant.) The infinitive in (4a) shows the full verb-forming suffix -ова- as used in nonpresent forms, and (4b-c) show that this suffix shifts to -у- in present tense forms. While this verb is not as simple as, say, читáть, it is conjugated in exactly the same way, and, therefore, it is not irregular in conjugation. Russian speakers do have to remember that it does have a peculiarity in conjugation, namely, the suffix -ова shifts to -у when conjugated. Having made that permutation, the conjugation of these verbs is normal. We may say these kinds of verbs are predictably unpredictable. Their idiosyncratic behavior is completely predictable.

Verbs formed by means of the suffix -ну- are also predictably unpredictable. They lose the vowel of the suffix in conjugation; -ну- becomes -н-:

(5) a. отдох -ну + т'   (отдохнýть)
    b. отдох -н -∅ -∅ + у   (отдохнý)
    c. отдох -н -∅ -о + ш   (отдохнёшь)

In (5a) the full verbal suffix is used, while it is truncated to {н-} in conjugated form (5b-c). Note also that the present suffix -й- is not used in -нуть verbs, so its place is filled with a {∅} in (5b-c). You may be wondering how to account for the soft н in отдохнёшь. Unlike the front vowels, the theme vowel {o} is not a phonological source of softness, and we have already rejected the possibility of positing {э} as the theme vowel, which would have accounted for softness. The answer to this question entails a separate area of study within linguistics, and due to its complexity, we will put off its discussion until Chapter 7, which is devoted to answering this and similar questions.

Other predictably unpredictable (not irregular) verb types are illustrated in (6).

(6)

INFINITIVE IN	PRES STEM	EXAMPLE
-ере́ть	-р	стере́ть: сотру́ сотрёшь соту́т
-ы́ть	-о	закры́ть: закро́ю закро́ешь закро́ют
-дава́ть -става́ть	-а	встава́ть: встаю́ встаёшь встаю́т
monosyllabic -ать, -деть	-н/м	оде́ть: оде́ну оде́нешь оде́нут
-ить	-∅	лить: лью льёшь льёт

Similarly, verbs in -чь, -сть/зть, and -ти have predictable stems. Once the stem is arrived at, these verbs, as well as those given in (6), are conjugated regularly.

Finally, a small set of verbs have unpredictable present tense stems. These verbs have stems which simply must be memorized; жить with pres tense stem {жив-} is a good example. These are "unusual" verbs since they have unpredictable stems. Still they are conjugated normally according to the rules discussed earlier; thus they are not "irregular," at least as far as their conjugation is concerned.

*A When there is a consonant mutation in 1st conj verbs, it affects all persons and numbers (скажу́, ска́жешь, ска́жет, ска́жем, ска́жете, ска́жут - сказа́ть). Why? (Hint: see the discussion on the source of mutations in some comparatives, section 5.8.)

*B Write in <u>morphological</u> transcription:

1. рабо́таю	5. рабо́таешь	9. закажу́
2. зака́жешь	6. собира́ю	10. пьёт
3. начну́	7. сове́тую	11. сове́туешь
4. закро́ю	8. закро́ем	12. забу́дут

*C Some say the 2nd conj verb чтить is completely irregular. How is it conjugated? What should the first sg be? Why isn't it?

Note that the morphological approach solves the problem discussed earlier regarding ю/ют occuring after consonants (бью, борю́сь, пошлю́). This approach states that there is only one first sg ending, namely {+ y} as seen in all types of 1st and 2nd conj verbs:

(7)   чит   -á -й -∅ + ́y
        б'   -∅ -й -∅ + y
        бор   -∅ -й -∅ + ́y + c'
        посл   -∅ -й -∅ + ́y

Verbal morphology allows us to see that endings are regularly added for all verbs. What makes one verb type unusual in comparison to another is whether or not it takes a verbal suffix or the present tense marker. We can now categorize verbs according to these parameters.

Since the stem structure of all 2nd conj verbs is constant (see section 6.3), we will consider here only the classes of 1st conj verbs. If normal is defined by the number of verbs belonging to a certain class, then the structure given in (3) above is normal. In that structure each verbal slot is filled (except for the theme vowel in the first sg and third pl). First conj verbs may lack a verbal suffix in conjugation, or they may lack the present tense marker {+й}, or they may lack both. These categories are illustrated in (8). In addition, we may refer to the presence or absence of a suffix in the past tense, or the permutation of a suffix from past to present such as in -ова ~ у. Since the presence (whether mutated or not) and absence of a suffix can be described by a binary system, and since we have two stems (past and present) we conclude there are four possible categories for 1st conj verbs. In (8) the plus sign indicates a suffix is present, a minus sign indicates no suffix. For the purposes of (8), the word "past" stands for both past tense and infinitive.

(8) +/+   suffix is present in both past and present:
          де́лал/де́лаю - thousands of verbs

    +/-   suffix is present only in the past: писа́ть/пишу́,
          би́ть/бью - about seventy verbs

    -/+   suffix is present only in the present: none

    -/-   suffix is not present in either present or past:
          нёс/несу́ - about two dozen

Thus the difference in conjugation between verbs such as писа́ть and де́лать is due to their morphological structure, not due to differences in conjugation, which is morphologically identical. Писа́ть is a +/- verb, or to be more precise, an a/∅ verb, while де́лать is a (+/+) or (a/a) verb. Танцева́ть is a +/+ verb, and its stem shows an alteration of the verbal suffix: {танц -ова + т'} - {танц -у -й + у}. The verb вы́тереть is a -/-, or to be precise, a ∅/∅ verb: {вы́тэрэ -∅ + т'} - {вы́тр -∅ -∅ + у}. Note that verbs like вы́тереть and нача́ть do not have a suffix in either past or present tense. Instead, they have an alternating stem. The a in the infinitive of нача́ть is part of the root, as is the н in the conjugated form: {нача -∅ + т'} - {начн -∅ -∅ + у́}.

*D Classify the following verbs as to their morphological structure. Indicate the present and past/infinitive suffixes. If no suffix is present, use the term ∅. Example: понима́ть is a/a.

1. страда́ть   8. улыбну́ться
2. сочиня́ть   9. стере́ть
3. старе́ть   10. дава́ть
4. оде́ть   11. мочь
5. откры́ть   12. укра́сть
6. пить   13. вести́
7. интригова́ть   14. снять

*E What distinguishes Ø/Ø verbs from other verb classes?

6.3 Second Conjugation morphology

The morphological structure of the present tense of 2nd conj verbs is much simpler than that of 1st conj verbs. It is composed of only three elements, all of which are always present: the root, verb-forming suffix (always -и- in the present tense, no matter what suffix is used in the infinitive), and ending. The example in (1) is for the verb говори́ть, an и/и verb.

(1) говорю́	<	{говор -и + у́}
говори́шь	<	{говор -и́ + шь}
говори́т	<	{говор -и́ + т}
говори́м	<	{говор -и́ + м}
говори́те	<	{говор -и́ + те}
говоря́т	<	{говор -и + а́т}

The third pl ending (-ат) differs from that of the 1st conj (-ут) due to the historical shift of the ProtoSlavic combination of и + нт (cf. ProtoSlavic *говори́нтъ, Old Church Slavic говоря́тъ, Modern Russian говоря́т) which caused palatalization of the preceding consonant. The problem with this structure, as with the palatalization of stem final в in живёшь, is finding an appropriate means to generate the soft quality of the root final consonant. For 2nd conj verbs, the verbal suffix serves this purpose nicely. This approach, however, requires some rule of the sort:

(2) и → Ø / ___ the ending -ат

The front vowel {-и} in the они form in (1) would be included only to acccount for the softness of the final consonant [гъвʌр'а́т]. Since the rule in (2) is not widely used throughout the language, we wonder if it really is a generalization of Russian. In Chapter 7 we will discuss an alternate approach to this problem.

Second conj verbs whose stems end in -р, л, н or a vowel have orthographic -ю for the first sg ending: я говорю́, я отделю́, я браню́, ястою́. Those whose roots end in a husher have orthographic -у, due to spelling exigencies: я спешу́, я учу́, я положу́, я обобщу́. All other 2nd conj verbs exhibit consonant mutation of the stem final consonant in the first person sg only. The mutations are from dental stops and dental fricatives to hushers, and the addition of an epenthetic л to labials:

(3)

	DENTALS	LABIALS
stem final consonant...	д т з с ст	п б ф в м
...mutates to →	ж ч ж ш щ	пл бл фл вл мл

After the hushers, the first sg ending is orthographic -у, after л the ending -ю is used. The mutations given in (3) occur in the present tense in the first sg form (and in the past passive participle). Recall that mutation in 1st conj verbs occurs in all forms of the present. That 2nd conj verbs have mutation only in the first sg is due to a sound change whereby unstressed и shifts to й when before a vowel, i.e., {ход -и + у} → {ход -й + у}. It is natural for the high front vowel [и] to become a glide [й] before a vowel since it allows two contiguous vowels to merge into one syllable.

The co-occurrence of a dental consonant and i-kratkoe results in mutation (see section 5.8). Since the verbal suffix и does not occur before other vowels in the present tense (with the exception of the third pl), there is no mutation in the rest of the present tense paradigm. Historically there was no mutation in the third pl, since

the verbal suffix -и- did not precede a vowel: ход -и +нт + ъ > ход' -и +нт + ъ > ход' -а +т + ъ > ход' -а + т > ход' + ат.

*A Write in morphological transcription:

1. бро́шу   3. смотрю́   5. встре́чу
2. бро́сишь   4. смо́тришь   6. встре́тишь

*B 1. When does the ending -ют/ут occur orthographically among 2nd conj verbs?
   2. Why is there no 2nd conj verb whose stem ends in a velar (к г х)?

3. Which conjugation, first or second, is simpler in terms of ease in predicting the stem?

6.4 The Infinitive and the Imperative

The infinitive form of most 1st conj and all 2nd conj verbs is arrived at by adding the infinitive suffix -ть (-чь, -ти) ({+т'}, {+ч}, {+ти}) to the past tense stem. This stem may be exactly like the present tense stem, or it may have a different suffix. In the following examples, the verb-forming suffix is in bold:

(1) **present tense stem**   **past tense stem**   **infinitive**

    рабо́т -а-   рабо́т -а-   {рабо́та + т'}
    пис -∅-   пис -а́-   {писа́ + т'}
    отдох -н-   отдох -ну́-   {отдохну́ + т'}
    чи́ст -и-   чи́ст -и-   {чи́сти + т'}
    смотр -й-   смотр -е́-   {смотре́ + т'}

For 1st conj stems that end in a velar, the infinitive ending is -чь ({+ ч}) and the velar is dropped: мочь < {мог + ч}. For 1st conj verbs that have do not have stress on the stem in the past tense and do not end in a velar, the ending is -ти несла́ → нести́ {нэс + ти́}.

There are three orthographic imperative suffixes: и, ь, and й. Their distribution is predictable orthographically from the present tense stem and is illustrated in (2).

(2) **present stem ends in...**   **imperative suffix (orthographic)**

    a vowel: й   чита́й
    two consonants: и   чи́сти
    one consonant
        stress on stem: ь   встре́ть
        stress on end: и   говори́, пиши́

Examples:

(3) рабо́тай, бо́йся, сове́туй, закро́й
    чи́сти, смотри́, отдохни́, пошли́ (< посла́ть)
    брось, заме́ть, забу́дь, встань
    говори́, неси́, положи́, закричи́

There are three orthographic endings for the imperative. Can we reduce this number by applying principles of morphology? We begin by determining the morphological transcription of imperatives. Many of the forms given in (3), including пошли́, забу́дь, and смотри́ suggest that the imperative is formed on the basis of the present tense, not on the past tense stem. If this is the case, then the present tense marker, if the verb has one, should also be present in the morphological variant. However, the theme vowel {о} in 1st conj verbs and the verbal suffix {и}, which serves as a theme vowel for 2nd conj verbs is not part of the stem for the imperative. Here are some stems ready to add the imperative ending.

(4) {рабо́т -а + й ... }   {чи́ст + ...}
    {бро́с + ...}   {говор + .:. }
    {нэс -∅ -∅ .:. }   {пис -∅ + .:. }

In (4), the dots represent the as yet unidentified imperative ending. What is the imperative ending? Consider the 1st conj a/a verbs.

(5) чита́ю < {чит -а́ -й + у} present tense suffix -й- is present
    чита́й < {чит -а́ -й + ?} present tense suffix -й- is present

*A What is the morphological representation of the imperative suffix for verbs whose present tense stems end in an i-kratkoe? In other words, what must "?" stand for in (5)?

*B Consider the forms брось, встань. Neither has a present tense suffix and both bear stress on the root. What is the morphological representation of the imperative for these? In other words, what does the "?" stand for in: {бро́с + ?}.

*C What is the imperative suffix for stems that end in a consonant but which have stress on the ending? What does the "?" stand for in {говор + ?}.

*D What is the morphological representation of the imperative suffix for verbs whose stems ends in two consonants, such as {чйст + ?}?

*E What do you conclude about the nature of the imperative ending?

6.5 Tense in Dialects

The manifold complex features of Russian verbal conjugation make it a perfect target for dialectal simplifications. As might be expected, complex verbal suffixes are simplified in many dialects. Thus, CSR ова/у type verbs become in dialectal form, as well as in beginning Russian classes, ова/ова verbs: трéбовают, прáзднуют. Regarding these forms, however, Bromlei warns: «Часть подобных образований распространена очень широко и носит просторечный характер». Bromlei lists several other instances where analogical "leveling" of the verbal stem takes place. Bromlei points out that the direction of analogy can be from present tense to past tense stem: CSR мáшет "he waves" > dialectal махáет (cf. махáть), or the opposite direction, from the past tense stem to the present tense stem: CSR жал "I pressed" > dialectal жмал (cf. жму). It is interesting to note the geographical location where most of these shifts occur:

Хотя рассмотренные процессы в глагольных основах встречаются на разных территориях распространения русских говоров, однако большинство этих процессов прошло в центральных говорах, на основе которых сформировалась система литературного языка, где представлены многие из таких новообразований. (стр. 106)

*A 1. On which geographical dialects is the standard literary language based?
2. Where do most of the dialectal shifts in verb stems occur?
3. What other kinds of simplifications or variations would you like to see in the Russian verbal system?

Speakers of German, French, or Spanish recognize the <u>pluperfect</u> form of the verb. It is used to indicate a past action that took place before another past action, and is often translated as "had" + past tense in English: "We <u>had just checked in,</u> when we found a note on our door." English uses the auxiliary word "had" (past tense of "have") and the past participle of the main verb to indicate pluperfect. A similar structure, the плюсквамперфе́кт (or давнопроше́дшее вре́мя), occurred in Old Russian. It too was formed with an auxiliary verb, often with simply the past tense of the verb бытъ plus the so-called "l-participle" of the main verb (=modern past tense):

(1) она была́ писа́ла   she had written

As in English, this form was used to speak about an action which occurred before another action in the past. Arvat states:

Плюсквамперфект обильно представлен во всех памятниках древнерусской письменности вплоть до XVII в. Например, в «Русской Правде»: Ярославъ былъ оуставилъ и оубити; в Ипатьевской летописи: крьстъ были цѣловали.

"Yaroslav had decided to kill...";   "they had kissed the cross"

The pluperfect is a verbal category in Ukrainian, and it still remains in several northern Russian dialects, particularly around Novgorod, Vologda, and the Archangel region. It is retained in the introductory phrase in fairy tales: Жи́ли бы́ли стари́к да стару́ха.

(2)   Она была жила. Ягоды росли были. Песни пела
        была, танцевала была, а когда замуж вышла--нет:
        дети пошли--некогда было.

        А в сентябре снег был высыпал, а октябрь был теплый.

        Он был до войны много заработал.

*B Translate the passages in (2).

*C How does any other language you know express the concept of pluperfect? If you don't know another language, ask a friend who does and start learning one yourself. What auxiliary verbs are used? What form does the main verb take?

Note that this combination continues to be used in standard Russian, but with a new meaning, the meaning of interrupted action. In addition, the auxiliary is now always in the neut sg:

(3) Я было пошел...   I was about to leave...
     Она было говорила...   She was about to speak...

Many central and northern Russian dialects show the absence of the present tense marker {-й} in present tense conjugation. For example:

(3)   играю, играшь, играт, играм, грате, играют
          {игр -á -∅ -∅ + ш}

In some northern dialects the verbal suffix is long, as if with the loss of the present tense marker, pronunciation of the verbal suffix spread to the theme vowel:

(4) думаашь, думаат, думаам, думаате   {дýм -а -∅ -а + ш}

*D Why is it possible for Russian to lose the present tense marker in these verbs? What new role does the person/number suffix (-шь, -т, etc.) play in these dialects?

6.6 Review

Morphology shows that 1st and 2nd conj verbs have much in common. They are formed with a stem, a verbal suffix (which may be missing in 1st conj verbs), and an ending. They are also quite different. Many 1st conj verbs have an alternate or unpredictable present tense stem, while the present tense stem is always predictable for 2nd conj verbs. The four verbs (and their derivatives) that are neither wholly 1st nor 2nd conj are: (1) хотеть (sg forms are 1st conj, pl forms are 2nd!). Dialects have хочý, хóчешь, хóчет, хóчем, хóчете, хóчут making this a regular 1st conj verb; (2) бежа́ть (the я and они forms are 1st conj, the rest are 2nd!); (3) есть and (4) дать have only person/number endings in common with 1st conj, and only somewhat resemble 2nd conj in the pl forms.

Having uncovered the morphological structure of nouns, adjectives, and verbs we may now ask what good we derive from this. Is there any relationship between morphological structure and stress? Does knowing morphological structure aid in forming and understanding related words, i.e., ти́хий - ти́ше - утиха́ть - ути́хнуть - тишина́? These questions are the topics of the next two chapters.

CHAPTER 7: Derivational Morphology and Morphophonemics

7.1 Morphemes vs. Phonemes

So far we have been mainly concerned with alternations of two types: phonological alternations (Chapters 1 through 4) and alternations in grammatical endings (Chapters 5 and 6). In this chapter we will discuss a third type of alternation, one that deals with changes within a morpheme. One specific question we want to answer is why the final consonant in the morpheme {жив} is pronounced soft when followed by the theme vowel morpheme {о} in conjugation, e.g., in {жив + о + ш} → [жыв'о́ш]. A morpheme (морфе́ма) is a sequence of sounds that bears grammatical or lexical meaning. For example, the sequence of sounds {стол} is a morpheme in Russian, as is the nom pl ending {+ы}, since they both bear meaning. In contrast the separate sounds [с], [т], [о] and [л] are phonemes but are not morphemes since they bear no meaning. We have seen that phonological alternations are automatic--they occur whenever a given environment is met, as with akan'e, for example. Morphophonemic alternations are predictable (automatic) and a few are unpredictable (not automatic). Phonological rules allow us to see one variant of a given sound alternation as basic (for example, between [ʌ] and [a], the latter is basic). The same is true for morphophonemic rules, which allow us to find one basic variant of related morphemes. Consider the underlined roots in the words in (1).

(1) a. пере<u>смотр</u>е́ть   b. пере<u>сма́тр</u>ивать

The verbs in (1) provide a good example of a morphophonemic alternation. The root in (1a) is {смотр}, and in (1b) the root has the form {сматр}. These two roots are related: they share the same meaning and are similarly composed. Which is basic and which derived? We know that both [о] and [a] are basic sounds in Russian. We can be sure that the vowel in the root in (1a) is [о] since that is how it sounds when stressed (смо́тришь). The differences in the vowel in the roots in (1) are due to a sound shift in the root, a shift that occurs before phonological rules have a chance to apply. The sound shift in the morpheme is not predicated by a nearby sound but *by another morpheme*.

When the verbal suffix {+ыва} is added to a root with the vowel {о}, then the {о} usually shifts to {a} as in:

(2) обрабóтать	обрабáтывать	work up
спросúть	спрáшивать	ask
уговорúть	уговáривать	persuade
устрóить	устрáивать	arrange
докóнчить	докáнчивать	finish

Morphophonemics is the study of the alternations in morphemes not due to contemporary phonological pressures. Morphophonemic rules express relationships between morphemes. Thus, we can write a rule to express the shift exhibited in (2), which is actually the result of an ancient phonological shift, whereby root {o} was lengthened to {ō} when adjacent to this suffix. Subsequently the sound {ō} shifted to {a}. Since contemporary Russian does not have long vowels our explanation of this alternation of sounds in the modern language cannot make reference to the historical {ō}. Instead we can say that the presence of the suffix {+ыва} triggers the sound change in an immediately preceding root morpheme; that is, there is a "morpho"--"phonemic" shift:

(3) $\{...o...\}_{root} \rightarrow \{...a...\} / \_\_\_ \{+\text{ыва}\}$

Nothing like assimilation can be seen involved in the shift in (3). We cannot justify the shift on the basis of any physiological trait of the environment. Morphophonemic rules account for shifts in morphemes that were once phonologically based but now cannot be so explained, due to the absence now of earlier occuring sounds. Another word for "related morpheme," whether related by rule or otherwise, is allomorph (алломóрф).

*A Note that stress always precedes the suffix {-ыва}. Vowels that were lengthened naturally attracted stress to them. Long vowels, however, are not a part of the composition of modern Russian. Yet stress remains on the root of verbs with this suffix, e.g., указáть → укáзывать. How can we explain this phenomenon, through phonological or morphophemic principles?

As illustrated above, morphemes may be composed of one or many sounds. A phoneme (фонéма) is a <u>single</u> sound that can bring about a change in meaning in a morpheme. For example, the final consonants in the following morphemes are phonemic (=phonemes) in English, since they alter the meaning of each pair: ha**t** - ha**d**, ha**s** - ha**th**, ha**m** - Ha**l**, ha**sh** - ha**tch**. In Russian, palatalization is phonemic--it can be crucial in differentiating meaning: мат - мать, угол - уголь, ломо́т "aches" gen. pl - ломо́ть "large slice of bread." Morphemes are composed of phonemes and other morphemes (in compound words).

Derivational morphology (словообразова́ние) investigates the processes of putting words together from morphemes. In Chapters 5 and 6 we saw how inflectional morphology interacts with morphemes to form declined or conjugated words. Further we saw how akan'e, ikan'e and spelling rules play an important role in this process; for example, 1st decl gen sg -о̲в̲ > -е̲в̲ after soft consonants and when not under stress. In morphophonemics we will see that in many instances shifts in morphemes are due to the presence of other morphemes rather than to phonological rules.

Words may be classified according to their "grammatical category," depending on how the word is generally used in a sentence. We will here be chiefly interested in the categories of noun, verb, and adjective. These kinds of words in Russian have the following structure (elements in parentheses may or may not be present in any given word):

(4) (prefix) = root + (suffix) + ending

Words have at least a root and an ending. Prefixes and suffixes may or may not be present. Examples:

(5) свобо́д + а   (root+ending)
     свобо́д -н + ый   (root+suffix+ending)
  о = свобод -и́ + ть   (prefix+root+suffix+ending)
  о = свобожд -е́ни + е   (prefix+root+suffix+ending)

In (5) the word свобо́да is composed of a nominal (=noun) root plus an ending. It is not a derived noun, since it neither contains a suffix nor is the grammatical category of the whole word different from that of the root. The other three words in (5) are derived: свобо́дный is an adjective derived from a noun base by means of the adjective-forming suffix -н̲-; освободи́ть is also derived from a noun and bears the verb-forming suffix -и̲- as well as a verbal prefix; освобожде́ние is a noun derived from the verb. Note its meaning is somewhat different from that of the original nonderived noun. Words may be nonderived or derived from nouns (denominal), from adjectives (deadjectival), or from verbs (deverbal). When a derived word is a different grammatical category from that of its root, then it is the result of a "cross-category" derivation. If a noun is derived from another noun, an adjective from an adjective or a verb from a verb and these derivations are made by means of a suffix, then the derivation is said to be "intracategory." Thus, морячо́к "little sailor" (denominal noun) is derived from моря́к "sailor" (also a denominal noun), which is derived from мо́ре "sea" (nonderived).

*B For each of the following write (a) the root, (b) its grammatical category, (c) the grammatical category of the given word, and (d) whether the given word exhibits intracategory derivation, cross-category derivation, or is not derived.

1. мо́ре	5. столи́чный	9. стари́к
2. сове́т	6. сове́тник	10. сове́товать
3. слова́цкий	7. перестро́йка	11. откры́ть
4. де́тство	8. учи́тельница	12. нау́ка

7.2 {*o}

It was suggested in Chapter Six that the basic endings for many 1st conj verbs have the theme vowel o̲: чита́ешь < {чита́й -о + ш}. One of the reasons for this suggestion is that when this vowel is under stress, it is pronounced as an o̲: встаёшь [фстʌйо́ш].

Now consider the stem of the word нести́. It presents a set of alternating stem morphemes:

(1) несу́ [н'ису́]   несёшь [н'ис'о́ш]
    нести́ [н'ис'ти́]   нёс [н'ос]

Judging strictly from the pronunciation of the various forms of the stem morpheme, as shown in (1), there are three possible candidates for the basic morpheme, the one from which the other two must be derived.

(2) {н'ис-} (ends in a hard consonant)
   {н'ис'} (ends in a soft consonant)
   {н'ос} (ends in a hard consonant, has the vowel <u>о</u>)

Earlier we evaluated this stem as having the base form #нэс#. It was suggested that none of the three stems listed in (2) represented the base form. Indeed, all the variations of the stems in (2) would be easily accounted for by taking {нэс} as the base form and applying several well-known historical phonological rules. In this account, the palatalized [н'] occurs before a front vowel, the palatalized [с'] occurs before the front vowel <u>э</u>, as in #нэс + <u>э</u> + ш# which subsequently would become <u>о</u> under stress and before a hard consonant. This is also the fate of the stem vowel <u>э</u> in the past tense masc form.

There is a critical weakness to this "historical" approach. In modern Russian the vowel <u>э</u> does not become <u>о</u> when under stress and before a hard consonant, or in any environment: нет, мéсто, лéто, бéгать. We recall that another historical rule accounts for the fact that some Russian <u>e</u>'s do not become ë. Historically the vowels in these stems were not <u>e</u>, but <u>ѣ</u>: нѣтъ, лѣто, etc. and this vowel never became ë. This line of reasoning, however, which continues to make reference to historical processes, is weak because crucial to its application is a sound which does not exist in modern Russian, namely <u>ѣ</u>. If the object of our study is modern Russian, then it may be suggested that reference to sounds that do not currently exist in the language is not allowed in our description. This purely theoretical statement is based on the idea that many native speakers of Russian have no idea what <u>ѣ</u> represents, or even that it existed. Linguists who are interested in learning and describing what speakers of modern Russian know must limit themselves to data that is available to those speakers. Information about previous stages of the language is not available to most natives learning Russian. Morphophonemics (морфонолóгия) makes no reference to historical rules, or what form a word took at an earlier stage of the language. It is limited strictly to sounds that are used in the language at the stage it is being studied. Morphophonemics suggests that sound changes are due not only to natural sound shifts (such as devoicing, akan'e and voicing assimilation), but also due to the pressure of certain morphemes on and in conjunction with other morphemes.

Returning to the underlying form of the root morpheme of the word нести́, morphophonemic theory states that one of the available, meaning "actually pronounced," roots in (2) must be basic. In no form of the word is the stem pronounced [нэс]. Since the first two variants reflect the phonological rule of ikan'e, they can be eliminated. This leaves only the third variant as the possible basis for the stem morpheme:

(3)   {н'ос + ý} → (ikan'e)   → {н'ис + ý} → [н'исý] "несý"

        {н'ос + Ø} →   no rules apply   → [н'ос] "нёс"

In (3) we have expanded the ikan'e rule to include o, thus allowing ikan'e to apply more generally to all nonhigh vowels:

(4) о, а, э → и,ь / С' ___
                         [-str]

The rule in (4) states that all unstressed nonhigh vowels are subject to ikan'e.

Since the back vowel o cannot motivate palatalization, morphophonemic theory requires underlying soft consonants in Russian, that is to say that morphemes can have either hard or soft consonants, as long as the consonant occurs hard or soft.

If the basic stem in (3) is {н'ос-} (this accounts for the final hard c in несý), then how does the c become palatalized in other forms of the present tense (несёшь, несёт, etc.)? We know that the theme vowel in 1st conj verbs is o, and, as is well known, back vowels do not motivate palatalization. In morphophonemics, morphemes can be responsible for a sound change, as we saw in root {o} shifting to {a} when concatenated with the suffix {ыва}. Accordingly, the theme vowel o in 1st conj verbs must be, like {ыва}, a specially marked morpheme. Simply stated, consonants are soft before it. Schematically:

(5)   {н'ос -*ó + ш}   → {н'ос' -*ó + ш} → [н'ис'óш]

In (5) *o indicates a specially marked morpheme which results in palatalization of a preceding consonant. Notice that no matter what consonant precedes this suffix, it will be palatalized: чту, чтёшь; встáну, встáнешь, etc. This shift is automatic and applies everywhere a consonant (excluding ж, ш, and ц) precedes {*о}. This kind of rule, formalized in (6) below, differs from phonological rules in that it does not present a <u>natural</u> reason for the physical variation observed. It is the result of natural processes that took place earlier in the history of the language but is now not a phonological shift.

Another way of viewing morphophonemics is to see that when a given phonological rule becomes active in a language it applies everywhere that the environment is met. Subsequent sound changes, however, make that phonological rule apply in a more restricted environment, or cause the rule not to apply at all. Yet the results of the rule may still be seen in the language, resulting in phonological alternations of the type we have been studying. The rule still seems to apply, but only in certain restricted environments, thus the exact places where the rule now applies must be stated. Thus, at one time the rule э → о was productive and applied throughout the language. By the time the rule ѣ → э became productive the former rule had stopped operating. We know this because the э from ѣ did not become о. But still the results of the former rule can be seen in various morphemes: несý ~ нёс, -ешь ~ -ёшь, смерть ~ мёртвый, etc. In most of these alternating forms we may posit an underlying <u>o</u>, and expand the ikan'e rule to include <u>o</u> as done in (4).

Morphophonemics allows us to see that the consonant softening rule now applies in fewer instances than earlier. This is because paired consonants in modern Russian may be hard or soft in underlying forms. Thus, consonant softening does not apply to palatalize the initial consonant of the root morpheme {н'ос-}. In addition, a morphophonemic rule exists in the form as given in (6).

(6) a.　　C → C' / _____ *o (verbal theme vowel)

　　b.　　K → Č / _____ *o (verbal theme vowel)

where <u>K</u> represents any velar and <u>Č</u> represents its palatal partner.

The base forms for morphemes which exhibit the <u>C ~ C'</u> alternation within the 1st conj present tense paradigm may now be written with an underlying <u>*o</u>:

(7) {н'ос -*ó + ш}　　{п'ок -*о + ш}

Morphemes which bring about a phonological change in another morpheme are marked by an asterisk.

*A Account for the alternations in the underlined segments in the following pairs. Give a historical explanation and a morphophonemic explanation for each alternation. In some instances the environment of the rule given in (6) will have to be expanded. This is a fairly complex assignment. Before looking at the key try to figure out what might be responsible for the observed changes.

    1. веду́ - ведёшь (hard - soft)
    2. река́ - речно́й (velar - palatal)
    3. друг - дружо́к (velar - palatal)
    4. смерть - мёртвый (э - о)

Nonpredictable morphophonemic shifts are represented in a different way. Consider the stem variations illustrated in (8):

(8) рука́   ручно́й   руча́ться

Recall that the combination husher + атъ derives historically from velar plus jat' (see section 4.5). But how should the root morpheme of these three related words be represented in a grammar which makes no reference to sounds which currently do not exist in the language? There appear to be two choices: {рук} or {руч}. The occurrence of руч in ручно́й is predictable: velars do not occur in combination with the adjectival suffix -н-, cf. те́хника - техни́чный, снег - сне́жный, у́хо - нау́шный, etc. We can say that in regard to this suffix, the alternation of velar with palatal is predictable on the basis of the adjectival suffix {-*/н} (where "/" is a place holder for a fleeting vowel). The morphophonemic rule given in (6b) would be expanded to include this environment. So, perhaps the root morpheme is {рук-}? Compare руча́ться with other verbs whose stem ends in a velar: сту́кать, бе́гать, отдыха́ть. Thus, {рук -а́ + т' + с'а} would yield *рука́ться. The alternation of к with ч in this environment is clearly not automatic. Yet the root morpheme is obviously related to that of the other two roots in (8). The roots рук- and руч- are variants, allomorphs, of a single morpheme, which we represent as: руК-. The capital К in the morpheme represents the two sounds к and ч, which occur in environments specified by morphophonemic rules. These rules state, for example,

(9) К → ч / _____ verbal suffix -a-

Thus the form сту́кать can be represented: {сту́к + а + т'}. The rule in (9) does not apply to this word. But the form руча́ться has the morphophonemic representation of {руК + а́ + т' + с'а}. What is unusual about the verbs руча́ться, молча́ть, крича́ть, etc. is not that the verbal suffix causes a shift in the root morpheme, but that the root morpheme itself has a split personality; it is made up of two variants (allomorphs): {рук-} and {руч-}. Morphophonemic rules such as the one given in (9) specify when each is used.

*B The roots in these derivationally related sets of words are underlined. Write the basic root morpheme for each. Give your reasoning.

1. <u>крик</u> "shout"   - <u>крич</u>а́ть "shout"
2. <u>нау́к</u>а "science"   - <u>нау́чн</u>ый "scientific"
3. <u>усло́в</u>ный "conditional"   - <u>усло́в</u>ие "condition"
4. <u>слуг</u>а́ "servant"   - <u>служ</u>и́ть "serve"
5. <u>у́лиц</u>а "street"   - <u>у́личн</u>ый "street"

Before moving on to word formation, consider the word печь. We suggested earlier that the root of this word is {п'ок-}. If this is the root, then how can we explain the vowel in the infinitive пе́чь? Recall that the о→ е spelling rule applies only to unstressed {о}. Historically the quality of the vowel in this word was due to the fact that a soft consonant followed the root vowel э: {п'эч}, so the э → о rule never applied. The same is true for words such as смерть (cf. мёртвый). In these words the roots are allomorphic: {п'Ок-}, and {м'Орт} which represent {п'эк-} and {м'эрт} when followed by a soft consonant.

7.3 Derived vs. Nonderived

Nonderived words are those that form verbs, nouns, and adjectives from verbal, nominal, and adjectival roots without a suffix. Examples are given in (1):

(1) **Root**	**Type**	**Forms**	**Gloss**
стол-	noun	стол	table
книг-	noun	книга	book
мор'-	noun	мо́ре	sea
б'эр-	verb	беру́	I take
п'ок-	verb	пеку́	I bake
чт-	verb	чту	I honor
стар-	adj	стар	old
молод-	adj	мо́лод	young
здоров-	adj	здоро́в	healthy

Since derivational suffixes are not involved in the formation of these words, we need not look for morphophonemic alternations.

Intracategory derivation is the formation of a noun from a noun, verb from a verb, adjective from an adjective by means of a suffix or prefix. Examples follow.

(2) **Stem**	**Type**	**Forms**	**Gloss**
стол-	noun	сто́лик	little table
кни́г-	noun	кни́жка	brochure
мо́р'-	noun	моря́к	sailor
б'эр-	verb	собира́ть	collect
п'ок-	verb	допе́чь	bake thoroughly
чт-	verb	чтить	to honor
ста́р-	adj	ста́ренький	somewhat old
мо́лод-	adj	молодо́й	young (long form)

More than one suffix may be added in this type of derivation, cf. the diminutive кни́жечка < {кни́г-*/к-*/к-а}. As can be seen in this example and the ones in (2), intracategory derivation may impinge on the structure of a root or stem. In the remainder of this chapter we will study those changes that affect the form of a root which are predictable on the basis of phonological and morphophonemic information. We leave to Chapter 8 questions dealing with shifts in stress.

*A Give the roots for the following words. Write N for nonderived words and D if the word is derived.

1. а́вгуст
2. ста́ну
3. и́щешь
4. ры́ба
5. мо́стик

6. земля́
7. дворе́ц
8. письмо́
9. рыба́к
10. ме́сто

*B What general alternation is observable in the shape of the roots of the following derivationally related words?

1. стол - сто́лик
2. ме́сто - месте́чко
3. ход - ходи́ть

4. брат - бра́тец
5. ры́ба - рыбёшка
6. род - ро́дина

7.4 Verb Formation

In this section we will examine how verbal derivational suffixes affect the structure of root morphemes. The following patterns are encountered:

(1) a. hard paired consonants are palatalized
   b. soft paired consonants become hard
   c. velars become palatals
   d. no modification

Verbal derivational suffixes are complex morphemes. The morpheme itself represents both nonpresent and present allomorphs. For example, the infinitive чита́ть, and present tense чита́ю have the morphophonemic structure:

(2) {чит -а́ + т'}   {чит -а́ -й + у}

The verbal suffix in both nonpresent and present tense forms is -a. Another way of representing this ending is a/a, where the suffix used for past tense and infinitive is given before the slash, the present (and simple future) tense suffix is given after the slash.

In this section we will examine the following suffixes:

(3) 1ST CONJUGATION

a/a	as in	чита́ть, отдыха́ть
ова/у		сове́товать, торгова́ть
a/∅		писа́ть, сказа́ть
e/e		боле́ть, име́ть
ну/н		отдохну́ть, взви́згнуть
∅/ну/н		поги́бнуть, пога́снуть
ыва/ыва		пересма́тривать, перечи́тывать

(4) 2ND CONJUGATION

и/и	as in	гото́вить, испра́вить
a/и		слы́шать, стоя́ть

7.4.1 Verbs in a/a

All types of consonants occur before this suffix. It is unusual among verbal suffixes, however, in that it triggers unpredictable mutations in velars:

(1) hard consonants:	обе́дать, де́лать, броса́ть
soft consonants:	гуля́ть, теря́ть, смея́ться
velars:	пуга́ть, пропуска́ть, пиха́ть
palatals:	продолжа́ть, руча́ться, слу́шать

Notice that the addition of this suffix causes no changes to the root morphemes of hard consonants or soft consonants: {обѐд -a + ...}, {гул'+а́+ ...}. Among velars the situation is not so straightforward. This morpheme may follow a velar causing no change or it may incite mutation as seen in the palatals: {про=долГ -a + ...}, {руК -a + ...}, {слуХ -a +...}. A morphophonemic rule such as (9) in section 7.2 will shift the final element of these morphemes to ж, ч, and ш respectively. This shift is not predictable on any synchronic basis. Other velars precede the suffix without mutation: пуга́ть {пуг -а́ + т'}.

Morphophonemic alternation is also visible in the following pairs (roots are underlined):

(2) заме́тить   -   замеча́ть   but   лета́ть
разряди́ть   -   разряжа́ть   обе́дать
пригласи́ть   -   приглаша́ть   броса́ть
уни́зить   -   унижа́ть   исчеза́ть

As the words in the third column above indicate, this suffix may follow hard dentals. Yet the second column indicates mutation of the dentals to palatals. Unlike the mutation of velars discussed above, the mutation of dentals to palatals is predictable and automatic. In other words, this alternation is not due to a morphophonemic rule but to a set of phonological rules which state that и shifts to й before a vowel and that dentals followed by й mutate to palatals. Example:

(3) замеча́ть is derived from: {за=мет -и -а + т'}
shift of и to й: {за=мет -й -а + т'}
shift of тй to ч: {за=меч -а + т'}

*A Where does the и come from in the above derivation?

The perfective form заме́тить is the basis of the derived imperfective замеча́ть. The same mutations seen in 2nd conj verbs with labials is repeated in the formation of these verbs as well: влюби́ть → влюбля́ть.

Here is what Zinovii A. Potixa has to say about perfective verbs in -ить with their derived imperfective counterparts in -ать:

Это устойчивый и употребительный пласт в системе русского глагола, но новые слова по этому типу не образуются. В глаголах типа «лишать», «бросать», «разрешать», «заземлять» ударный суффикс -а (-я) является показателем несовершенного вида. Коррелятивные глаголы совершенного вида имеют суффикс -и: лишить, бросить, разрешить, заземлить.

*B According to Potixa, how many new imperfective verbs would y o u expect to be formed on the basis of perfective -ить counterparts?

*C According to Potixa, where does stress fall on derived imperfectives in -ать when the perfective counterpart ends in -ить?

*D Write out the derived imperfective forms of the following:

1. зарази́ть	5. сооруди́ть
2. отве́тить	6. разреши́ть
3. пригласи́ть	7. упрости́ть
4. вста́вить	8. округли́ть

7.4.2 Verbs in ова/у

All morphophonemic alternations are automatic with this suffix. When it is added to hard paired consonants or velars there are no shifts: сове́товать, кома́ндовать, образова́ть, атакова́ть, торгова́ть, страхова́ть. When added to a soft paired consonant, a palatal, or ц, then the suffix-initial o shifts to e according to the spelling rule: трелева́ть (cf. трель), горева́ть (cf. го́ре < {го́р' + о}), ночева́ть, танцева́ть, свежева́ть, бушева́ть.

The verb танцева́ть illustrates an automatic morphophonemic shift with this suffix: fleeting vowels in the root morpheme are fugitive:

(1) танцева́ть   <   {тан(е)ц + ова + т'}
    кольцева́ть   <   {кол(е)ц + ова + т'}

Some verbs that end in -евать do not take the suffix -у in the present tense; instead, they are a/a verbs: надева́ть, навева́ть "to blow," зева́ть. These verbs do not have the suffix -ова. The sequence -ев is part of the root morpheme, e.g., {зев + а + т'}.

Another set of verbs takes the suffix -ва/ва, as ослабева́ть (ослабева́ю, ослабева́ешь, etc.), затвердева́ть, одолева́ть. The final consonants in the root morphemes in these words are soft. They derive from verbal forms, which in turn are derived from nouns or adjectives:

(2) base morpheme: {слаб}   (cf. сла́бый)
    verb formation: {слаб -э + ...}
    palatalization: {слаб' -э + ...}   (phonological)
                          ↓↓↓
base morpheme for deverbal
        derivation: {слаб'э}
    verb formation: {о-слаб'э -ва + ...}

*A Write out in morphophonemic transcription and in normal orthography the infinitive based on the following root morphemes (they are all normal -ова/у verbs):

1. {слэ́д-} cf. след
2. {п'йа́нств-} cf. пья́нство
3. {та́н/ц} cf. та́нец
4. {врач-} cf. врач
5. {тоск-} cf. тоска́

6. {бэ́дств-} cf. бе́дствие
7. {брак-} cf. брак
8. {свин/'ц-} cf. свине́ц
9. {бэсэ́д-} cf. бесе́да
10. {имэн-} cf. имя, имена́

7.4.3 Verbs in -a/∅

Root morphemes taking this suffix always end in a hard paired consonant or velar. All morphophonemic shifts are automatic and predictable from the suffix: писа́ть (я пишу́, ты пи́шешь, etc.). Dental stops mutate in the present tense, including dentals preceding л. Labials add an epenthetic л, and velars mutate to palatals in the present tense:

(1) писа́ть - пишу́   write
     слать - шлю   send
     ре́зать - ре́жу   cut
     глода́ть - гложу́   gnaw
     лепета́ть - лепечу́   babble

With this suffix fleeting vowels disappear in the nonpresent tense forms. This is expected because the nonpresent tense morphophoneme is a vowel. In the present tense forms fleeting vowels are present. This is also expected since the present tense morphophoneme is a nonvowel:

(2) стлать < {ст(е)л -a + т'}   but
     стелю́ < {ст(е)л -∅ + й + у́}

*A Why isn't звать, an a/∅ verb, conjugated: я *зовлю, ты *зовлешь, etc.? In other words, what is there about its present tense structure that removes the possibility of mutation? What else is strange about the present tense conjugation of звать?

7.4.4 Verbs in -e/e

This complex morpheme is composed of two occurrences of the morphophoneme {э}. Hard paired consonants are palatalized before them: слáбый → ослабéть, зуб → обеззýбеть. Many verbs formed by means of this suffix are derived from adjectival roots and bear the meaning "to be(come) X": белéть, ржавéть, робéть.

No mutations occur with this suffix, although palatals in base morphemes do occur: свéжий → свежéть, i.e., there is no *<u>свег</u>, or *<u>свед</u>. Similarly no root morphemes ending in a velar co-occur with this suffix.

7.4.5 Verbs in -ну/н and -∅/ну/н

Verbs that have the suffix <u>-ну</u> in the infinitive belong to one of two subgroups. In both subgroups this suffix loses the vowel in the present/future tense: отдохнýть, я отдохнý, ты отдохнёшь, etc. The two subgroups differ in that in one subgroup the suffix <u>-ну</u> is present in the past tense:

(1) -ну/н verbs	**infinitive**	**past**	
	клю́нуть	клю́<u>ну</u>л	peck
	вернýться	вернý<u>ла</u>сь	return
	двúнуть	двú<u>ну</u>ло	move
	подчеркнýть	подчеркнý<u>ли</u>	underline

In the other subgroup the suffix <u>-ну</u> disappears completely in the past tense (thus ∅/ну/н means past tense/infinitive/present tense):

(2) -∅/ну/н verbs		
infinitive	**past**	
привы́кнуть	привы́к	be accustomed
затúхнуть	затúхла	abate
сóхнуть	сóхло	be parched
подóхнуть	подóхли	die

The addition of the suffix -∅ to root morphemes entails no morphophonemic shifts. The other suffixes (<u>-ну, -н</u>) admit no hushers (one exception: качну́ть "to rock, pitch, stagger"), thus, this suffix does not trigger mutation. Interestingly enough, soft paired consonants are hard before this suffix, with the exception of {л'}, which remains soft. (We will see that л remains or becomes soft in conjunction with other suffixes that begin with -н.) Examples: ныря́ть {ныр'-} ~ нырну́ть, грязь {гр'аз'-} ~ погря́знуть. This shift is automatic: all soft consonants (except л') become velarized (hard) before this suffix, e.g., {по-гр'а́з' - *ну + т'}, where the morpheme {*ну} deletes preceding softness. Root morphemes ending in a palatalized л' retain this softness before -н: стреля́ть {стр'эл' -а́ + т'} and стрельну́ть {стр'эл' -ну́ + т'}.

The adherence of -нуть verbs to the -∅/ну/н subgroup is predictable on the basis of the following:

(3) a. stress falls on the root morpheme AND
   b. the root morpheme ends in a consonant AND
   c. the verb is imperfective OR the verb is prefixed

For examples see (2) above. If a -нуть verb has stress on the suffix or the root does not end in a consonant, then it is a -ну/н verb. There are six exceptions to (3): вспы́хнуть, всхли́пнуть, приплю́снуть, проти́снуться, взви́згнуть, all of which should be ∅/ну/н verbs, but which take the suffix in the past. The sixth exception is увя́нуть "to fade" which has past увя́л, etc. An important caveat to (3) is that prefixed derived verbs of -ну/н verbs are always -ну/н: кли́кнуть (perf) → восклиќнуть (восклиќнул).

*A Give the past tense masc of the following.

1. сла́бнуть (impf)	6. захлебну́ться
2. просну́ться	7. поги́бнуть
3. привы́кнуть	8. пры́гнуть (perf)
4. замёрзнуть	9. дви́нуть (perf)
5. щёлкнуть (perf)	10. поддёрнуть

The past tense of поддёрнуть is поддёрнул, but it is derived from дёрнуть (perf, hence ну/н). Zinovii Potixa explains that a difference in meaning also separates the two subgroups in this class:

(ну/н-) Это единственный продуктивный суффикс со значением совершенного вида; он присоединяется к бесприставочным глаголам несовершенного вида и придает им добавочное значение--энергичность, резкость, а также моментальность, однократность действия. ... Глаголы несовершенного вида обозначают «постепенный переход из одного состояния в другое»и характеризуются тем, что основа настоящего времени оканчивается на -н- (мёрзну, киснy), а в формах прошедшего времени суффикс -ну- полностью исчезает (мёрз, кис). Ударение в глаголах [несовершенного вида] с суффиксом -ну- всегда падает на слог, предшествующий этому суффиксу.

*B According to Potixa's characteristics for each subgroup, which of the following should have -ну- in the past tense and which -∅-? Do exercise *C before checking your answers.

    1. взви́згнуть to let out a scream, to squeal
    2. обману́ть to deceive
    3. дости́гнуть to achieve
    4. дро́гнуть to be chilled; to quaver, falter
    5. пры́гнуть to leap
    6. цы́кнуть   to shut someone up
    7. ви́снуть   to hang, droop
    8. га́снуть to go out, be extinguished
    9. засну́ть to fall asleep
    10. гло́хнуть to become deaf; subside, die away

*C Based on your answers in *B what should the verbal aspect be for each of the verbs in *B? What can you conclude regarding the semantic characteristics suggested by Potixa?

7.4.6 Verbs in -ыва-

This suffix is used to form derived imperfectives from prefixed perfectives. It also occurs in two variants, but the second variant, -ива-, can be predicted on a phonological basis; following velars, vowels, and hushers and when the root morpheme ends in a soft consonant, the -ива- variant is written.

This suffix has two more interesting features. First, stress always falls on the syllable preceding it. Second, the root morpheme vowel -o after hard paired consonants usually shifts to -a in conjunction with the suffix -ыва. (See section 7.1.) Examples:

(1) пересмотре́ть   >   пересма́тривать   revise
    закопа́ть   >   зака́пывать   bury
    обрабо́тать   >   обраба́тывать   work up
    разлома́ть   >   разла́мывать   break down

An apparent exception to the shift of o to a comes from verbs with a base morpheme ending in the suffix -ов(а):

(2) запакова́ть   >   запако́вывать   pack
    реорганизова́ть   >   реорганизо́вывать   reorganize
    преобразова́ть   >   преобразо́вывать   transform
    завоева́ть   >   завоёвывать   conquer
    зарисова́ть   >   зарисо́вывать   sketch

And, consider the vowel in the root morphemes of the following:

(3) оскрёбывать < оскреба́ть   but   подде́лывать< подде́лать
    захлёбывать < захлебну́ть   дочёрпывать< дочерпну́ть
    замётывать < замета́ть   подре́зывать< подреза́ть

Since Russian does not now have an э → o rule, we must assume that the underlying vowel in the left-hand column of (3) is o: {оскр'о́б + ыва + т'} {оскр'об + а́ + т'}, with ikan'e applying in the perfective. The base vowel in the right-hand column is э: {подд'э́л -ыва + т'} {подд'э́л -а + т'}. In regard to the presence of o or a in the stems in (1), the alternation is due to a morphophonemic rule, which states that root vowel o following a hard paired consonant becomes a before the suffix -ыва, but no other o's do, as illustrated by (2) and (3).

We are now ready to look at what happens to the final consonants of root morphemes when this suffix is attached.

Velars and dentals are not modified.

(4) затра́гивать, докла́дывать

However, mutations of dentals and labials do occur if the morpheme from which the imperfective is derived contains the verbal suffix -{и}. In conjunction with the initial vowel of {+ыва} the {и} shifts to {й} resulting in mutation of dentals and labials:

(5) доха́живать < {до=ход -и -ыва + т'} < доходи́ть
    просве́чивать < {про=све́т -и -ыва + т'} < просвети́ть
    перемора́живать < {пере=моро́з-и-ыва + т'} < переморо́зить
    угота́вливать < {у-гото́в -и -ыва + т'} < угото́вить

*A Is the mutation illustrated in (5) phonological or morphophonemic? Why?

*B The alternation of д with ж in the first example in (5) suggests that the root morpheme should be written {хоД-}. True or false? Why?

*C Here are some verbs which derive imperfective partners with the suffix {+ыва}. Write out in normal orthography the derived imperfective for each.

1. огороди́ть	6. допры́гать
2. обусло́вить	7. договори́ть
3. залечи́ть	8. заточи́ть
4. недове́сить	9. вы́растить
5. упакова́ть	10. перечита́ть

7.4.7 Verbs in и/и

This suffix forms 2nd conj verbs. Hard paired consonants are softened ((a) examples below) phonologically, and velars are palatalized ((b) examples below) morphophonemically. Thus, the suffix involved here is {*и}, which effects mutation of velars. No change for soft paired consonants ((c) examples below).

(1) (a) руби́ть   < {руб -*й + т'}
        Palatalization is phonological before {и}.
        освободи́ть   < {о-свобод -*й + т'}
        чи́слить   < {чи́сл -*и + т'}

(b) обслужи́ть   < {об-слуг -*и́ + т'}
     Mutation is morphophonemic
     смягчи́ть   < {с=м'агк -*и́ + т'}
     оглуши́ть   < {о-глух -*и́ + т'}

(c) гвозди́ть   < {гвозд' -*и́ + т'}
     Palatalization present in root
     цари́ть   < {цар' -*и́ + т'}
     матери́ть   < {матэр' -*и́ + т'}

7.4.8 Verbs in а/и

The root morpheme of all but two verbs taking this suffix ends in a husher. Not all husher final verbs take this suffix, however, cf. отвеча́ть. The two verbs that do not end in a husher are: гнать (гоню́, го́нишь) and спать (сплю, спишь). The paradigm of гнать indicates that this suffix triggers the loss of fleeting vowels in the nonpresent and the presence of fleeting vowels in the 1st sg form (the и becomes non-vocalic й). The presence of the fleeting vowel in the other forms of the present tense is due to analogy or to the fact that they are stressed. Nearly all the verbs in this class are intransitive (except слы́шать and держа́ть) and denote something to do with noise. Examples follow.

(1) -ЧАТЬ

молча́ть	be quiet	мчать	rush, whish
урча́ть	rumble	крича́ть	cry
звуча́ть	sound	ворча́ть	growl
рыча́ть	snarl	бурча́ть	mumble
стуча́ть	knock	бренча́ть	jingle
журча́ть	babble	мыча́ть	moo

-ШАТЬ

шурша́ть	rustle	слы́шать	hear

-ЩАТЬ

вереща́ть	squeal	треща́ть	crackle

-ЖАТЬ

дребезжа́ть	tinkle	жужжа́ть	buzz
брюзжа́ть	grumble	визжа́ть	squeal, yelp

*A Many of the words in (1) are derivationally related to words whose
root morpheme ends in a velar (молк-, звук-, стук, to name just a
few). Assuming that the morpheme {+a} is the same as found in a/a
verbs, what will the morphophonemic representation of these words be
like?

*B Given the following data, write
      (a) the complex verbal suffix used for each verb
      (b) the morphophonemic representation of the infinitive
      (c) an explanation for observed alternations

Infinitive	1st sg	2nd sg	Related
1. плáкать	плáчу	плáчешь	плáкса
2. платúть	плачý	плáтишь	платёж
3. решáть	решáю	решáешь	решúть
4. просвещáть	просвещáю	просвещáешь	просветúть
5. облегчáть	облегчáю	облегчáешь	лёгкий
6. трещáть	трещý	трещúшь	треск
7. упакóвывать	упакóвываю	упакóвываю	упаковáть
8. глянцевáть	глянцýю	глянцýешь	гля́нец
9. ослéпнуть	ослéпну	ослéпнешь	слепóй
10. разы́скивать	разы́скиваю	разы́скиваешь	искáть

*C Give the derived imperfective in -ыва or -ива for the following:

1. образовáть	6. выхолостúть
2. спросúть	7. показáть
3. доигрáть	8. навéсить
4. оправдáть	9. загадáть
5. затрóнуть	10. устрóить

7.5 Noun and Adjectival Derivation

In verbal derivation we saw that different types of morphophonemic
shifts are predicated on the complex verbal suffix. Most of these shifts are
automatic, since they always occur with a given verbal suffix. The
phonological properties of suffixes, on the other hand, were found to have

little to do with the modifications of the root morpheme. In this section we will review some of the morphophonemic changes that occur in noun and adjectival derivation. They are:

(1) a. hard paired consonants are palatalized
 b. velars become palatals
 c. soft consonants become hard
 d. no modification

Dental consonants do not mutate in nominal and adjectival derivation, as they do in verbs. We will study the following suffixes:

(1) NOUN SUFFIXES

1. -ец	6. -ок, -ёк, -онок
2. -ик, -ник, -чик, -щик	7. -ость
3. -анин	8. -ств(о)
4. -к	9. -тель
5. -н(ие)	

ADJECTIVAL SUFFIXES

1. -н(ый)   2. -ск(ий)

7.5.1 Nouns in -ец

This suffix forms agentive nouns, diminutives and nouns showing residency or nationality (e.g., гаваец "Hawaiian"). At an earlier stage in the language, it contained a lax front high vowel, -ьц, which was lowered to e in strong position. Front vowels caused softening of hard paired consonants and mutation of velars. We are able to see the results of these phonological changes in the modern language:

(1) гордéц "arrogant person" < гордь́ць
 запорóжец "Zaporozhian Cossack" < запорóгьць

Palatalization of hard paired consonants and of velars is automatic with this suffix in the modern language, but mutation of velars no longer is:

(2) саўдовец "Saudi"   < {саўдов -эц}
    чика́гец "Chicagoan"   < {чика́г -эц}
    ньюйо́ркец "New Yorker"   < {ньюйо́рк -эц}

Since the vowel of this suffix goes back to a jer, it now shows up as a
fleeting vowel. The presence of the fleeting vowel accounts for the
palatalized quality of the root morpheme's final consonant. For those
ending in a velar the data in (2) suggest that the fleeting vowel insertion
rule must specify / → э / ___ ц. Thus the alternations involved here are not
morphophonemic in nature but phonological. However we must still
account for the shift of г to ж in forms such as лжец "liar" and
норвѐжец "Norwegian," cf. лгать, Норве́гия. These words contain
allomorphs, made up of the morphemes {лГ-} and {норвеГ-}. A
morphophonemic rule similar to the one in (9) in section 7.2 then chooses
the correct allomorph in the right environment:

(3) Г → ж / ___ noun suffix {+эц}

where Г stands for any morpheme final velar (Г: г ~ ж), (К: к ~ ч), (Х:
х ~ ш). We shall see below that the environment for this shift is much
wider.

7.5.2 Nouns in -ик, -ник, -чик, -щик

The suffix {+ик} forms agentive nouns, diminutives, and affectionate
forms. It causes fleeting vowels to disappear. As expected for a suffix
beginning with a front vowel, paired consonants are softened before this
suffix by phonological processes. The following combinations do not
occur: -гик, -кик, -хик, and apparently never did, since there are no
instances of -жик, -чик, -шик derived from the former. Instances of the
latter do not have velar counterparts:

(1) о́рлик   -   softening, loss of fleeting vowel (cf. орёл)
    ёжик   -   no modification, derived from ёж.
    мужи́к   -   no modification, derived from муж.
    ко́вшик   -   no modification, derived from ковш.

The loss of the fleeting vowel is an automatic mophophonemic shift.

The suffix {чик} is built upon {+ик}. It has the morphophonemic structure {*чик}, where the ч derives from a historical (ьк), as in {ьк + ик}. Nevertheless, paired consonants (except л) are hard before this suffix (cf. го́лубь > голу́бчик). As we might expect velars do not occur before this suffix, instead there are two palatals:

(2) перебе́жчик - no modification, derived from перебежа́ть

    обтя́жчик - no modification, derived from обтя́жка

This suffix also causes preceding л to be palatalized, and so is morphophonemically marked (*):

(3) бока́льчик - softening of л, derived from бока́л

The morphophonemic rule operating here is:

(4)   л → л' / ___ {-*чик}

By now it should be apparent that the stars we have been using to mark morphophonemically active suffixes are redundant if the morphophonemic rules state which morpheme is being represented in the environment of the rule. Thus, the verbal theme vowel {*o} really need not be marked by a star, since the morphophonemic rule involving this suffix states explicitly that the shift of C → C' occurs in conjunction with this particular morpheme, not just any {o}. We will retain the use of the star, however, since it provides a good reminder that a morphophonemic shift may occur.

The suffix -ник has several interesting characteristics. Velars become palatals before it and, though it contains a vowel, fleeting vowels do occur in preceding morphemes. Examples:

(4) соба́чник - mutation, derived from соба́к(а)

    бу́лочник - fleeting vowel, derived from бу́лк(а)

              {бу́л(о)к + ник}

There is no phonological basis for the shift of a velar to palatal before н, cf. окно́. This shift actually first occurred when the suffix contained a front jer (-ьн + ик), the first element of the suffix being the adjectival suffix (cf. бу́лочная). This adjectival suffix fused with the noun forming suffix -ик, to form the new suffix -ник. Like -чик, the letter л is always soft before -ник. We are able to account for velar mutations in conjunction with this suffix by the automatic application of a morphophonemic rule. The environment of the rule must include this suffix, and, incidentally, all suffixes that start with the consonant -н. This implies that the suffixes are responsible for the velar mutations here, not a synchronically unaccountable, unpredictable shift in the root morpheme. This is similar to the verbal suffix {*o}, which causes palatalization of any paired consonant preceding it. Suffixes which begin with н do not permit preceding velars. All velars become palatals before it. Thus, the suffix -ник must be marked to bring about such a change: {*ник}. The marking on this suffix can be interpreted:

(5) к,г,х,л → ч,ж,ш,л' / _____ *ник

The suffix -щик acts like -ник. It causes fleeting vowels to appear (у́голь/у́гля - у́гольщик) and causes morphophonemic л to be soft (игла́ - иго́льщик). No velars or palatals occur with this suffix. Finally, paired consonants are hard before this suffix (фона́рщик). Fleeting vowels appear only if followed by a consonant.

*A Form nouns using the suffixes given in parentheses.

1. молоко́ (+ник)   6. обману́ть (+щик)
2. игла́ (+ник)   7. паке́т (+ик)
3. парово́з (+ник)   8. пиро́г (+ник)
4. бесе́да (+чик)   9. котёл (+щик)
5. наём (+ник)   10. ходьба́ (+щик)

7.5.3 Nouns in -анин

The addition of this suffix to morpheme roots results in nonautomatic shifts. Paired consonants may or may not be softened:

(1) final -в: молдава́нин   but   славяни́н
    final -м: мусульма́нин   армяни́н
    final -т: пурита́нин   египтя́нин
    final -р: лютера́нин   северя́нин

Consequently those roots which do undergo softening must be so marked: {слаВ-}, {сэвэР-}, etc. A morphophonemic rule which states that marked nonvelars become palatalized before certain suffixes will then operate to produce the observed forms.

In some words with this suffix a trace of the suffix -и which joticized before the initial vowel of the suffix (i.e., ианин → йанин) and caused mutation of velars and dentals is evident. Examples:

(2) final -в: древля́нин　from {древ -и -анин}
　　final -д: горожа́нин　from {город -и -анин}
　　final -х: палеша́нин　from {палех -и -анин}
　　final -г: южа́нин　from {юг -и -анин}
　　final -ст: мещани́н　from {мест -и -анин}

Whether or not the и (→ й) is present, however, is unpredictable from a synchronic point of view, as shown in (1). The root morphemes are accordingly marked for mutation with the suffix {анин}: {дреВ}, {гороД}, etc.

7.5.4 Nouns in -к

This suffix is added to nouns to create diminutives and to form nouns from verbs. It causes hardening of soft paired consonants (сеть - се́тка, нить - ни́тка), except for soft л (земе́лька, неде́лька). Velars automatically become palatals before this suffix (кни́жка). Another suffix, -лка, used to derive nouns from verbs, does not have a palatalized л, as in скака́ть "jump" > скака́лка "jump rope."

7.5.5 Nouns in -ние

The suffix {ний} is used to form abstract (neut) nouns from verbal stems ending in a vowel. If the verbal stem ends in a consonant (нес-, тек-, etc.) then a filler vowel е is added between the consonant and this suffix: несе́ние, тече́ние, etc. This filler vowel, morphophonemically {*э}, softens paired consonants (phonologically) and mutates velars (morphophonemically). When the suffix -н(ие) is added to a stem ending in a vowel no changes occur, except for shift of stress (see Chapter 8). Examples follow.

(1) опозда́ние   <   опозда- (vb)   <   позд (adv)
     поруга́ние   <   поруга- (vb)
     воздержа́ние   <   воздержа- (vb)

The 2nd conj verbal suffix {-и} is not dropped when forming nouns with this suffix. But the filler vowel e̲ is added to the suffix and и + э yields й + э. Consequently, mutations normally seen in 2nd conj verbs are repeated here. Thus, dentals mutate to palatals, and labials add an epenthetic л̲. (Recall that no stem final velars exist in 2nd conj verbs.)

(2) тормози́ть   >   торможе́ние   {тормоз -и -э́ -ний +о}
                                     braking
     броди́ть   >   броже́ние   fermentation
     укрепи́ть   >   укрепле́ние   strengthening
     отпра́вить   >   отправле́ние   sending
     сгусти́ть   >   сгуще́ние   thickening

7.5.6 Nouns in -ок, -ёк, -ек, -о́нок

Velars do not occur before these suffixes, the first three of which are morphophonemically {*/к}, the final suffix being {*он/к}. Instead an automatic morphophonemic shift occurs which mutates them to palatals: снежо́к, овра́жек, скачо́к, смешо́к, казачо́нок. The suffix -оно̲к causes paired consonants to soften (automatic) and causes fleeting vowels to disappear: кит - китёнок, козёл - козлёнок. A few dentals mutate to palatals before the suffix -оно̲к. This is an unpredictable shift: ле́бедь - лебедёнок, but медве́дь - медвежо́нок. The latter form derives from {медвеД' + *о́н(о)к} (cf. also верблюжо́нок). Otherwise, no changes, except for stress: городо́к, уголёк, кошелёк.

7.5.7 Nouns in -ость

No changes are observed in derivation with this suffix: ра́дость, бла́гость, ги́бкость. Root-morpheme final hushers are due to previous derivations: похо́жесть < похо́жий, тя́жесть < тя́жкий. Forms in -ность are secondarily derived from adjectives in -н̲-, as акти́вность < акти́вный̲.

7.5.8 Nouns in -ство

Velar stems become palatals and a filler vowel e̱ follows mutated velars: ра́бство, схо́дство, божество́, му́жество, кня́жество, оте́чество, чуда́чество. Soft paired consonants except л' become hard: зве́рство, изда́тельство.

7.5.9 Nouns in -тель

No changes occur. This suffix fuses with verbal suffixes to derive agentive nouns: нагрева́тель, свиде́тель, исправи́тель.

*A Form nouns from the base words given below. Use the suffix given in parentheses. Be ready to write each derived word in morphophonemic transcription.

1. вдова́ (ец)
2. глаз (ок)
3. гриб (ок)
4. Ри́га (анин)
5. чертёж (ик)
6. загото́вить (ние)
7. обогрева́ть (тель)
8. развести́ / разведу́ (чик)
9. ёлка (ка)
10. бес (ёнок)
11. бе́дный (ость)
12. ка́мень (щик)
13. зверь (онок)
14. моги́ла (щик)
15. оговори́ть (щик)
16. осёл / осла́ (онок)
17. кружи́ть (ние)
18. опа́сный (ость)
19. па́ртия (ец)
20. подру́га (ка)
21. друг (ок)
22. голла́ндия (ец)
23. зате́я (ник)
24. твори́ть (ние)
25. кни́жный (ость)
26. сапо́г (ник)
27. га́лка (ка)
28. дру́жный (ость)
29. штук (ка)
30. кри́тика (∅ suffix)

7.5.10 Adjectives in -н

This is one of the most productive suffixes in Russian. As expected for a consonantal suffix, it causes fleeting vowels to appear (су́то̱чный). Velars mutate and л is palatalized: язы́чный, ме́сячный (< {мэ́с'аЦ + н + ый), шко́льный. Soft consonants become hard: гря́зный, слова́рный.

These are morphophonemic shifts. With the exception of stress, no shifts are observed among other consonants: досту́пный, безво́дный.

7.5.11 Adjectives in -ский

This is another widely used suffix. Velars rarely occur before this suffix, instead the corresponding husher is found followed by the filler vowel е: челове́ческий, куби́ческий, педогоги́ческий, бо́жеский, дру́жеский, мона́шеский. A few irregular morphemes do not take the filler vowel: во́лжский, пра́жский (< {волГ -ск + ий}, etc.). Soft paired consonants (except л') are hard before this suffix: апте́карский, ца́рский, де́тский. Soft л' retains softness and hard л becomes soft: чита́тельский, а́нгельский, се́льский. As with other consonantal suffixes, fleeting vowels appear: неме́цкий (< {нем(е)ц + ск + ий}).

*A What nouns derive the following adjectives?

1. нау́чный	4. во́дочный	7. оши́бочный
2. коне́чный	5. де́нежный	8. автомоби́льный
3. ство́льный	6. оте́ческий	9. биологи́ческий

*B Form adjectives by means of the suffix -н-.

1. ме́сто	4. грусть	7. культу́ра	10. доро́га
2. успе́х	5. ме́сяц	8. семья́	11. мы́ло
3. грех	6. тетра́дка	9. вкус	12. ружьё

7.6 Regionalisms

One of the richest aspects of Russian dialectology concerns not the way words are pronounced from area to area, but the various words that are used from region to region. In linguistics, "word" variations are often refered to as "lexical" (лекси́ческие) variations. There are literally thousands of lexical variations in Russian and these numbers may be greatly multiplied if other Slavic languages are considered. Lexical variations often deal with interesting "folk" or "common" items that reveal local color and folk traditions.

Lexical variations themselves may be broken down into two major categories: different words for the same thing, or one word is used in different areas but with different meanings. An example of the first category is the CSR word петух "rooster." In the northwest part of Russia the word for rooster is петун. In some northern dialects it is певун or пёвун. In a southwest dialect it is пёвень. The latter three retain a trace of the word from which петух originated: петь. In addition, петух is related to the name Петя--from Пётр), but in a large area south and east of Moscow from Belgorod in the south to Kostroma in the north this farmyard animal is referred to as кочет, derived from the Common Slavic word for rooster, *кокотъ (cf. Polish koczot), and related to French coq and English cock. CSR петух meaning "rooster" must have started with only one speaker. But the usage seems appropriate, and the popularity of this word for "rooster" grew to become standard, making the original form кочет, now dialectal.

The word мост provides a good example of how one word may have different (if related) meanings in varying dialects: a) bridge, b) floor of any building, c) floor of an entry way, d) any entry way.

Lexical variations often deal with aspects of life that are important to a particular geographical area. These might include terminology for weather, farm implements, hunting and fishing, planting and harvesting, local celebrations, clothing, and food. CSR does not have a single word for "harvested field" or "mowed field." Areas where harvested fields are an important part of the landscape, however, do have a special word for this: жнивьё, жнитво, жнёвенье, жнёвник, жнивняк. Here are other dialectal variations of words dealing with "harvest:"

(1)

dialectal	meaning	CSR
жатвина (Archangel)	"reaping time"	время жатвы
жатвина (Archangel)	"ploughed field"	пашня
жальья (Penza)	"reaper"	жнец

The dialect of Russian Old Believers in Alaska also contains several lexical innovations. They include americanisms such as бебечка "baby," гарбач "garbage," and гринхаус "greenhouse." Other words are variations of standard Russian words, such as братаник "cousin," жись "life," лесина "tree."

7.7 Review

Pronunciation rules seem to have a life cycle of their own. They come into existence hesitantly in rapid speech and colloquial usage and as characteristics of dialectal speech. They may then become fully operative throughout most of the language as full-fledged phonological phenomena. Then new sound changes may occur that restrict and ultimately nullify the previous changes. Often a trace of earlier sound shifts can be seen as "irregularities" in the language. We account for such irregularities by means of morphophonemic rules.

The fate of jers in weak position is a good example of this process. In rapid speech jers in weak position were lost. One can imagine an Old Russian wondering why the youth of her day said [с'м'э́р'т'] instead of [съм'э́р'ть]. In strong position jers became fully vocal. It is likely that at one time both [от'ьц'ь] and [от'э́ц'ь] were heard. Modern Russian contains a trace of these changes in its system of fleeting vowels. But original jers no longer exist in the language and to treat modern fleeting vowels as jers implies that modern speakers have an understanding at some level of linguistic competence of these historical processes. This seems unlikely. When confronted with the fleeting vowel question most well-educated Russians say that these are simply exceptional forms which must be learned. Morphophonemics shows us that these exceptions occur only in certain restricted and definable, environments. Fleeting vowels are not expected anywhere and everywhere throughout the language. Some morphemes trigger the presence or absence of fleeting vowels, given the ability of another morpheme (root or suffix) to display a mobile vowel. Morphophonemics allows us to describe many of the changes that occur in the modern language when various segments are concatenated to form words. Why these changes, based on long-dead or dying phonological rules, continue to be observed in the language is a question which deserves attention. An area that appears to be closely involved with morphophonemics is the stress system, the subject of the next chapter.

CHAPTER 8: STRESS

8.0 Introduction

Of all the difficulties involved in learning Russian, stress is one of the most trying. Students learn that stress is not very predictable and that paying attention to stress while speaking leads to uneven or halting speech. Students who attempt to strengthen vocabulary by reading are continually presented with new words, the meanings of which may be determined by roots and context, but the pronunciation of which may be unclear due to uncertainty about stress locus. Though the meaning of the word may be known students find themselves looking up the word in a dictionary just to find its stress.

Many students learn stress simply by repetition and assimilation. This currently is probably, after all, the most efficient way to learn stress, but an understanding of the stress system may facilitate this process. In addition, a study of Russian stress helps us become better acquainted with this critical factor in the way Russians communicate. What role does stress play in speech? What do Russians intuitively know about stress? Are there ways in which learners of Russian could more easily master this seemingly intricate system? This chapter attempts to answer these and other questions dealing with stress, and to present a method for predicting stress.

Since stress is closely related to the morphophonemic structure of words, we will use morphophonemic transcription throughout this chapter, including the following conventions. Prefixes are set apart from roots by the equals sign, as in {в=клад}. Suffixes begin with a dash and endings begin with a plus sign, as in бе́дный {бэ́д -*/н +ый}.

8.1 A Portrait of Russian Stress

Stress (ударе́ние) in Russian involves the question of how vowels are pronounced. Stress, sometimes called accent, is the relative lengthening of a vowel in relation to how long that vowel is usually pronounced and relative to the length of neighboring unstressed vowels. This lengthening may be accompanied by a slight increase of amplitude (loudness - гро́мкость) and tone or pitch (тон). Because of akan'e and ikan'e, unstressed <u>o</u>, <u>e</u>, or <u>я</u>, and to a lesser degree unstressed <u>a</u> are pronounced noticeably differently, i.e., reduced, than when they are stressed. Though such reduction does not occur for unstressed <u>и</u>, <u>ы</u>, and <u>у</u> or <u>ю</u>, these vowels still stand out when they are stressed, even if neighboring vowels do not show akan'e or ikan'e, as in у́ксус "vinegar" the initial vowel stands out more than the second vowel due to stress.

In writing, stress is indicated by the acute accent mark, as in по́нял, or by two dots in the letter ё, as in встаёт. The two dots mark thus fills two functions: it distinguishes the pronunciation of this letter and it marks stress. Therefore, there is no need to mark an acute stress mark on the letter ё. It is always stressed.

Since stress is a relative phenomenon, it means little to speak of stressed or unstressed vowels in isolation. As the morpheme is a major player in locating stress in Russian, we may refer to stressed or unstressed roots, suffixes, or endings. Since morphemes are made up of one or more syllables, we may also refer to stressed or unstressed syllables.

Stress in Russian is usually called "free." This means that stress may fall on any syllable of any given word. Thus stress may be on the first syllable, second syllable, etc., of a given word, whether it is a noun, adjective, or verb, as illustrated in (1).

(1)

1st syllable:	ко́локол	то́лстый	де́лать
2nd syllable:	ана́лиз	краси́вый	писа́ть
3rd syllable:	крокоди́л	основно́й	выбира́ть
4th syllable:	авторите́т	передвижно́й	перегрузи́ть

To make matters more complex, there is another dimension to the possible location of stress in Russian words. The words in (1) have been given in the nom sg masc, nom sg masc long form, and in the infinitive. But when words are inflected, stress may or may not shift from one syllable to another. Thus, ко́локол "bell" becomes колокола́ "bells." The stress shifts to the ending in the short form fem of то́лстый "fat" to толста́. And stress shifts from the second syllable in писа́ть "to write" to the first in пи́шет "she writes." While this kind of mobility in stress is limited to a small percentage of words, simply knowing that it exists often causes hesitancy in the speech of students learning Russian.

Even a cursory study of the words in (1) suggests that stress in Russian does not follow a simple syllable counting system such as Polish, where stress nearly always falls on the second to last syllable, or penultimate. Other forces appear to be at play. For example, is it just coincidence that

the nouns рыбáк "fisherman" and чудáк "eccentric" both have stress on
the suffix, which is the same in both words (-ак)? Since stress seems to be
capable of falling on any syllable and since some syllables seem to be
involved with stress in a peculiar way, it may be suggested that it is
impossible to state simply that stress in Russian falls on any numbered
syllable, counting either from the beginning or from the end of the word.

Regarding stress location, Lebedeva writes:

> Другой отличительной чертой русского ударения является его
> разноместность и подвижность, представляющие собой
> важный аспект обучения иностранцев. Разноместность
> ударения, являющаяся признаком дифференциации значений
> словв русском языке (мукá - мýка, дорогóй - дорóгой, парóм -
> пáром, целýю - цéлую), с большим трудом воспринимается
> иностранными учащимися.

> Для учащихся неродственных языков ошибки по месту
> ударения в русских словах становятся возможными едва ли не
> в каждом многосложном слове, так как отсутствуют какие-
> либоправила, которые могли бы установить или объяснить, в
> каких словах ударение падает на первый слог, в каких--на
> второй, и т.д.

*A 1. The word водá "water" has one of the shifting patterns mentioned
by Lebedeva. In the acc sg stress shifts to the initial syllable: вóду. If
you neglect to make this stress shift in pronouncing a sentence such as:
Я хочу пить воду, what does it sound like you are saying?

2. What rules are there, according to Lebedeva, that may help foreign
students of Russian place stress correctly?

While Lebedeva (where is the stress in this name?) accurately stated
some of the difficulties regarding stress for foreigners, her statement that
there are no rules to aid the learner in predicting stress is no longer
completely true, thanks to advances made in the theory of accentuation. In
the remainder of this chapter we will discuss methods and principles by
which stress can be predicted for most words. Even so, many words defy
the categorizations presented here. But we can use the principles discussed

as a foundation upon which apparent irregularities can be further elucidated.

Good dictionaries give the stress of entries for all their inflected forms. In order to save space, however, a system is used in most dictionaries in which the stress of any inflected form of a word is only given if it differs from the stress of the dictionary entry, or from the stress of the last form given. Thus, Ozhegov gives the following partial entries:

(2) читáть, -áю, -áешь   = stem stress throughout
     снéжный, -ая, -ое, -жен, -жна   = stem stress throughout
     давáть, даю́, даёшь   = ending stress throughout
     смешнóй, áя, óе, -шóн, шнá   = ending stress throughout
     шкóла, ы   = stem stress throughout

*B Do the following have stress on stem or ending throughout their inflected forms? Which do you think are not likely candidates for stem stress? Refer to a dictionary if necessary.

1. злой	4. роднóй	7. крýпный
2. стать	5. отдохнýть	8. жить
3. молчáть	6. удóбрить	9. простúть

*C Given the following dictionary entries, tell if the following have stress fixed on the stem or on the ending.

1. прирóда, -ы	6. завестú, -едý, -едёшь; -ёл, -елá
2. наéздить, -зжу, -здишь	7. чудéсный, -ая, -ое; -сен, -сна
3. инструмéнт, -а	8. умножáть, -áю, -áешь
4. индю́к, -á	9. статья́, -й
5. звонóк, -нкá	10. враг, -á

8.2 Predicting Stress

Modern Russian stress is the result of a thousand or so years of language development. The observed complexities are due to many historical shifts in stress as well as to historical sound shifts in the language. Some of these stress shifts will be discussed in section 8.3. But the net result of these changes is the impression of a complete hodgepodge of stress possibilities. For the majority of words, however, stress can be predicted correctly by means of a two-step process. The first step in this process is to determine the stress on the basic form of the word. For nouns the basic form is the nom sg. For adjectives the basic form is the nom sg long form. For verbs the basic form is the infinitive. The following sections present an overview of this two-step process. Due to space limitations we will not be able to review all possibilities here, but the material presented should provide a good foundation for understanding how this account of the stress system works and for making correct predictions.

The second step in the process of predicting stress is to determine the stress pattern of each word in question. This allows the prediction of stress on any inflected form of a word. In the great majority of cases stress is fixed on the same syllable as in the basic form. Many high-frequency words, however, do exhibit shifting stress patterns. Methods for determining stress in these words will be presented in section 8.8.

We have seen that stress can fall on any syllable of a given word. And words with the same root may have different stress loci:

(1) РЯД "order/row/rank"   →   ря́д, ряди́ться
    РЫБ "fish"   →   ры́ба, рыба́к
    ПРЫГ "jump"   →   пры́гать, прыгу́н
    МУЖ "man"   →   му́ж, му́жество, мужи́к
    ЛИК "face"   →   лицо́, ли́чный

On the other hand some roots occur only under stress.

(2) КОЛЕ́Н "knee"   →   коле́но, коле́нце
    ИНЖЕНЕ́Р "engineer"   →   инжене́р, инжене́рша
    КРАХМА́Л "starch"   →   крахма́л, крахма́лить

Finally, some roots rarely or never occur under stress.

(3) ЗР "see, view"   →   зре́ть, зре́ние, зрачо́к
    ДРАЗ "irritate"   →   дразни́ть, раздража́ть
    ПРЯМ "direct, straight"   →   прямо́й, прями́ть, прямота́

One way to account for these facts is to suggest that some roots are somehow attractive to stress. In a sense, the roots in (2) and many others (see Appendix 2) are "strong" as far as stress is concerned, that is, in normal circumstances they attract word stress. Strange to say, there also seem to be roots that are weak in regard to stress. For example, stress seems to avoid the roots in (3). Finally, there is a large set of roots that are neither weak nor strong, but, like the words in (1), are sometimes stressed and sometimes not stressed. These seem to be ordinary roots without any particular attachment or aversion to stress.

It is easy to see that if one knows that a root is strong, then one will know the stress of any word that the root occurs in. This may not, at first blush, be very satisfying. We ask, why not just memorize the stress of these words? Why worry about the notion "strong?" Actually, this is exactly what must be done. But there are other forces at play in Russian accentuation that can be readily explained if we assume that these (strong) roots are different from the others. Luckily, there are not very many high-frequency strong roots and most of them are polysyllabic or borrowed, thus, they are easy to spot.

Similarly it is easy to see that if a root is weak then stress must fall elsewhere in the word. Again this may seem like a cop-out. Some may ask, why not just learn the stress of these words and forget about this strong/weak nonsense. As you learn that certain roots never bear the stress, you are learning that they are weak. And as for both weak and strong roots, there are important rules involved in the placement of stress that require just this information.

It turns out that most polysyllabic roots are strong. In their dictionary of morphemes, Kuznecov and Efremova list about 915 polysyllabic roots. Of these, the majority (about 650) are stressed on the final syllable, e.g., ЛИМО́Н. Nearly all of these roots are strong. About 200 roots are stressed on the second to last syllable, eg., КА́ВЕРЗ, ГО́РОД, А́ДРЕС. Of these, however, about 45 are TORT forms and may be considered, from an accentual point of view, as monosyllables (see section 8.3). Most TORT forms are not strong. However, the great majority of non-TORT form roots in this list of 200 roots are strong. Finally, about 65 polysyllabic roots appear to be weak in regard to stress, e.g., МОЛОК-, ЕРУНД-, КОНОП.

Interestingly enough only two roots have stress on the third to final syllable (ГУ́СЕНИЧК- "caterpillar" and КИ́НОВАР- "cinnabar"), both of which end in what looks like a suffix. A handful of others with stress on the third to final syllable contain TORT formations and may be considered

disyllabic: жа́воронок, пе́репел, ко́локол, щи́колот and four others.
There exist only a couple of four syllabic roots, and none are stressed on
the fourth to last syllable. If we were to try to state the general location of
stress in Russian, the data from the polysyllabic roots would suggest that
generally speaking stress tends to fall towards the end of a word. This is
confirmed by the stress of "artificial" words such as abbreviations and
acronyms: СНГ, МГУ, США all have end stress (эс-эн-гэ́, эм-гэ-у́, сэ-
ша-а́) as do acronyms such as исполко́м, комсомо́л, ГАЙ, госизда́т.
Finally the bias towards the end of the word can also be seen in compound
words where the second element of the compound always receives the
primary stress, with secondary stress (marked by a grave accent) falling on
the first: дѐревоплита́, кру̀пноголо́вый, желѐзобето́н.

If there is a general tendency to stress towards the end of words, then
this tendency should be observable in words composed of ordinary roots,
where stress is not influenced by strong or weak roots. Consider the words
in (4), all of which are composed of ordinary roots (neither strong nor
weak in regard to stress). Note that when a suffix is added to these roots,
stress falls on the suffix or even on the ending in some cases:

(4) снег   снежо́к   снежни́к   снегово́й
    свет   света́ть   светля́к   освети́ть
    мо́лот   молото́к   молоти́ть   молотово́й
    мёртвый   мертве́ц   мертви́ть   мертвя́к
    ро́вный   ровня́ть   равни́на   ровнота́

We see in (4) that stress is not on ordinary roots when these vowel-
bearing suffixes fall to the right of the root. Instead the suffix is stressed.

*A Write in morphophonemic transcription the first three words of
each column in (4).

*B Given the stress tendency discussed above, where would you expect
stress to fall in the following? (Words in parentheses are given for
comparison.)

1. (см. бе́лый) белеть   3. (го́рдый) гордец
2. (тёмный) темнеть   4. (А́фрика) африканский

5. (све́тлый) светлеть
6. (ЧИТ-) читать
7. (лезть) влезать
8. (мост) мостить
9. (мя́гкий) смягчить
10. (крест) крестить
11. (о́стрый) острить
12. (ры́ба) рыбец

13. (во́лос) долговолосый
14. (А́нглия) английский
15. (ночь) ночевать
16. (исто́рия) исторический
17. (испра́вить) исправление
18. (послу́шать) послушание
19. (хо́лод) холодный
20. (ры́ба) рыбак

Consider the stress of the following:

(5) a. <u>nouns</u>   b. <u>adjectives</u>   c. <u>verbs</u>

солда́т	здоро́вый	рабо́тать
кероси́н	бога́тый	печа́тать
конта́кт	краси́вый	обе́дать
мунди́р	девя́тый	лука́вить
маши́на	угрю́мый	отве́тить
свобо́да	дешёвый	увели́чить
оре́х	соля́рный	дежу́рить

Consider first the nouns in (5a). Stress falls on the final syllable in most of the words in (5), but not all. In some words the final syllable is the nom sg fem ending -a, and here it is not stressed. In spite of this difference, stress in all the nouns in (5a) is located in the same position, namely, stress falls on the <u>final stem syllable</u>.

The stress of the adjectives in (5b) is similar to that of the nouns, where stress falls on the last syllable of the stem. It would be nice if whatever rule that accounts for stress of the nouns in (5a) would also account for stress in the adjectives. The more words a single rule covers the more valuable it is. If the nouns have stress on the final stem syllable, we can see that that applies to most of the adjectives in (5b) as well: {здоро́в +ый}, {угрю́м +ый}. But what about those whose stem ends in the suffix {-*/н-}: {соли́д -*/н +ый}. This stem ends in an adjectival suffix which contains a place holder for a fleeting vowel, but no vowel is present in this form. Stress cannot fall on this suffix in this word, since only vowels can be stressed. A preliminary version of the rule that assigns stress in the words in (5a) and (5b), then, might have the form:

(6) V → [+stress] / _____ (C) +

Rule (6) states that the vowels of final stem syllables are pronounced stressed. This rule accounts for stress in each word in (5a) and (5b). Schematically:

(7) a. свобод +a   →(6)→   свобо́д +a
    b. угрюм +ый   →(6)→   угрю́м +ый
    c. солид -*/н +ый   →(6)→   соли́д -*/н +ый

Since stress cannot fall on a nonvowel, as in the syllable -*/н in (7c), some principle must be in operation that causes the stress to fall onto another syllable. For a start we may state the following principle:

(8) If stress falls on an unvocalized /, stress shifts to the left by one syllable.

The operation of rule (6) in combination with the restriction in (8) can be seen in hundreds of words:

(9) подро́бный   изве́стный   ска́льный
    спосо́бный   нау́чный   огро́мный
    заба́вный   разли́чный   стекля́нный
    ежедне́вный   отде́льный   язы́чный

Some readers may recognize that there must be something else involved in the assignment of stress in these kinds of adjectives and in other words since not all words have stem final stress, cf. за́падный, обще́ственный, зубно́й, го́род, голова́. We will discuss the stress in these words shortly. The huge majority of adjectives ending in -ный, however, have stem final stress.

The rule assigning stem final stress apparently does not apply to the verbs in (5c) since no verbal suffix in these stems is stressed (stems in (10) are underlined):

(10)   раб о́т -а+ть   печ а́т -а+ть

The stress falls on the stem in the words in (10), but not on the final stressable vowel in the stem, as it does, however, in words such as those given in (11):

(11) чит -а́+ть   хват -а́+ть   ис= чез -а́+ть

The verbs in (11) show that stress can fall on the verbal suffix, and stress falls on these final stem syllables normally. There appears to be something unusual about the roots in the verbs in (10) that discourages stress from falling on the final stem vowel. One obvious difference between the verbs in (10) and (11) is that the roots of the verbs in (10) are polysyllabic, while the roots in (11) are monosyllabic. In fact, nearly all verbs in -ать which do not contain other derivational suffixes, e.g., -ир ов-, -ыв-, and are monosyllabic have stress on the verbal suffix as given in (11). This includes polysyllabic verbs in -ать which are composed of prefixed monosyllabic roots:

(12) возника́ть   воз ник а́ ть   arise
      воспита́ть   вос пит а́ ть   educate
      достига́ть   до стиг а́ ть   reach, attain
      напада́ть   на пад а́ ть   attack
      обнима́ть   об ним а́ ть   hug
      открыва́ть   от крыв а́ ть   open
      понима́ть   по ним а́ ть   understand
      сообща́ть   со общ а́ ть   communicate

However, it is not enough to state that these kinds of verbs have suffix stress if the root is monosyllabic and root stress if the root is polysyllabic. There are a number of verbs with monosyllabic stems with stress on the root:

(13) ве́шать   жа́ждать   ню́хать
      дёргать   ла́ять   пры́гать
      ду́мать   ку́шать   пры́скать

These verbs, as well as the several with polysyllabic roots (there are not many--and most are very low frequency) contain roots that seem to "draw" stress to themselves. In short, they are exceptions to (6). These roots are strong. The fact that most of these roots retain stress **no matter** what suffix is attached supports the hypothesis that they are attractive to stress. For example, the root ДЁРГ- is **always** stressed. Kuznecova and Efremova list 37 words based on this root. Each has stress on the root. Of the 61 words with the root ДУМ-, all but four have stress on the root. The four which do not have stress on the perfective verbal prefix вы́-, which is always stressed in perfective verbs (вы́думать, etc.). The four words built on the root ЖАЖД- have stress on the root. A similar fixity of stress on the roots can be seen in the other verbs in (13), and in most other -ать verbs with stress on the root.

We must conclude that some roots are simply always, or nearly always, stressed. (Appendix 2 contains a list of high frequency roots and their accentual weight.) These are strong roots, or more specifically, strong syllables within roots, and they attract stress in defiance of the generalization expressed in (6). The rule which assigns stress to strong syllables may be formalized:

(14)   V → [+stress] / ___
                        S   where S=strong syllable

The rule in (14) states that strong syllables are stressed. This is illustrated in (15):

(15)   дум -а+ть → (14) →   ду́м -а+ть
         S

These premises entail two further assumptions. First, since Russian has only one primary stress per word, there must be some restriction that keeps multiple stresses from appearing on words. This principle is formalized:

(16)   Stress cannot be assigned to a word that already has stress.

Thus, once the rule which assigns stress to strong syllables applies, the restriction stated in (16) disallows any other rule from assigning stress.

The second conclusion arising from the facts presented above is that the two rules which assign stress must apply in the following order:

(17)　　a. Stress strong syllables -- rule (14)
　　　　　b. Stress final stem syllables -- rule (6)

The two rules, or stress principles, given in (17) and the principles given in (8) and (16) account for the stress in tens of thousands of words. Some fine-tuning of these rules will be needed in order to include many thousands of other words into their predictive web. This fine-tuning will take the form of answering the following questions, which will be discussed in subsequent sections:

(18)　　　a. What happens when a word contains two or more
　　　　　　　strong syllables?

　　　　　b. What happens when a word is composed of all weak
　　　　　　　syllables?

　　　　　c. What happens when a word is composed of a mixed
　　　　　　　bag of strong, ordinary, or weak syllables?

*C Mark stress according to the statements given in (8), (16), and (17). Recall that generally speaking polysyllabic roots have final strong syllables.

1. парад	11. колымага	21. угрюмый
2. кинжал	12. кукуруза	22. откровенный
3. виноград	13. железо	23. знаменитый
4. лейтенант	14. колено	24. подобный
5. форма	15. болото	25. блаженный
6. культура	16. полотенце	26. равнять
7. система	17. кресло	27. хватать
8. мимоза	18. взрослый	28. отрицать
9. капуста	19. могучий	29. кувыркать
10. микстура	20. нелепый	30. запрягать

*D The stems of the following word pairs are strong on the syllable as shown in the first column. Determine the stress of the second member in each pair.

1. стака́н	стаканчик	6. коле́но	подколенный
2. у́жин	ужинать	7. мёрзлый	замерзнуть
3. дежу́рная	дежурить	8. ме́сяц	месячина
4. де́ньги	обезденежеть	9. овра́г	овражистый
5. карма́н	карманчик	10. сою́з	союзничество

8.3 The Stress of TORT forms

Recall that TORT forms are words which have one of the following combinations in the root (where C=any consonant):

(1) C оро C	го́род, сто́рож, во́рон
C ере C	бе́рег, те́рем, че́реп
C оло C	мо́лот, го́лод, го́лос

The stress of nonderived TORT forms can usually be determined from the inflectional ending of their basic form. If the word is masc and has a null ending, then stress falls on the initial vowel of the TORT form; see all the examples in (1). If the basic form is fem or neut, then stress falls either on the final vowel of the TORT form or on the inflectional ending:

(2) берёза	"birch"	боло́то	"swamp"
воро́на	"crow"	желе́зо	"iron"
доро́га	"road"	борозда́	"furrow"
коро́ва	"cow"	сторона́	"side"
теле́га	"cart"	голова́	"head"

In regard to the masc nouns, we may conclude that the final syllable of the root is weak in the nonderived basic form. When stress is assigned by rule, stress in masc nouns falls on the stem final stressable vowel. In masc TORT forms, this is the initial vowel. Thus all the roots in (1) are either weak or ordinary. For some reason the words горо́х, моро́з, поло́н, and холо́п do not follow the majority of masc TORT forms, instead they have final stress, and all are strong except ПОЛОН-, as seen in полони́ть.

Similarly a few neut nouns have initial stress: зо́лото, де́рево, both ordinary roots.

In general TORT forms with initial stress are ordinary or weak roots. Those with final stress are strong. This divergence has its explanation in historical accentology.

Common Slavic not only had stress, but also tones. Leftovers of the tonal system can still be seen in some dialects of Serbian and Croatian, and in related Baltic languages. Modern Lithuanian and Latvian retain tone, at least it is marked in dictionaries if it is often lacking in speech. Stress was a secondary factor, a by-product, in this ancient system--it correlated to the highest pitch in any given word. As tones were lost, stress began to migrate to various positions within words, depending on the dialect in question. In Polish, for example, stress eventually moved to the penultimate syllable. In Czech stress finally settled on the initial syllable. In Russian, as we shall see, stress became associated with morphological segments and boundaries, ostensibly resulting in a "free" stress system.

Some words in Common Slavic had a rising pitch (the "acute") and others had a falling pitch (the "circumflex"). In Old Russian, stress that had been associated with these pitches remained on the same syllable after pitch was lost. TORT forms with initial stress (i.e., for the most part masc nouns), reflect the old falling pitch on the syllable. TORT forms with stress on the second vowel show the old rising pitch:

(3) <u>Russian</u>   <u>Common Slavic</u>

    зо́лото   *зậлто   (falling intonation)
    хо́лод   *хậлдъ   (falling intonation)
    го́лод   *гậлдъ   (falling intonation)

    коро́ва   *ко́рва   (rising intonation)
    моро́з   *мо́рзъ   (rising intonation)
    боло́то   *бо́лто   (rising intonation)

We may therefore associate the terms "weak" and "ordinary" (read: movable) with the old falling intonation, and the term "strong" (read: fixed) with the old rising intonation.

The few exceptions to the generalizations outlined above regarding stress in TORT forms, eg., коро́ль, поло́н, and чере́д, should, like золото and дерево, be memorized as exceptional.

Finally, it should be noted that in some cases in conjunction with certain derivational suffixes TORT forms act like monosyllabic roots. This is not surprising given the historical source of these words (see sections 4.3 and 8.7.3).

*A The following words have TORT form roots which are not strong. According to the principles of stress placement discussed in the previous sections, where should stress fall in these words on the left? Words on the right are given for comparison.

1. молодчага "fine fellow"	мо́лод "young" short form masc
2. черепаха "tortoise"	че́реп "skull"
3. городище "huge town"	го́род "town"
4. молоток "hammer"	мо́лот "hammer"
5. золотить "to gild"	зо́лото "gold"
6. воротничок "collar"	во́рот "neckband"
7. насторожить "to set a trap"	сто́рож "guard"
8. голодать "to hunger"	го́лод "hunger"
9. голосить "to cry out"	го́лос "voice"

*B In each blank of the following place a ∅, or a according to the stress of the root.

1. ко́лоб___	6. соло́м___
2. берёз___	7. коро́в___
3. сторон___	8. теле́г___
4. сто́рож___	9. по́лоз___
5. шо́рох___	10. доро́г___

8.4 Stress of Derivational Suffixes

We have seen that roots may be strong; they attract stress over the general rule which stresses stem final syllables. Russian also contains some roots that are weak, which means they refuse to be stressed under most circumstances. Stress in nonderived words with weak roots falls on the ending or even jumps off the word altogether:

(1) слон   слонá (gen sg)
    четвéрг   четвергá (gen sg)
    головá   нá голову (acc sg)

We will discuss these kinds of weak nonderived words in section 8.8.1. We will now be interested in how roots interact with various suffixes.

It turns out that suffixes exhibit the same tripartite stress orientation that roots do. Suffixes may be strong, weak, or ordinary. In the next three sections we will review how suffixes of different valencies (weak, strong, ordinary) interact with roots of different valencies in what Zaliznyak, a foremost Russian accentologist, called "the competition for stress." Since roots and suffixes may be either strong, weak, or ordinary, there are nine different avenues for positing stress onto three possible positions: root, suffix, or ending. Stress on the ending occurs only rarely with derived words, so we will here be most interested in root or suffix stress and will discuss ending stress later. The following table summarizes the possible combinations of roots and suffixes and the stress that normally results in the basic form.

(2)

ROOT IS	SUFFIX IS	STRESS FALLS ON THE
STRONG	**STRONG**	SUFFIX
STRONG	weak	ROOT
STRONG	ordinary	ROOT
weak	**STRONG**	SUFFIX
weak	weak	ROOT OR SUFFIX
weak	ordinary	SUFFIX
ordinary	**STRONG**	SUFFIX
ordinary	weak	ROOT
ordinary	ordinary	SUFFIX

In the next three sections we will review the data that supports the predictions given in (2). Before doing so, however, let us make a few general observations about the distribution of stress in (2). When a morpheme contains a strong syllable, stress falls on that morpheme. If two or more strong morphemes are present stress falls on the one to the right, toward the end of the word. When a weak morpheme is present stress does not fall on it. When the word is made only of weak morphemes, stress usually falls on the root in nouns and on the suffix in verbs and adjectives. In all other cases stress falls on the stem final syllable. We will discuss each of these generalizations in more detail below. Space does not permit a thorough review of all combinations of roots and suffixes. However, in the following sections we will discuss many of the most common suffixes and integrate them into the theory of stress assignment so far developed. This is an overview of how the stress system works according to the theory outlined above. Students who use this theory for predicting stress, as they read, for example, should note where the theory makes incorrect predictions. For the majority of cases, however, correct stress will be obtained by following the guidelines offered here.

8.5 Derived Words with a Strong Suffix

Russian has several strong suffixes, but only a few of them are very widespread, particularly in conjunction with genuine Russian roots. Here is a list of the strong suffixes most likely to be encountered:

(1) -ýн	-ёнок/-я́т	-а́нт	-и́рова(ть)
-ýч(ий)	-а́к	-а́льн(ый)	-и́н(ый)
-ýш(а)	-ня́к	-а́ч	-и́тель
-ýх(а)		-а́нин	-и́ческ(ий)
		-а́/а́*	

*This is the derived imperfective suffix.

In all cases when the suffix is strong and the root is weak or ordinary stress falls on the suffix. When a strong suffix is added to a strong root, stress still falls on the suffix. This is in keeping with the general tendency observed above for stress to fall towards the end of the word. In a sense the two strong stresses cancel each other out and the stress rule assigning stem final stress applies. These generalizations are summarized in (2):

(2) STRONG ROOT + STRONG SUFFIX → stress falls on the suffix
WEAK ROOT + STRONG SUFFIX → stress falls on the suffix
ORDINARY ROOT + STRONG SUFFIX → stress falls on the suffix

As an example of this generalization, consider the suffix {-ант}. This suffix is normally a part of foreign words but it also may be added to roots which have been Russified (e.g., квартúра). Note that stress seems to jump to it no matter where the stress is on the root:

(3) a. концéрт   →   концертáнт   performer
мýзыка   →   музыкáнт   musician
квартúра   →   квартирáнт   tenant

b. none

c. комéдия   →   комедиáнт   actor, hypocrite
курс   →   курсáнт   student
оркéстр   →   оркестрáнт   orchestra member
дебю́т   →   дебютáнт   debutant

Examples in 3a have strong roots, in 3b weak roots, and 3c contains examples of ordinary roots. This same order will be followed in giving examples throughout the remainder of this and the following two sections.

With one exception (курс), all the roots in (3) are polysyllabic and all are of foreign origin. The roots in 3a retain stress throughout declension (acc sg мýзыку, gen sg мýзыки, etc.) and when combined with weak or ordinary suffixes they retain stress: квартúрник. However, when combined with a strong suffix, the suffix is stressed as shown in (3). This can be seen with other strong suffixes as well, as with the suffix {-ал'н}, which forms музыкáльный, машúна becomes машинáльный, фигýра -- фигурáльный. In these last three examples, the suffix -áльн(ый) is added directly to the stem. When this suffix is added to verbs, the verbal suffix is truncated: рисовáть → {рис ов -áл'н +ый} → рисовáльный. Truncation of verbal endings in conjunction with adjective- or noun-forming suffixes is the rule, rather than the exception. In any event, the strong suffix attracts the stress.

The suffix -ят- {-*ат} replaces -ёнок in the pl (телёнок-телята). In addition to being used in the pl for nouns in -ёнок, it is used in combination with other suffixes (never independently): курятник, перепелятник. Since the suffix -ник is ordinary, we would expect stress to fall on it if -ят were not strong.

The suffix {-*óн/к} derives nouns denoting the young of animals and humans (осёл - ослёнок, казáк - казачóнок, цыгáн - цыганёнок). The motivating stem for these derived nouns is always a noun. Regardless of the stress of the stem it is deleted in conjunction with this strong suffix:

(4) a. бýйвол → буйволёнок baby buffalo
   цыгáн   цыганёнок gypsy child

 b. лисá → лисёнок fox kitten
   осёл   ослёнок donkey foal

 c. сóкол → соколёнок baby falcon
   ýтка   утёнок duckling
   зверь   зверёнок wild animal baby
   тигр   тигрёнок baby tiger

We can be confident that this suffix is strong because it draws stress away from other strong suffixes: ребята → ребятёнок "baby."

The morphological structure of the suffix is {-*он -/к} with stress falling on the initial vowel of the polysyllabic suffix (cf. gen sg лисёнка). Why does stress fall on the initial vowel of this suffix? For now we may simply say that in polysyllabic suffixes the first syllable is strong, the second weak (with the single exception of the suffix -анý(ть)). Further examples of this are given below.

Another polysyllabic suffix which is strong on the initial syllable is {-йтэл'}. Like {-*он/к}, the final syllable of this suffix is never stressed. The entire morpheme, however, is considered strong, as it draws stress to it from preceding strong syllables; see examples in (6a). This suffix forms agentive nouns from 2nd conj verbs. It shouldn't be confused with the suffix -тель, which forms agentive nouns from 1st conj verbs (see section 8.6.4). In conjunction with the suffix -ѝтель, verbs truncate the verbal suffix (-и- or -е-):

(5) уч и -ит эль →(truncation of и)→ уч -ит эль → stress → уч -и́т эль
    S   S   S

(6)   a. избáвить →   избави́тель   deliverer
            довéрить   довери́тель   principal
            поздрáвить   поздрави́тель   well-wisher
            мы́слить   мысли́тель   thinker

        b. замести́ть →   замести́тель   substitute
            посети́ть   посети́тель   visitor
            обвини́ть   обвини́тель   accuser
            вручи́ть   вручи́тель   message bearer

        c. учи́ть   →   учи́тель   teacher
            смотрéть   смотри́тель   supervisor
            води́ть   води́тель   driver

The words мнóжитель and дви́житель are exceptional.

    As a final example of the generalizations given in (2), consider the following.

(7)   a. рéзать   →   резáк   tool for cutting
            Сиби́рь   сибиря́к   person from Siberia
            Áвстрия   австрия́к   Austrian

        b. чýдо   →   чудáк   eccentric person
            свéжий   свежáк   strong ocean wind
            простóй   простáк   simpleton

        c. мóре   →   моря́к   sailor
            ры́ба   рыбáк   fisherman
            лéвый   левáк   leftist; racketeer

    Students who learn that the suffixes in (1) are strong should have no difficulty in stressing any word that bears these suffixes. The data given in this section also bear out the assertion that stress tends to move toward the end of the word, if it moves at all.

The suffix {-анин} is two suffixes fused into one: {-ан} and {-ин}. Many words end in the sequence -ан, but these are part of foreign polysyllabic roots (караван, хулиган, ресторан). A handful of noun and adjective roots add the suffix {-ан} to form nouns: голова → голован, кожа → кожан "leather coat; large bat," великий → великан, критик → критикан. These derived words illustrate the accentual strength of this suffix. The suffix {-ан} occurs, however, in a much more productive way in combination with the suffix {-ин}, which denotes a single member of a group. (In the pl of these nouns the suffix {-ин} is deleted: крестьянин nom pl крестьяне.) The noun-forming suffix -ин- also occurs independently but sporadically: господь → господин, Грузия → грузин (with truncation of final -ий). Note thel final stress in nouns of this type. This is also the case for nouns related to adjectives: славянин → славянский, дворянин → дворянский, гражданин → гражданский. The final stress rule is exhibited in both the deriving and derived partners of these pairs. This is probably the case in чужой → чужанин "stranger," as well.

When {-ан} and {-ин} are used, they form the compound suffix {-*анин}, which is used to form nouns from noun and verb stems. As with most other compound suffixes, the initial syllable of this suffix is strong. A variant of this compound suffix is {-чанин}. It normally occurs after vowels: англ и(й) -чан -ин and sporadically after в.

As illustrated in (9), the suffix -анин is morphologically {-*анин}, since stem final velars and dentals mutate before this suffix. This also accounts for the palatalized р in северянин. In addition to молоко, a few borrowed roots derive nouns without palatalization, that is, the suffix {-анин} is used: молоканин, пуританин, магометанин.

(8) a. Волга   →   волжанин   Volga native
        Прага   пражанин   native of Prague

     b. молоко   молоканин   Molokanin

     c. приходить   →   прихожанин parishioner
        север   северянин   northerner
        город   →   горожанин   city person

With a handful of "ancient" roots, this suffix is ordinary: афи́нянин, ассири́янин, карфеге́ниянин, лати́нянин, but египтя́нин, критя́нин. These, however, are technical terms and most Russians would use in their place афи́нец, ассири́ец, etc.

*A Mark stress.

1. землянин
2. персиянин
3. рижанин
4. ростовчанин
5. римлянин
6. харьковчанин
7. древлянин
8. полянин
9. соборянин
10. каторжанин

*B Derive nouns in -анин. Mark stress.

1. Во́лга
2. Росси́я
3. армя́нский
4. У́глич
5. крестья́нский
6. Пари́ж
7. Варша́ва
8. мир

The suffix -ан- also occurs in combination with other suffixes: {-ан/к}, {-ан/ц}, as in турча́нка, америка́нка, америка́нец. See sections on the suffixes {-/к}, and {-/ц} for how these suffixes interact.

Finally, consider the polysyllabic suffix -и́ческ(ий), which forms adjectives from noun stems. It attracts stress from all roots. If the deriving stem ends in -ик or -ий, these are truncated: исто́рия → истори́ческий, педаго́гика → педагоги́ческий, меха́ник → механи́ческий, геро́й → герои́ческий. Note, however, that adjectives in -нический may be derived from nouns ending in -ник, and therefore may have presuffixal stress (see sec. 8.6.6).

*C Derive words by means of the suffixes given. Mark stress.

1. оле́нь {-*он/к}
2. болта́ть {-ун}
3. прое́кт {-ант}
4. ду́ра {-ак}
5. пла́вать {-учий}
6. за́яц cf. за́йчик {-*он/к}
7. мышь {-*он/к}
8. консульта́ция {-ант}

9. трясти́ {-учий}
10. ко́пия {-ироват'}
11. копи́ровать {ал'н}
12. увели́чить {-итэл'}
13. гря́зный {-уха}
14. я́стреба {-ин(ый)}

15. здоро́вье {-ак}
16. скрипе́ть {-ач}
17. пла́кать {-ун}
18. рекла́ма {-ироват'}
19. па́па {-уша}
20. осве́домить {-итэл'}

8.6 Weak Suffixes

Unlike strong suffixes, weak suffixes are common. They form all grammatical categories. Weak suffixes are those which under normal circumstances do not bear stress. The ones most often seen are given in (1).

(1) -ий   -ов(а)/у   -ость
    -ик   -ыв(а)   -тель
    -чик   -ств(о)
    -щик   -ск(ий)
    -чив(ый)

In cases where the suffix is weak and the root is ordinary or strong, stress falls on the root. When a weak suffix is combined with a weak root then the grammatical category of the word being formed plays a role in stress assignment. In summary:

(2) STRONG ROOT + WEAK SUFFIX → stress falls on the root
    WEAK ROOT + WEAK SUFFIX → stress falls on the root if the motivating stem and the suffix are nominal; otherwise stress falls on the suffix
    ORDINARY ROOT + WEAK SUFFIX → stress falls on the root

In most cases weak suffixes imply stress on the root. A major exception to this comes from adjectival and verbal suffixes where a weak root plus a weak stem results in stress on the suffix (or ending).

8.6.1 The Suffix -ий

The suffix {-ий} is one of the most productive and widely used in

Russian. It is nearly always weak. The only general exception to this is when the word, usually with a foreign root, refers to sickness, medicine, or the professional activities of physicians. (There are a handful of nouns that have final stress that are not medically related, e.g., драматургия, литургия, телеметрия, and a couple of medical terms that have stem stress, e.g., контузия, микроцефалия.) In these medical words, all of which are fem, the suffix is ordinary and final stress is assigned: аллергия, терапия, атрофия, хирургия. This does not include scientific fields that have a bearing on medicine: биология, химия, физиономия. In the latter, and in masc (критерий, суппозиторий) and neut nouns (сидение, наказание) the suffix -ий- is weak. Stress does not fall on it. Since this suffix is so widespread, it is worthwhile to examine how it is used in more detail.

2ND DECLENSION NOUNS. The suffix is used in combination with several other suffixes, and attached to bare roots, nearly all of which are foreign, and, strange to say, none of which are strong. The only instance where this suffix concatenates with a strong morpheme is if the latter is a suffix, as in (3a) and (3b). These compound suffixes are strong on the initial syllable while the formant {ий} continues weak. The suffix {лог} is actually inherently weak, as биолог, астролог and a host of others show. However, when fused with the weak suffix {ий}, it becomes strong: фраза → фразеология. This follows the general trend already noted that the initial syllable of polysyllabic suffixes is strong.

(3) a. сигнализация   {сигнал -из -ац -ий +a}   signaling
        религия   {рэлиг -ий +a}   religion
        энергия   {энэрг -ий +a}   energy
        армия   {арм -ий +a}   army
        мелодия   {мэлод -ий +a}   melody

    b. биология   {би о -логий +a}   biology
        орнитология   {орнит о -логий +a}   ornithology
        астрология   {астр о -логий +a}   astrology

    c. none

*A Mark stress.

1. стипендия	6. эмбриология
2. академия	7. эмбриолог
3. компания	8. фобия
4. невралгия	9. ориентация
5. педиатрия	10. паталогия

FOURTH DECLENSION NOUNS. The suffix {-ий} is used to form abstract neut nouns from verbs and nouns. When formed from a verb whose stem ends in a vowel, an -н- is added: держáть → держáние. This suffix is expanded further to {-эний} when preceded by a consonant or the verbal suffix -и: несéние. This last example shows that the first part of the expanded suffix is stressable, or strong.

Consider the stress variation shown in (5):

(4) снúзить → снижéние

The stem from which снижéние is formed is strong (снúжу, снúжешь). How do we account for the stress in the derived noun? The morphophonemic structure of снижéние gives us a clue: {снúз + и + эний + о}. The shift of the verbal suffix {и} to {й} before a vowel results in the combination of dental + й, which results in palatalization of the dental and subsequent loss of й. This loss, or truncation, of a salient part of the stem results in the loss of the stress valency associated with the stem. The resultant stem, {сниж...}, has no stress marking, that is, it is now an ordinary stem as far as stress is concerned. The stress rule will then assign stress to the strong element in the expanded suffix in the sequence {сниж + эний + о}. We will see that the loss of stress on a stem due to truncation is fairly common. (See sections 8.6.3, 8.6.5, and particularly 8.6.7 where this phenomenon is formally discussed.) Truncation occurs in the formation of several words where there is no loss of strong stress on the root: вúдение (but cf. видéние) and пýдрение. These are exceptions, possibly due to the fact that the roots of these words are not mutated. The following are truly exceptional: they undergo mutation and strong stress is retained on the root: мурáвление, повéшение, уравновéшение and крáшение (but cf. normal украшéние).

The suffix -ий- is productive in forming nouns from verbs, most of which are themselves derived. When derived words are used as a base for further derivation, the stressed syllable of the base is always strong (see 8.6.7). Thus, all of the examples given in (5) have strong stem syllables, either because they are inherently strong or strong due to derivational processes.

(5) a. Verbal stems with inherently strong roots

тре́бовать → тре́бование {трэ́б -ов -а -ний +о}

		requirement
печа́тать	печа́тание	printing
сма́зать	сма́зывание	lubrication
пла́вать	пла́вание	swimming

b. Verbal stems with inherently weak roots (but derivationally strong)

изобрази́ть →	изображе́ние	representation
собра́ть	собра́ние	meeting
течь	тече́ние	flow; course
трясти́	трясе́ние	shaking
стро́ить	строе́ние	structure

c. Verbal stems with inherently ordinary roots (but derivationally strong)

молча́ть →	молча́ние	silence
жела́ть	жела́ние	desire
спи́сывать	спи́сывание	copying
раздели́ть	разделе́ние	division

Note that strong roots retain stress when the suffix is not polysyllabic as in (5a). In the first two words in (5c) stress falls on the verbal suffix, which is ordinary and stressable.

Verbs formed by the suffix {-ну} drop this suffix. If the resultant stem ends in a consonant it takes the expanded suffix {-э́ний}. As with 2nd conj verbs that truncate the verbal suffix, verbs in -нуть also exhibit loss of strong root stress, although this is not crucial since the right-most strong morpheme will receive stress. Compare the shifts in stress shifts for nouns formed from -ить and -нуть verbs:

(6)	свéргнуть	свержéние	overthrow
	двúнуть {двиг-}	движéние	movement
	тúскнуть	тискнéние	stamping; imprint
	освéдомить	осведомлéние	notification
	зачúслить	зачислéние	inclusion
	устрóить	устроéние	organization
	напрáвить	направлéние	direction
	отпустúть	отпущéние	remission

*B Form nouns in {-(э)(н)ий}. Mark stress.

1. плáвать
2. настáивать
3. осмáтривать
4. образовáть
5. слéдовать

6. достúгнуть
7. положúть
8. учúть
9. ослáбить
10. исполнить

*C What is exceptional about покаяние and послушáние?

Verbal roots in -ы- and -М/Н- add т to the suffix: {-тий}.

(7) закры́ть	→	закры́тие	closing
взя́ть		взя́тие	capture
поня́ть		поня́тие	concept
пожа́ть		пожа́тие (руки́)	handshake

A number of nouns in -ий are formed from noun roots, and a few from other verbal stems and from phrases: бессою́зие, двоемы́слие, чу́вствовать → чу́вствие, любить женщин → женолю́бие. In these instances the suffix {-ий} is weak.

8.6.2 The suffix -ств(о)

So far we have seen that stress falls on the root of a word if the suffix is weak and the root is strong or ordinary. What happens when both the root and suffix are weak? When this occurs and the motivating stem is a noun and the derived word is a noun, then stress falls on the weak syllable to the left. We will refer to this as the w+w (weak plus weak) principle. Formally:

(1) If the stress rule assigns stress to the second of adjacent
    weak syllables, stress falls there unless it is a nominal
    morpheme, in which case stress falls on the first syllable.

In (1), "nominal morpheme" means that it forms nouns.

This is the normal reaction when two weak "nominal" syllables are contiguous: стол + ик → сто́лик.

The suffix {-*(э)ств} forms abstract or collective neut nouns from all grammatical categories. Its extended form is used when the stem ends in a husher: язы́чество "paganism." Stem final velars and dentals mutate to hushers (студе́нчество). Motivating stems with strong or ordinary syllables retain stress. Words such as садо́вник, руководи́ть in (1a) are strong by derivation. Stems with weak syllables have stress on the stem as well, due to the w+w principle.

(1) a.	садо́вник	→	садо́вничесто	gardening
	това́рищ	→	това́рищество	fellowship
	руководи́ть	→	руково́дство	leadership
	ко́нсул	→	ко́нсульство	consulate
b.	ца́рь	→	ца́рство	kingdom
	язы́к	→	язы́чество	paganism
	уби́ть	→	уби́йство	murder
c.	друг	→	дру́жество	friendship
	вели́кий	→	вели́чество	majesty
	член	→	чле́нство	membership

For a number of words with weak roots (Zaliznjak, 1981 lists 28), the suffix -ств(о) appears to be ordinary, instead of weak. In these words stress falls on the desinence instead of on either stem or suffix, e.g., мастерство́, существо́, вдовство́. These words are all *singularia tantum*; they do not form the pl. Since many are deverbal (торжество́) or deadjectival (волшебство́), the entire group should be considered exceptional.

*A Mark stress in the following. If you are not sure about the location of stress on the root, find a word containing the root in question in a good dictionary. Indicate whether the stem contains a (s)trong, (w)eak, or (o)rdinary root.

1. ябедничество
2. мужество
3. производство
4. соперничество
5. монашество

6. лесничество
7. государство
8. строительство
9. мастерство
10. общество

8.6.3   The suffixes -ик, -щик, and -чик.

These suffixes are all weak, with the exception of {-ик}, which is ordinary and stressable (see 8.7) when concatenated with adjectival and verbal roots. With nominal roots, however, it is weak. Thus these suffixes are normally not stressed. Strong roots retain stress, ordinary roots receive stress by rule, and weak roots receive stress by virtue of the w + w principle.

(1) a. завóд   →   завóдчик   factory owner
        билéт   билéтик   ticket (dim.)
        жáлоба   жáлобщик   plaintiff
        áтом   áтомщик   atomic war monger

     b. гроб   →   грóбик   little coffin
        молодóй   молóдчик   rascal
        упаковáть   упакóвщик   packer

c. счастли́вый	счастли́вчик	lucky man
сара́й	сара́йчик	small barn
проглуля́ть	прогу́льщик	absentee

The suffix {-чик} is a variant of {-щик}, which normally does not occur after stems ending in one of the dentals т,д,с,з. Instead -чик occurs after these consonants. This suffix also occurs independently as a diminutive- or agentive-forming suffix and as such occurs after other consonants as well, e.g., сара́йчик. Both versions of the suffix {-чик} are weak, even when the motivating stem is adjectival. Thus, -чик is never stressed when occupying the final position in a word.

The final example in (1b) and (1c) show that verbal suffixes are truncated in conjunction with these noun-forming suffixes. As we have seen earlier, truncation is accompanied by the erasure of stress, whatever its weight, and stress is assigned according to the weight of the suffix. This can be seen in the following:

(2) разлива́ть	разли́вщик	pourer
заказа́ть	зака́зчик	customer
разводи́ться	разво́дчик	separator
гоня́ть	го́нщик	racer

Truncation can also be seen in words whose motivating stems end in -ий or -ик. Like the derivations in (2), stress is reassigned by the general stress rule after truncation erases both final suffix and stress weight from the motivating stem:

(3) дистрофи́я {дистроф -и́й + а} → дистро́фик
    бота́ника {бота́н ик + а} → бота́ник

*A Mark stress. What words are these derived from?

1. ежик	6. солдатик	11. вагончик
2. тазик	7. пакетик	12. доносчик
3. рублик	8. зубчик	13. сигнальщик
4. академик	9. разведчик	14. танцовщик
5. фонарик	10. мизинчик	15. заговорщик

8.6.4 The suffixes -ость and -тель

These suffixes, which both end in a soft consonant, are extremely productive in modern Russian. The suffix {-тэл'} forms nouns from verbal stems. The suffix {-тэл'} is added to the verbal suffix -a, and the expanded suffix {-итэл'} is added to the verbal suffix {-и}. This expanded (polysyllabic) suffix is strong on the initial syllable and therefore attracts stress, even from ordinary stems (see section 8.9 for {-итэл'}. Compare:

(1) слу́шать   слу́шатель
     дви́гать   дви́гатель
     подде́лывать   подде́лыватель

but

     осла́бить   ослаби́тель {осла́б -и -итэл'}*
     изба́вить   избави́тель
     упра́вить   управи́тель

*The verbal suffix и is truncated, which results in the loss of strong stress on the root. Stress is then assigned by rule. The word сказӥтель "teller of folk tales" verifies the existence of the variation {-итэл'}.

The suffix {-ост'} is used to form nouns from adjectival stems. In the overwhelming number of nouns with {-ост'}, stems are strong by having been previously derived (see section 8.6.7). Those that are ordinary or weak have stress on the final stressable stem vowel, i.e., on the vowel preceding these weak suffixes, or due to the w+w principle.

(2) a. изме́рить →   измери́тель   gauge
        иссле́довать   иссле́дователь   researcher
        уро́дливый   уро́дливость   deformity
        дове́рить   довери́тель   principal

    b. тупо́й   →   ту́пость   bluntness
        сухо́й   су́хость   dryness
                       (none in -тель)

c.	читáть	→	читáтель	reader
	писáть		писáтель	writer
	любúть		любúтель	lover

Thus, given a word in -ость, we may be sure stress is not on the final suffix and that if other adjectival suffixes intervene between the suffix and the root, then stress is likely to fall on the root. If no suffix intervenes stress is on the final root syllable. (Exception: мóлодость.) Given a noun with the suffix -тель, if the vowel preceding the suffix is а or я stress is the same as in the verb. If the vowel is и, stress falls on the и (with two exceptions: мнóжитель, двúжитель).

*A Form nouns in -ость or -тель. Mark stress.

1.	солидáрный	6.	молчалúвый	11.	достáвить
2.	трéпетный	7.	всáсываемый	12.	запóлнить
3.	мелодúчный	8.	болóтистый	13.	опры́скивать
4.	грóмкий	9.	усúлить	14.	предáть
5.	похóжий	10.	заместúть	15.	собирáть

8.6.5 Verbal suffixes -ов(а), -ыв(а)

The suffix {-ов} forms verbs on the basis of verbal roots and noun stems, which may be strong (they retain stress in derivation), weak (stress falls on the final syllable of the suffix according to the w+w principle), or ordinary (stress falls on the final root syllable).

The suffix {-ыв} forms imperfective verbs from perfective verbs ending in the verbal suffixes -а, -ну, -е, -и, and ending in -ороть and -олоть with truncation of the stem final vowel, sometimes having been involved in the mutation of preceding dentals. Truncation is accompanied by the loss of stress marking (strong or weak), in effect turning verbs into stems with ordinary syllables. Thus stress is assigned by rule and always falls on the syllable preceding the suffix {-ыв}.

(1) a.	ТРÉБ-		→	трéбовать	require
	дéйствие			дéйствовать	act
	задýмать			задýмывать	conceive

b. ПАК-　→　паковáть　　　pack
зимá　　　зимовáть　　　hibernate
РИС-　　　рисовáть　　　draw
омолодúть　омолáживать　rejuvenate

c. СЛЕД- →　слéдовать　　follow
чéсть　　　чéствовать　　honor
расколóть　раскáлывать　disrupt
подыгрáть　поды́грывать　accompany

*A Mark stress on the verbs you form from the following.

1. размолóть
2. снизáть
3. ЦЕЛ- (w)
4. ЖАЛ- (о)
5. ДАР- (w)

6. перечитáть
7. окопáть
8. отбросáть
9. тоскá
10. подписáть

11. опечáтать
12. обрабóтать
13. ПРОБ- (о)
14. рáбство
15. свидéтельство

8.6.6 The suffixes -ов(ый) and -ск(ий).

The suffix {-*ск} expands to {-*эск} when following a stem final husher (мýжеский) unless nationality or place of origin is referred to (вóлжский). This suffix is expanded further to {-*ичэск} when the motivating stem is a foreign word, or ends in the sequence {-ик} or the suffix {-ий}. Like other polysyllabic suffixes, the initial syllable of this expanded suffix is strong. See section 8.5 for discussion of the strong expanded version of this suffix.

The adjective-forming suffix -ов(ый) occurs as ёв(ый) when stressed and following a palatalized consonant (рублёвый). In conjunction with either variant a stem syllable is stressed by virtue of its being strong or ordinary. The weak suffix {-ов}, however, is stressed with a weak root syllable, as a result of the w+w principle.

(1) a. итóг　　→　итóговый　　　total
рóза　　　　рóзовый　　　　rose; pink
Сувóров　　сувóровский　Suvorov military academy
Узбéк　　　узбéкский　　Uzbek
Лéнин　　　лéнинский　　Lenin

b. дуб   →   дубо́вый   oak
    рубль   рублёвый   ruble
    плод   плодо́вый   fruit
    ТОРГ-   торго́вый   commercial
    раб   ра́бский   slave
    язы́к   язы́ческий   pagan

c. кро́лик   →   кро́ликовый   rabbit
    знак   зна́ковый   sign
    обря́д   обря́довый   ritual

In effect the weakness of this suffix keeps stress from falling toward the
end of the word. However, as illustrated in (1b), roots with weak syllables
do not retain stress. Words such as дубо́вый, then, receive stress by rule,
the same rule that assigns stress to words such as обря́довый. The latter
has a root composed of an ordinary syllable. Stress falls there since the
suffix is weak. In the former, stress falls on the suffix since the root is
weak. Remember that the w+w principle applies in (1b) to allow stress to
fall on the suffix, since it is not a noun-forming suffix.

Finally, there are a number of adjectives in {-ов}, which have
monosyllabic ordinary or weak roots and desinential stress (compare with
(1b) above):

(2) гробово́й   ключево́й   рядово́й
    грозово́й   корнево́й   восково́й

And there are a handful of finally stressed adjectives in -ско́й, for example:

(3) городско́й   мужско́й
    морско́й   донско́й

The words in (2) and (3) are exceptions to the theory of stress assignment
outlined here.

*A Form adjectives in -овый. Stems that have stress on a suffix in the
nom sg or on the ending in the nom sg or gen sg are considered weak
(e.g., острога́ → острого́вый). If you do not know the gen sg of the
masc words, check a dictionary. Mark stress on the adjectives you

form.

1. четве́рг	6. ро́за	11. ту́ндра
2. дождь	7. пята́к	12. двор
3. съезд	8. ледни́к	13. костёр
4. нож	9. шёлк	14. кит
5. берёза	10. ла́мпа	15. дворе́ц

*B Form adjectives in -ский, or one of its variations. Mark stress on the adjectives you form.

1. ара́б	6. купе́ц {куп/'Ц-}	11. Коре́я
2. Кана́да	7. оте́ц {от/'Ц-}	12. мона́х
3. бог	8. Алба́ния	13. Кавка́з
4. сосе́д	9. славяни́н	14. Дуна́й
5. друг	10. апте́карь	15. свет

8.6.7 Multiply-derived Words and Derivationally Strong Suffixes

Many suffixes may be added to a single root in Russian. For the most part the interaction of multiple strong, weak, and ordinary morphemes proceeds as outlined above. However, in some derivations, another factor seems to be at play. Consider, for example, the stress of the words in (1). In (1) and (4) below the letters in parentheses stand for (s)trong, (w)eak, and (o)rdinary, and refer to the accentual weight of each syllable.

(1) I   II   III

шут (w)   →   шу́тка (w+o)   →   шу́точка (w+o+o)

                     шути́ть (w+o)   шу́точный (w+o+o)

The weak stress of шут is revealed when it is inflected (gen sg шута́, etc.). We account for the stress of the words in column II by means of the stress rule which applies in both words. In шу́тка stress falls on the stem final vowel by the stress rule. But how do we account for stress in the words in III? We might expect the stress rule to apply to give *шуто́чка, *шуто́чный.

Russian words have a hierarchy of places where stress is likely to fall. We have seen that at the top of this hierarchy are strong morphemes. Next on the hierarchy is the final stressable stem vowel. When a word consists of only weak morphemes, stress still tends to fall on the final stem vowel, except for weak noun suffix combinations, when stress falls on the root. Recall that some roots are polysyllabic. Some polysyllabic roots are stressable on the initial syllable (áдрес), others on a noninitial syllable (анáлиз). The place holder for stress in these roots is associated with just one syllable.

In addition to forming words by adding suffixes to roots, words may be formed by adding a suffix to a complex stem, that is, a stem that already has a suffix. In this case, stress remains on the same syllable as found in the complex stem. In addition, this stress becomes strong. Thus, the effect of multiple derivation is to lock stress onto the deriving complex stem.

The words in column III illustrate this process. The diminutive шýточка is morphophonemically: {шут -оч -/к +а}, composed of w+o+o syllables. The underlined morphemes make up the derivational base-- derived from {шут -*/к +а}. Stress then falls on the strong syllable of the stem. That syllable is determined by earlier derivation of {шут -/к +а}: шýтка. Thus, the addition of other ordinary suffixes does not affect the location of stress. This explains the lack of words ending in -óчка, -éчка. These words are multiply-derived and therefore have stress on a syllable preceding the compound suffix.

The concept of maintaining the stressability of polysyllabic derived stems can be formalized by considering these stems strong in regard to further derivation. According to this principle, syllables may become strong by the addition of other suffixes.

(2) Stressed stem syllables in derived words are strong in subsequent derivation.

The words in the final column in (3) provide another example of the "derivationally strong" principle given in (2):

(3) стрелá   →   стрéлка
                       стрелóк   →   стрелóчек
                                          стрелкóвый

The difference in stress between шýточек and стрелóчек is due to the difference in stress of the words they are derived from: шýтка and стрелóк. In both, stress falls on the final stressable syllable and those syllables become strong in further derivation. The word стрелкóвый shows that the accentual strength of the derived syllable is lost when the fleeting vowel it is attached to is not vocalized. In (4) syllables which have become strong via derivation are underlined:

(4) a.   стрелá (w) → {стрэл -*/к} (w+o) → стрелóк

    b.   стрелóк (w+s) → {стрэл -*/к -*/к} (w+s+o) → стрелóчек

    c.   стрелóк(w+s) → {стрэл -*/к -ов + ый} (w+s+w) → стрелкóвый

In (4b) the suffix {-*/к} becomes strong due to additional suffixation. It receives stress. In (4c) the derivationally strong suffix loses accentual weight since the fleeting vowel is not vocalized. Stress is awarded according to the w+w principle:

(5) стрел -/к -ов + ый
    w   ś   w
    w   w

Here is a final example of a word which shows multiple processes of derivation. In мéстничество "regionalism," the root, МЕСТ- "place" is ordinary. When the ordinary adjectival suffix {-*/н} is added, stress falls on the final stressable stem vowel: мéстный "local." Since further derivation, including the addition of ordinary suffixes, does not affect the stress of this derived word, we assume that the stem местн- has become strong due to derivation: мéстничество. Schematically:

(6) мéст + o →   мéст -/н +ый   →   мéст -/н -ик -*(е)ств +o
    o   o   o   s   o   o   w

*A Determine stress given the base words in parentheses.

1. (леснúк)	лесничество	5. (чулóк)	чулочек
2. (чудáк)	чудачество	6. (телёнок)	теленочек
3. (садóвный)	садовничество	7. (минýтка)	минуточка
4. (удáрить)	ударничество	8. (крючóк)	крючочек

8.7 Ordinary Suffixes

(1) <u>noun</u>   <u>adjective</u>   <u>verbal</u>
   ик   */н   a/a
   ник   ов(ый)   a/и
   /к   a/∅
   /ц   и/и
                                   e/e

These are suffixes that take the stress if a preceding strong syllable is not present.

8.7.1 The suffix -н

In his authoritative work on Russian word formation, Townsend states that -н is the most important adjective-forming suffix in Russian. In addition to being important in its own right in terms of adjective formation, thousands of words are created on the foundation of adjective stems bearing this suffix. The adjective- forming suffix {-*/н} builds adjectives mostly from noun stems but also from a few verb stems. Strong root syllables are not affected by this suffix. Adjectives built on ordinary or weak noun stems have stress preceding this suffix. The stress rule assigns stress to the final stressable syllable of the stem, which will always be on the syllable preceding the suffix -н, since the suffix {-*/н} is not vocalic in the basic form.

Interestingly enough, of the 10,255 adjectives in -ный listed in Zaliznjak, fewer than ten are built upon verbal stems. Nearly all of the 585 adjectives in -ной, however, are built upon verbal stems. This distribution provides the basis for altering the principle regarding the direction stress takes when it is assigned to a nonvocalic suffix. This principle must be something like:

(1) If stress falls on an unvocalized /, stress shifts to the right by one syllable if the stem is verbal, otherwise it shifts to the left by one syllable.

The difference in stress between во́дный and проводно́й is thus attributed to the grammatical category of the stem. Adjectives built on verbal stems reflect the inability of stress to fall on the stem or on the nonvocalic suffix. Instead, stress, by virtue of (1), falls on the ending. Consider, for example, the derivation of резнóй "carved, fretted."

(2) рéзать (s) →   резнóй   { рез -á -*/н + ой } (o+o)

The strong stress of the root is deleted upon truncation, leaving an ordinary stem. Stress is assigned by stress rule to the final suffix and the "nonvocalic" principle given in (1) applies to direct stress onto the ending. Examples are:

(3)	посéять	→	посевнóй	sowing
	призывáть	→	призывнóй (возраст)	draft
	вклáдывать	→	вкладнóй	depository
	наградúть	→	награднóй	award

Послýшныйand слышный, both derived from verbs, are exceptional. In addition, a few weak noun stems form the adjective in -нóй (губнóй < губá, зубнóй < зуб). These are also exceptional.

The huge majority of adjectives in -н, however, are not built on verbal stems. Even the lexicalized passive participles have an adjectival suffix inserted between the verbal root and the suffix: обсуждённый {об сужд -ен -*/н + ый). Presuffixal stress is the norm for these adjectives, except when the root is strong.

Weak denominal roots are still stressable according to the nonvocalic principle given in (1) above.

(6) a.	квартúра	→	квартúрный (-ая плáта)	rent
	рáдуга	→	рáдужный	iridescent
	скáзка	→	скáзочный	fabled
b.	грозá	→	грóзный	stormy
	гарáж	→	гарáжный	garage
	водá	→	вóдный	watery
c.	óзеро	→	озёрный	lake
	истéрика	→	истерúчный	hysterical
	хóлод	→	холóдный	cold

An extended variant, -ичн- is also ordinary. It truncates stem final -ий or -иц, which results in the stem being marked as ordinary. This is the meaning of (s→o) in (7). Stress therefore shifts to the suffix if truncation occurs.

(7) ри́тм (o)	→	ритми́чный	rhythmic
иро́ния (s→o)	→	ирони́чный	ironic
исто́рия (s→o)	→	истори́чный	historical
я́годица (s→o)	→	я́годичный	berry
столи́ца (s→o)	→	столи́чный	capital (city)

*A Mark stress. Recall that derived stems are strong. Stems are ordinary, unless otherwise stated.

1. местный (w)
2. памятный (s)
3. совестный (s)
4. воздушный
5. лодочный (s)

6. пословичный (s)
7. публичный
8. фабричный
9. символичный
10. единогласный (w)

8.7.2 The suffix -ик

The suffix {-*ник}, meaning "person or thing that accomplishes or receives the action of the verb," forms nouns from verbal stems. Nearly all words with this suffix are stressed on a syllable before the suffix. Do not confuse nouns in ник with nouns in ик derived from adjectives in {*-/н} (лесни́к < лесно́й, see next paragraph. In fact, the overwhelming majority of words with the sequence -ник are derived via an adjectival suffix: {-*/н -ик}. Nouns in -ник, however, are formed from verb stems and from a few noun and bare adjectival stems: рабо́тать → рабо́тник "worker," полково́й → полко́вник. This suffix is weak.

A few nouns end in -ик but are not derived, e.g., тю́бик, ку́бик, ло́бзик, кро́лик, астма́тик. These all have polysyllabic strong root syllables. Most nouns ending in -ик, however, are derived. If the motivating stem is a noun, then this suffix is weak (section 8.6.3). With adjectives other than those with the suffix -ов, this suffix is ordinary, but rarely occurs: го́лый → голи́к, прямо́й → прями́к, шу́стрый (strong) → шу́стрик, ста́рый → стари́к. The overwhelming majority of words with

-ик are added to adjectival stems ending in -н, such as сли́вочный →
сли́вочник. The compound -*/н-ик need not be confused with the suffix
-ник, since the latter usually occurs with verbal stems.

Nouns in -(н)ик that are built from a derived adjectival stem in -н,
retain stress on the (derivationally strong) syllable of the stem in these
words:

(1) a. ры́бный   →   ры́бник   fishmonger
        монта́жный   монта́жник   erector
        шко́льный   шко́льник   schoolboy
        ко́жный   ко́жник   dermatologist

    b. ста́рый   →   стари́к   old man
        ше́стеро   шестери́к   type of yoke
        по́стный   по́стник   person fasting
        насле́дный   насле́дник   heir

    c. сы́рный   →   сы́рник   frittered curds
        грузово́й   грузови́к   truck

8.7.3 The suffix -ец

Some words contain the sequence -ец as an integral part of the word,
that is, the word is not derived: пе́рец, па́лец, та́нец, огуре́ц.
Consider the following words that do take the suffix {-*/ц}:

(1) a. расска́зец   b.   оте́ц
        парти́ец   вдове́ц
        латви́ец   дворе́ц
        ло́ндонец   волче́ц
        китобо́ец   бое́ц
        чудотво́рец   творе́ц

The data in (1) tell us two things. First, the suffix {-*/ц} is not strong: it
does not always bear stress. Second, it is not weak, i.e., it may bear stress.
We therefore conclude that it is ordinary. Preceding strong syllables retain
stress (ло́ндонец). But why is stress in some words with ordinary roots
on the root and on the suffix in others? Since this suffix contains a fleeting

vowel (отéц--отцá) and is preceded by palatalization of velars (петербýрг--петербýржец, лгать--лжец), the morphophonemic transcription of this suffix is {-*/ц}.

The words in (1a) have roots that are not strong: рассказáть РАССКАЗ- (о), пáртия (ПАРТИЙ-) (о), áрмия (АРМИЙ-) (о), писáть (ПИС-) (о), творúть (ТВОР-) (w), БИЙ/БОЙ- (w). The root ЛÓНДОН- is strong and so attracts the stress. Stress is assigned to the rest of the words in 1a and all the words in 1b by the same stress rule. Stress seems to shift back one syllable, however, in words that have a polysyllabic root. Schematically:

(2) лат вий */ц (о+о)
  vocalization of /: лат вий *эц
  stress rule: лат вий *э́ц
  putative retraction: лат вúй *эц

The principle involved in the placement of stress in words in (1a), however, is not really one of stress retraction. It only appears to be retracted when we compare word pairs such as боéц and китобóец. We can account for the differing stress in these two words by suggesting that the suffix {-*/ц} is weak when attached to ordinary polysyllabic stems (including prefixal or compound elements). In other words, when connected to polysyllabic stems the suffix {-*/ц} is not stressed, even though the / ultimately is vocalized to e̲. When connected to polysyllabic stems with a weak root, then the suffix remains ordinary (образéц).

Given the weakness of the suffix {-*/ц} when combined with ordinary polysyllabic stems, the stress of the words in (1a) and of the words in (1b) is assigned by the same rule and no reference to stress retraction is necessary:

(3) {раз= сказ -*/ц} (о+w) {вдов -*/ц} (w+о)
vocalization of /: {раз= сказ -*эц} {вдов -*эц}
  stress: {раз= скáз -*эц} {вдов -*э́ц}

In both instances the final stressable syllable is stressed.

Strong syllables retain stress with this suffix. For ordinary and weak syllables stress is assigned to the final stressable syllable of the stem. For polysyllabic roots stress falls on the syllable prior to the suffix {-*/ц}, since the latter is weak in connection with ordinary polysyllabic roots. For monosyllabic roots, the suffix is ordinary and except for a handful of words, stress falls on it, as shown in (4).

(4) a. лени́вый   →   лени́вец   lazybones
       торго́вый   торго́вец   merchant
       ми́лостивый   ми́лостивец   gracious person
       ре́зать (s→o)   резе́ц   cutting tool

    b. зуб   →   зубе́ц   tooth; cog
       хромо́й   хроме́ц   lame person
       скупо́й   скупе́ц   miser
       молодо́й   молоде́ц   fine fellow

    c. заказа́ть   →   зака́зец   order
       ю́ный   →   юне́ц   youth
       мёртвый   →   мертве́ц   corpse
       ПИС-   →   писе́ц   scribe
       живопис-   →   живопи́сец   painter
       хо́лод   →   холоде́ц   fish in aspic

*A Mark stress on the following words. None has a strong syllable.

1. ловец	6. красавец	11. конец
2. земледелец	7. гордец	12. борец
3. зубец	8. европеец	13. змееборец
4. трезубец	9. кузнец	14. хитрец
5. лукавец	10. украинец	15. американец

Recall that TORT form roots are considered monosyllabic for accentual purposes (молоде́ц, холоде́ц, вороне́ц, зелене́ц). True exceptions to the monosyllabic -ец rule described above are: не́мец, хло́пец, ста́рец, бра́тец, го́рец, where the stress is expected on the suffix and деле́ц, which has a strong root. Stress in these words must be memorized.

8.7.4 The suffix -к, -ок.

The suffix {-*/к} derives masc and fem nouns from nouns (forming diminutives) and verbs. It is weak when concatenated with verbal stems.

(1) a. чи́стить   →   чи́стка*   cleaning
        рабо́тать   рабо́тка*   small work
        пото́м   пото́мок   descendant
        пионе́р   пионе́рка   girl scout

  b. ого́нь   →   огонёк   small light
      причеса́ть   причёска*   haircut
      грех   грешо́к   peccadillo

  c. мо́лот   →   молото́к   hammer
      поступи́ть   посту́пок*   deed
      знак   значо́к   pin
      обломать   обло́мок*   fragment
      морко́вь   морко́вка   carrot
      упада́ть   упа́док*   decline
      по́рох   порошо́к   powder

*The root of this word has become ordinary via truncation.

The first two examples in (1a) are examples of how truncated verbal roots acquire ordinary stress valency in derivation. The suffix {*-/к} is weak with verbal roots so stress never falls on it when it is combined with a verbal root:

(2) связа́ть {связ -á + ть}   →   {связ -á -*/к + а} →
    {связ -*/к + а} (o+w)   →   свя́зка

We know that the suffix is weak with verbs since the nonvocalic principle does not apply (see sec. 8.7.1). When the fleeting vowel appears, however, stress falls naturally on the suffix by the application of the stress rule:

(3) {молот -*/к} →   {молот -ок} (o+o)   →   {молот -о́к}

This suffix is often reduplicated:

(4) гриб → грибóк → грибóчек(гриб -*/к -*/к)

In (4), the final syllable of грибóк is derivationally strong, so stress remains on this syllable upon further derivation.

*A Form nouns in -ок or -ка. Strong stems are marked. Mark stress.

1. монáх (s)	6. снимáть
2. друг	7. покупáть
3. кни́га	8. сын
4. сапóг	9. провéрить (s)
5. дéвка (s)	10. гóлос

8.7.5 Verbal Suffixes

Unlike adjective- and noun- forming suffixes, most verbal suffixes are ordinary. Stress falls on them when there is no strong preceding syllable. In the two cases where the suffix is weak (ов/у and ну/н), stress falls on the root with strong stems and ordinary stems. Stress falls on the suffix with weak stems. One suffix, и/и, is ordinary in the nonpresent and weak in the present (discussion below). Finally, the derived imperfective suffix -á/á is strong (see 8.5). Table (1) gives examples of each suffix. Note that strong stems are the exception, not the rule, for each suffix. In addition they are, with a few prominent exceptions, usually low frequency verbs. For the sake of comparison, the three weak verbal suffixes are included.

(1) a. <u>Strong Roots</u>:

a/a   бéгать, дéлать, обéдать, вéдать, сту́кать, ты́кать, царáпать, щу́пать, ку́шать, слу́шать

в/й   none--the three roots that take this suffix are weak (see below)

a/и   слы́шать (this is the only one with a strong root)

a/Ø   ре́зать

е/е   (very few) крова́веть, бере́менеть, румя́неть

и/и   стро́ить, спо́рить, ве́рить, зна́чить, гото́вить,

ыв/ыв (weak)   переде́лывать, вре́зывать, зада́вливать

ов/у (weak)   тре́бовать, же́ртвовать, чуда́чествовать,
                      де́йствовать, бесе́довать,

ну/н (weak)   бры́знуть, поги́бнуть, дви́нуть, пры́гнуть

   b. Weak Roots:

а/а   понима́ть, посыла́ть, прогоня́ть, разбира́ться, чита́ть

в/й   дава́ть, встава́ть

а/и   шурша́ть, треща́ть, мурча́ть, стуча́ть, крича́ть, лежа́ть

а/Ø   нажа́ть, нача́ть

е/е   молоде́ть, густе́ть, просте́ть, сироте́ть, золоте́ть

и/и   глуши́ть, винти́ть, строчи́ть, труди́ть, гневи́ть

ыв/ыв (weak)   none: all are derivationally strong
                      (омола́живать, про́игрывать)

ов/у (weak)   целова́ть, зимова́ть, чарова́ть, рисова́ть

ну/н (weak)   отдохну́ть, толкну́ть, черпну́ть, верну́ть

   c. Ordinary Roots

а/а чита́ть, жела́ть, хрома́ть, улыба́ться, лета́ть

в/й none--all roots that take this suffix are weak

а/и дыша́ть, держа́ть

а/∅ сказа́ть, писа́ть, глода́ть, иска́ть

е/е беле́ть, красне́ть, слабе́ть, але́ть, боле́ть, умне́ть, ясне́ть,

и/и проси́ть, носи́ть, тащи́ть, молоти́ть, вози́ть, серди́ть

ыв/ыв (weak) перепи́сывать, расска́зывать

ов/у (weak) че́ствовать, усе́рдствовать, пира́тствовать

ну/н (weak) сла́бнуть, щёлкнуть, га́снуть, до́хнуть

While stress may shift in conjugation, stress in the infinitive and first sg is always on the same syllable, except колеба́ть: я колéблю. Verbs in -чь, -ти, -ереть, and -олоть have final stress in the infinitive and final (desinential) stress in the first sg.

*A What is exceptional about the stress of махну́ть? The imperfective, from which it is derived, is маха́ть.

*B Here are pairs of infinitives and first sg forms. Use this information and the information in (1) to predict stress <u>on the infinitive</u>. Strong and weak stems are marked.

1. хромать (хромаю)
2. замазать (замажу) (s)
3. опоздать (опоздаю)
4. лысеть (лысею)
5. стареть (старею)
6. царить (царю)
7. будить (бужу)
8. мыслить (мыслю) (s)
9. оценить (оценю) (w)
10. прыгнуть (прыгну) (s)
11. посягнуть (посягну) (w)
12. сунуть (суну)
13. защитить (защищу)
14. изобразить (изображу) (w)
15. удобрить (удобрю) (s)
16. присутствовать (присутствую)
17. наследовать (наследую)
18. волновать (волную) (w)
19. организовать (организую) (w)
20. жаждать (жажду) (s)

8.8 Nonderived Words and Inflected Words

In most cases derived words retain the stress of the basic form when conjugated or declined. A cover term for both conjugation and declension is "inflection" (словоизменéние). In this section we will review those having a shifting stress pattern and discuss the stress of nonderived words.

Many words in Russian do not have a derivational suffix. These are bare roots used with appropriate inflectional endings. The stress of the basic form for these words may be determined by the rules discussed above. However, when inflected many of these words exhibit movement in stress from one syllable to another, for example, nom sg избá, with a weak root syllable, but nom pl úзбы. We will refer to this as mobile or shifting stress (подвúжное ударéние). We cannot simply ignore these words, since most are of very high frequency. Fortunately, the movement in stress in these words follows certain patterns. In addition, it is usually easy to identify words that exhibit one of the shifting patterns, since, as stated, they are mostly nonderived words, i.e., words that do not contain a derivational suffix.

Each grammatical category can be characterized as having major inflectional oppositions. For nouns, this opposition is between sg and pl. For adjectives the opposition is between long form and short form, and for verbs it is between present and nonpresent. It is precisely across these oppositions that stress shifts in nonderived words.

Since shifting stress moves from stem to ending or from ending to stem, we can describe these shifts by means of a binary system, using the terms A and B. The term A stands for stress on the stem. The term B stands for stress on the first syllable of the ending. The two positions possible for each grammatical category are defined in (1):

(1)   <u>1st Position</u>   <u>2nd Position</u>

Nouns	singular	plural
Adjectives	long form	short form
Verbs	nonpresent	present

Thus we can characterize nouns with fixed stem stress throughout the sg and pl as AA nouns, where stress is on the stem in the sg (first position) and on the stem in the pl (second position). Adjectives with fixed stress on the stem in the long and short form have AA stress, as do verbs with stress on the same vowel in the present and nonpresent. Given these definitions, the following stress patterns are possible.

(2) AA   fixed on stem syllable throughout the paradigm
   BB   fixed on the ending throughout the paradigm
   AB   stress on the stem in the 1st position and on the ending in the 2nd
   BA   stress on the ending in 2nd position and on the stem in the 1st

A few (less than 20) high frequency nouns, such as голова́ (acc sg го́лову) have patterns that do not wholly fit into this scheme. Here we will be concentrating on the patterns given in (2), plus one other pattern, the AC pattern. In <u>nouns</u> with this pattern, stress falls on the initial vowel of the word throughout the sg and in the nom pl. In the rest of the pl stress falls on the ending. In <u>adjectives</u> with the AC pattern, stress falls on the stem throughout the long form and the short forms, except for the short form fem, which has stress on the end. In <u>verbs</u>, the AC pattern implies stress is on the verbal suffix in all forms of the nonpresent and on the ending in the first sg, but stress is on the immediately preceding syllable throughout the rest of the sg. Thus, the oppositions given above are skewed somewhat for words with the AC pattern:

(3)

	NOUNS	ADJECTIVES	VERBS
1st position	sg and nom pl	long form and other short forms	verbal suffix and 1st sg ending
2nd position	other pl	fem short form	other pres conj

Most words have the AA pattern. This is true because nearly all derived words (with some notable exceptions, discussed below) have fixed stress. Nonderived words tend to take one of the other patterns listed in (2). Happily, even here, a certain amount of order can be observed. Certain kinds of words fall generally into one pattern, other kinds of words fall generally into another. We will briefly review each grammatical category and discuss features of each that are symptomatic of stress locus.

*A Mark stress according to the indicated stress pattern.

1. бе́лый (AC): белая, бела, бело, белы
2. вокза́л (AA): вокзала, вокзалы, вокзалов
3. везти́ (BB): везу, везешь, везут, везла, везли
4. ветвь (AC): gen sg ветви, nom pl ветви, ветвей
5. пье́са (AA): пьесу, о пьесе, nom pl пьесы, пьесами
6. гара́ж (BB): гаража, в гараже, гаражи, гаражей
7. гру́бый (AC): грубое, груба, грубо, грубы
8. боло́то (AA): gen sg болота, nom pl болота, болот, болотах
9. стать (AA): стану, станешь, станут, стала, стали
10. петь (AB): пою, поешь, поют, пела, пели
11. купи́ть (AC): куплю, купишь, купят, купил, купила, купили
12. дар (AB): дара, даром, дары, даров
13. зуб (AC): зуба, зубом, зубы, зубов
14. письмо́ (BA): gen sg письма, о письме, nom pl письма
15. сро́чный (AA): срочная, срочное, срочен, срочна, срочно
16. скамья́ (BB): скамью, gen sg скамьи, о скамье, nom pl скамьи
17. клева́ть (AB): клюю, клюешь, клюют, клевал, клевала

8.8.1 Nouns

Here are some examples of what is regular in the distribution of stress for nonderived nouns. Read through each column carefully and see if you can determine what the words in each column have in common. Dots in a column indicate that there are no nouns with that stress pattern for that gender.

(1) Masculine Nouns

AA	BB	AB	BA	AC
банк	гриб	го́род	.	ка́мень
грамм	дождь	рог	.	па́рень
фильм	плод	шаг	.	но́готь
грипп	враг	глаз	.	ко́рень
рома́н	топо́р	по́езд	.	зуб
това́р	сапо́г	сто́рож	.	бог
стадио́н	коро́ль	учи́тель	.	волк

(2) Feminine nouns

AA	BB	AB	BA	AC
ба́ба	.	.	жена́	о́бувь
бу́ква	.	.	труба́	па́мять
ба́ржа	.	.	глава́	по́мощь
ло́гика	.	.	звезда́	пло́щадь
а́збука	.	.	игра́	власть
соло́ма	.	.	семья́	по́весть

(3) Neuter Nouns

AA	BB	AB	BA	AC
блю́до	.	сло́во	лицо́	.
ве́ко	.	по́ле	гнездо́	.
ле́то	.	мо́ре	число́	.
я́блоко	.	ме́сто	зерно́	.

Regularities:

1. Nonderived masc nouns with AA are mostly words of foreign origin. Stems are strong or ordinary. Fem and neut nouns with stress on the stem which ends in a hard consonant also take the AA pattern. Both strong and ordinary roots can be found with the AA pattern.

2. The nouns in BB are usually monosyllabic masc nouns. Polysyllabic masc nouns with the BB pattern have stem final stress in the nom sg. Some fem nouns do take this pattern, but except for a handful of nouns (скамья́, мечта́, черта́), they are of so low frequency that you may never encounter them. They are obsolete or generally obscure church related words. A large set of derived nouns, however, exhibits the BB pattern. These are masc nouns whose stress in the basic form falls on the derivational suffix, e.g., стари́к. Nonderived stems that take the BB pattern are weak.

3. Masc nouns with the AB pattern usually either take the nom pl ending -á, or take the loc-2 ending -ý. They have initial stress in the sg

(except учи́тель, профе́ссор, дире́ктор, and рука́в). A handful of neuts take this pattern, including the neut -мя nouns. These roots are accentually ordinary.

4. There are no BA masc nouns. This is the normal pattern for fem nouns with -а́ or -я́ in the nom sg and for neut nouns ending in -о́ or -e in the nom sg. There are a few BØ (no pl forms) nouns, but no true nonderived BB neut nouns. The BA pattern implies the root is accentually weak.

5. The stress of most 3rd decl nouns can be predicted on the basis of whether or not the word has a suffix. If a suffix is present then stress is fixed and its location is determined by the accentual weights of the suffix and root. If the word is not suffixed, then stress can be determined from the final (palatalized) consonant. <u>Nonsuffixed</u> stems have AC stress if the word does not end in a stem final -нь or -ль. If the word ends in -нь or -ль, then expect stem final AA stress (cf. меда́ль, гастро́ль, акваре́ль, бандеро́ль). Nonderived stems with the AC pattern are weak.

*A Mark stress using the regularities given above as guidelines.

1. год (в э́том году́): года (nom pl)
2. война́: во́йны (nom pl)
3. звезда́: звезду́, звезды (nom pl)
4. ме́лочь, ме́лочи, мелоче́й
5. о́стров, nom pl острова́: острово́в

6. ключ: ключа́
7. вдова́: вдо́вам
8. си́ла: си́лу, си́лой
9. бана́н, бана́ны
10. го́род, nom pl города́: городо́в (gen pl)

8.8.2 Adjectives

Here is the distribution of stress among derived and nonderived adjectives. Derived adjectives are included since they may or may not have a mobile stress pattern. Recall that for adjectives the second position in regard to stress opposition is the short form. There are only a handful of true AB adjectives (горя́чий, хоро́ший, здоро́вый, тяжёлый, мудрёный). Instead a large number of high frequency adjectives exhibit the AC pattern, which have stress on the stem in all forms of the long form and short form except the fem short form which has stress on the ending.

For example: бе́лый / бел, бела́, бе́ло, бе́лы. Similarly, there is no BA pattern among adjectives. Instead, we will review the BC pattern which reflects final stress in the long form and in the short form fem, and stem stress in other short forms (живо́й, жив, жива́, жи́во, жи́вы).

(1)

AA	BB	AC	BC
здра́вый	злой	до́лгий	плохо́й
а́лый	чудно́й	бе́лый	дорого́й
вя́лый	смешно́й	гла́дкий	живо́й

AA	BB	AC	BC
я́рый	больно́й	гро́мкий	немо́й
упру́гий		жа́лкий	хромо́й
гото́вый		кра́ткий	слепо́й
суро́вый		ти́хий	скупо́й
румя́ный		я́сный	тупо́й
неле́пый		кра́сный	косо́й
спосо́бный			просто́й

Regularities:

1. Zaliznjak lists over 7,000 adjectives with the AA or A∅ pattern; adjectives in -ский are A∅--they take no short form. The vast majority of these are polysyllabic and have derived stems. Only seven adjectives ending in -кий have the AA pattern, however. Nonderived stems may be strong or ordinary.

2. Basically all the BB adjectives are given in (1). Roots with this pattern are weak.

3. Adjectives that end in -кий (not -ский) take the AC pattern. Adjectives with this pattern have ordinary stems.

4. Stems with the BC pattern are weak, so stress falls on the ending. There are about fifty adjectives of this type.

5. The main regularity involving adjectives is that if the adjective stem is derived or polysyllabic then chances are excellent it will have the AA pattern. Adjectives with monosyllabic roots ending in -кий (not -ский) and a number of others which are frequently encountered, including adjectives in -ный with monosyllabic roots, exhibit the AC pattern.

*A Mark stress.

1. красный	красен	красна	красны
2. смешной	смешон	смешна	смешны
3. старый	стар	стара	стары
4. физический	-	-	-
5. жаркий	жарок	жарка	жарки
6. низкий	низок	низка	низки
7. живой	жив	жива	живы
8. гордый	горд	горда	горды
9. волшебный	волшебен	волшебна	волшебны
10. снежный	снежен	снежна	снежны

8.8.3 Verbs

Most verbs are derived and so have a derivational suffix. Here is the distribution of stress among both derived and nonderived verbs. Departing from traditional nomenclature, we will call all verbs with fixed stem stress, including fixed stem stress on a suffix, AA. This is by far the largest stress category among verbs. There are no BA verbs, that is, verbs with final stress on the ending in the nonpresent and on the stem in the present. The AC pattern, with shifting stress in the present, is widespread among 2nd conj verbs: любить, люблю, любишь, etc. Other variations than the ones given below occur only rarely, cf. понять, which is a CB verb (stress acrobatics in the past), and обнять, which is a CC verb. See Levin for more details.

(1)

AA	BB	AB	AC
делать	нести	давать	писать
проигрывать	везти	плевать	сказать

AA	BB	AB	AC
рабо́тать	течь	верну́ть	купи́ть
ку́шать	жечь	отдохну́ть	смотре́ть
ве́рить		смея́ться	обману́ть
отве́тить		запере́ть	кури́ть
чита́ть		грызть	носи́ть
конча́ть		попа́сть	коло́ть
гля́нуть		жать	
боле́ть			
сове́товать			
говори́ть			
гляде́ть			

Regularities:

1. The vast majority of verbs in Russian take the AA, AB, or AC pattern. Only a handful take the BB pattern, and these can be determined from their infinitive form (-ти, -чь, -олоть, -ороть). Verbs with the BB pattern have accentually weak roots.

2. The AB pattern is limited to verbs that delete all or part of a suffix in the present tense: дава́ть--present tense stem is {да-'}, верну́ть, with future tense stem {верн-'}. Suffix mutation in these stems does not cause the root to become accentually ordinary, which is a morphophonemic, not inflectional phenomenon.

3. When stress falls on a root vowel, the verb will have the AA pattern. This occurs with strong root vowels or when a weak suffix is present. When stress falls on the verbal suffix, stress remains on the verbal suffix if the root is ordinary, such as чита́ть, or weak, such as говори́ть. These verbs also exhibit the AA pattern.

4. When stress falls on the verbal suffix *and the root is ordinary*, we usually see the AC, or shifting stress pattern. This is illustrated below. However, it must be stated that the shifting stress pattern in the present/future tense is an area fraught with exceptions. Generally speaking, the shifting pattern is observed when the root is *verbal*. In a sense, this

combination, verbal root plus shifting, defines "accentually ordinary" for verbal roots. With the exception of a handful of adjectives in -ой (e.g., сухо́й, туго́й, тупо́й), adjectival roots do not form verbs with the shifting pattern, no matter what the accentual weight of the root. Noun roots that are accentually ordinary normally do form 2nd conj verbs with the shifting pattern, but there are exceptions here as well; шут (w) → шути́ть (shifting). In short, the shifting pattern in the present/future tense continues to present problems. However, the generalizations presented here account for the majority of verbs with shifting stress.

Second conj, therefore, is either AA or AC. AA has stress fixed on the root (polysyllabic or strong roots) or on the suffix (weak noun roots, or ordinary adjectival roots). Generally speaking, AC verbs have ordinary verbal or noun roots and stress is mobile in the present. Mobility is illustrated in (2c).

The suffix и/и is ordinary in nonpresent conjugation and weak in present/future conjugation. All verbal endings are also weak, with the exception of the first sg ending {+y}, which is ordinary.

The distribution of stress in 2nd conj verbs is illustrated in (2):

(2)   a. Fixed stem stress (AA with strong root):

избавить	{из=ба́в -и + т'} (s+o)	→	избавить
	{из=ба́в -и + y} (s+w+o)	→	избавлю
	{из=ба́в -и + ш} (s+w)	→	избавишь

b. Fixed end stress (AA with weak root):

прости́ть	{прост -и + т'} (w+o)	→	прости́ть
	{прост -и + y} (w+w+o)	→	прощу́
	{прост -и + ш} (w+w)	→	прости́шь (w+w principle)

c. Shifting stress (AC with ordinary root):

дари́ть	{дар -и + т'} (o+o)	→	дари́ть
	{дар -и + y} (o+w+o)	→	дарю́
	{дар -и + ш} (o+w)	→	да́ришь

купи́ть	{куп -и + т'} (о+о)	→	купи́ть
	{куп -и + у} (о+w+о)	→	куплю́
	{куп -и + ш} (о+w)	→	ку́пишь

Contrast the distribution of shifting stress among 2nd conj verbs (2c) with that of 1st conj verbs, where the theme vowel {o} is weak:

(3)   a. Shifting stress (AC with ordinary root):

писа́ть	{пис -а + ть} (о+о)	→	писа́ть
	{пис -∅ -й + у} (о+w+w+о)	→	пишу́
	{пис -∅ -й + о + ш} (о+w+w+w+w) →		пи́шешь

Stress falls on the endings of 1st conj verbs when stems are weak and the w+w principle is invoked: сдава́ть-сдаю́, сдаёшь, etc.

*A Given the following information about the accentual properties of the root, mark stress.

1. СТУП- (о)	ступить	ступлю	ступишь	ступила
2. СТРОЙ- (s)	построить	построю	построишь	построила
3. МЯГ- (w)	смягчить	смягчу	смягчишь	смягчила
4. ВИД- (s)	видеть	вижу	видишь	видела
5. НИМ- (о)	понимать	понимаю	понимаешь	понимала
6. ТРЯС- (w)	трясти	трясу	трясешь	трясла
7. ПРОС- (о)	просить	прошу	просишь	просила
8. РЕШ- (w)	решить	решу	решишь	решила
9. СТАВ- (s)	поставить	поставлю	поставишь	поставила
10. ЛОГ- (о)	положить	положу	положишь	положила

8.9 Predicting Stress: Reprise and Exercise

Stress in Russian can usually be predicted correctly on the basis of the structure of the word and accentological weight of the root. Inferences about stress can be enhanced by means of the general stress rule and stress principles discussed in this chapter. If the generalizations presented above are correct, then they not only may represent something close to what native Russian speakers learn as they acquire their language, but also something close to what they use as they speak.

While the presence of a suffix nearly always implies fixed stress, the question of where stress will fall in a word with a suffix is much more complex. The approach presented here assumes that most roots are neither weak nor strong. But it is important to know which roots and suffixes are accentually weighted. It may be suggested that this is exactly what Russians do as they learn their own language. Given a morpheme in combination with any number of suffixes or alone, certain conclusions can be made about its relationship to stress. The wider the morpheme is used, the more often its stress characteristics are verified, until usage becomes automatic. Perhaps a similar process could be followed for non-natives learning Russian.

Still, students should not attempt to memorize these rules and then employ them as they speak, since it would be counterproductive to pass mentally through a list of rules and principles for every word one uses. Instead, these rules could be valuable as guidelines for students who want to exercise vocabulary and understand the dynamics of stress, so that when they do speak the correct stress comes from force of habit. Stress rules can also be of use when reading where a word's meaning can be determined by its root and context, and its proper pronunciation can be determined by phonological and stress rules. For most words stress can be predicted via the suffix. If the word is nonderived, stress can usually be predicted on the basis of the regularities presented in the previous section. Other predictive mechanisms can be employed; for example, in some words stress can be predicted by the way the word is spelled. This is due to the spelling rule which specifies that unstressed o is written e after hushers and ц. Consequently:

(1) stress falls on any o following a husher or ц:

большо́й, отцо́в, карандашо́м, шо́рох, чащо́ба, плечо́, дружо́чек

Other rules based on the suffixes involved could be written. For example:

(2) Nouns ending in -ие or -ия usually have stress on the vowel preceding this syllable. (See sec. 8.6.1)

(3) Nouns ending in consonant+ка in the nom sg usually have stress on the first vowel preceding the consonant. (Sec. 8.7.4)

(4) Words with polysyllabic or foreign roots are usually stressed on the last vowel of the root. (Sec. 8.2)

(5) Nouns ending in consonant+<u>ость</u> or consonant+<u>ность</u> usually have stress on the vowel preceding the suffix. (Sec. 8.6.4)

(6) The suffix -<u>ыва</u> is always preceded by stress. (Sec. 8.6.5)

(7) The AC pattern is frequent among nonderived 3rd decl nouns. (Sec. 8.8.1, number 5)

(8) Masc nouns with stress on the final suffix in the nom sg have the BB pattern. (Sec. 8.8.1, number 2)

(9) Most fem nouns encountered with stress on the desinence in the nom sg (-<u>á</u>, -<u>я́</u>) have the BA pattern. (Sec. 8.8.1, number 4)

(10) Masc nouns that take the nom pl ending -<u>á</u> or the loc2 ending -<u>ý</u> usually have the AB pattern. (Sec. 8.8.1, number 3)

Exceptions to these generalizations should not be considered "irregular," but simply show that the generalizations given here are neither complete nor exhaustive.

ADDITIONAL EXERCISES

*A Give the stress pattern (AA or BB) of the following. Refer to a dictionary if needed. In which words is the end-stress pattern not a logical choice, given the nom sg form?

1. звук	5. знак	9. биолог
2. рецéпт	6. труд	10. дождь
3. кирпи́ч	7. факт	11. живóт
4. архитéктор	8. двор	12. падéж

*B Which stress pattern do the following exhibit, AA, BB, or AB? Refer to a dictionary if necessary.

1. бе́рег
2. язы́к
3. и́скренний
4. чи́стить
5. гото́вый

6. о́стров
7. встре́тить
8. го́лос
9. мести́
10. ра́зный

*C What is the stress pattern of the following, AC or BC? You shouldn't need to use a dictionary.

1. плохо́й
2. гро́мкий

3. просто́й
4. стра́нный

*D Identify the stress pattern of the following nouns. Make a guess, before referring to a dictionary.

1. а́дрес
2. бе́дный
3. дуб
4. произнести́
5. произноси́ть
6. це́рковь
7. холо́дный
8. смерть
9. мя́гкий
10. гость

11. изба́
12. гнило́й
13. коне́ц
14. пра́во
15. янва́рь
16. четве́рг
17. сосна́
18. приня́ть
19. ме́сто
20. сказа́ть

*E Consider the following <u>nom pl</u> masc words. Write out the words in the given cases and mark stress for each.

1. номера́: gen sg, gen pl, inst pl
2. образа́: nom sg, inst sg, prep pl (This is образ "icon.")
3. колокола́: nom sg, prep sg, gen pl
4. кондуктора́: dat sg, gen pl, prep pl
5. голоса́: acc sg, acc pl, gen pl

*F Write out the case forms of the following and mark stress.

    1. мораль: nom sg, gen sg, nom pl, gen pl
    2. мелочь: nom sg, gen sg, nom pl, gen pl
    3. часть: acc sg, prep sg, acc pl, gen pl
    4. мысль: inst sg, nom pl, gen pl
    5. церковь: nom sg, gen sg, nom pl, gen pl

*G Indicate stress pattern.

	nom sg	acc sg	nom pl	gen pl	prep pl
1.	о́стров	о́стров	острова́	острово́в	острова́х
2.	язы́к	язы́к	языки́	языко́в	языка́х
3.	пляж	пляж	пля́жи	пля́жей	пля́жах
4.	гора́	го́ру	го́ры	гор	гора́х
5.	зима́	зи́му	зи́мы	зим	зи́мах
6.	ночь	ночь	но́чи	ноче́й	ноча́х

*H Predict stress. Fill in the blanks without referring to a dictionary.

nom sg	acc sg	prep sg	nom pl	gen pl	ptrn
большо́й					
	певца́				
мост	мост	на мосту́			
			паспорта́		
				богаче́й	BB
сла́вный					
ключ					
о́бласть					
ко́рень					
			ве́тви	ветве́й	
		бро́ви	бро́ви		AC
го́лубь					

*I What is the stress of the following words. What is the stress of the gen
    sg and nom pl forms of the nouns?

1. мышоночек
2. ка́мень (masc.)
3. по́езд (nom pl. поезда)
4. молоде́ц
5. свисту́н
6. морозилка
7. орнитология
8. приготавливать
9. значок
10. дружба

11. лицо
12. гость
13. коза́
14. аборда́ж
15. мост (на мосту́)
16. благочестие
17. моложавость
18. багаж
19. словарь
20. плечо

*J Write out the underlined words. Mark stress.

1. Это интересная <u>поговорка</u>. У русских много <u>поговорок</u>.
2. У меня нет <u>ключа</u>. Все <u>ключи</u> были на <u>столе</u>.
3. Мне нравится эта изба́. Все другие <u>избы</u> сгорели.
4. <u>Купцы</u> гуляли в <u>саду</u>. Там собрались все <u>семьи</u>.
5. Сколько <u>карманов</u> в этом костюме? Нет ни одного <u>кармана</u>.
6. Это приятное село́. Здесь все <u>села</u> красивые.
7. Это большая гора́. Мы сегодня едем в <u>горы</u>.
8. Такие красивые <u>голоса</u>! У нее тоже красивый <u>голос</u>.
9. Он нашел старый буква́рь. А что он нашел в <u>букваре</u>?
10. Если он троглодит, тогда и она <u>троглодитка</u>.

*K Be prepared to read the following passage from Lev Tolstoy's <u>Набег</u>
   aloud in class. You should be able to predict stress on the underlined
   words and explain what stress principles are involved in each, even if
   the principle is simply, "I already knew the stress of this word."

Вода была <u>лошадям</u> по <u>груди</u>, с <u>необыкновенной</u> силой <u>рвалась</u>
между <u>белых</u> камней, которые в иных <u>местах</u> <u>виднелись</u> на <u>уровне</u>
воды, и <u>образовывала</u> около ног <u>лошадей</u> пенящиеся, шумящие
<u>струи</u>. <u>Лошади</u> <u>удивлялись</u> <u>шуму</u> воды, <u>подымали</u> головы,
<u>настораживали</u> уши, но <u>мерно</u> и <u>осторожно</u> <u>шагали</u> против
<u>течения</u> по <u>неровному</u> дну. <u>Седоки</u> <u>подбирали</u> ноги и <u>оружие</u>.

Пехотные солдаты, буквально в одних рубахах, поднимая над водою ружья, на которые надеты были узлы с одеждой, усилием старались противостоять течению.

Как скоро переправа кончилась, генерал вдруг выразил на своем лице какую-то задумчивость и серьезность, повернул лошадь и поехал по широкой, окруженной лесом поляне.

В лесу виднеется пеший человек в черкеске, другой, третий... Кто-то из офицеров говорит: «Это татары».

8.9 Review

The seemingly chaotic state of stress in Russian yields grudgingly to attempts at simplifying the number of patterns involved and at discovering rules which permit prediction of stress locus. Perhaps further attempts will be successful in unraveling the secrets of stress assignment. Here historical principles have proven largely useless since they are based on features such as tone, which are no longer found in the language. When faced with this problem in regard to phonology, as with soft [н'] before [o] in нёс, linguists turned to morphophonemics. The approach presented here is a kind of accentual morphophonemics. This system provides a fairly accurate account of the stress of most Russian words. It makes use of the interaction of morpheme stress valencies. Strong morphemes attract stress while weak morphemes tend to repulse stress. Other morphemes may or may not be stressed depending on neighboring morphemes. A set of principles regulates whether or not a given morpheme receives stress. A stress rule assigns stress to strong morphemes or to morphemes marked for stress. Stress patterns among both derived and nonderived words emerge and predictions about stress based on these patterns can be made.

Languages leave in the wake of change irregularities which are easily enough learned by children. Adults learning a foreign language need not founder on these irregularities. Structural descriptions can illuminate and simplify some language learning tasks. Other tasks require memorization. As we continue to observe and learn about speech, one of the most human of human activities, perhaps in addition to acquiring practical information we will discover more about ourselves and our own abilities.

APPENDIX 1: KEY TO THE EXERCISES

Chapter 1

1.1

*A.

1. Only <u>o</u> and <u>т</u> represent more than one sound. In молоко́, the first two o's sound more like a's. In чита́ть there is a hard т and a soft one.
2. The following in (1) represent only one sound: м, л, к, ё, я, ч, и, а
3. Soft т is represented in (1) before ё, (2) before я, and (3) before ь.

*B.

Using as many Cyrillic letters as possible, here is one of many possibilities:

   a. мↆлↆко, where ↑=an "a" sound
   b. ToTa, where T=soft т
   c. читаT

1.2

*A

1. губны́е: б, в, п, ф, м
2. зубны́е: д, з, л, н, р, с, т, ц
3. нёбны́е: ж, ч, ш, щ
4. йод: й
5. задненёбны́е: к, г, х

*B

1. и → ы after hushers (нёбны́е) and velars (задненёбны́е)
2. ю, я → у, а after hushers (нёбны́е), velars (задненёбны́е) and ц
3. unstressed о → е after hushers (нёбны́е) and ц.

*C.

1. nasal cavity - полость носа
b. lips - губы
c. teeth - зубы
d. alveolar ridge - альвеола
e. hard palate - твёрдое нёбо
f. soft palate - мягкое нёбо

g. tongue - язык
h. vocal chords - голосовые связки
i. lungs - лёгкие

*D.

1. б	6. г
2. п	7. х
3. т	8. к
4. с	9. д
5. ж	10. ф

1.3

*A.

1. Vowels present little or no obstruction to the air flow, consonants present significant obstruction.

2. voice

3. Like vowels they are all voiced, and although they present an obstruction to the flow of air, in the case of м and н, air still flows freely (through the nasal cavity). In the case of р and л, the air flow is only slightly restricted.

1.4

*A.		
	1. пять	7. тётю
	2. судьба	8. тень
	3. пить	9. лицо
	4. дети	10. дынь
	5. письмо	11. тюбик
	6. труба	12. мыть

*B.		
	1. [суйо́т]	5. [л'а́гу]
	2. [л'эс]	6. [с'эл]
	3. [с'ол]	7. [кл'уйу́]
	4. [сто́ит]	8. [им'эт']

*C. You're on your own on this one.

1.5

*A.				
	1. кино	6. читают	11. ноги	16. гуляю
	2. печь	7. жён	12. руке	
	3. чищу	8. идёт	13. цен	
	4. руки	9.клён	14. пять	
	5. шёл	10.живой	15. ясный	

*B.   1. [чи́стый]   6. [м'эч]
        2. [глуш]   7. [мыш]
        3. [жыво́т]   8. [цыкл]
        4. [л'ул'к'и]   9. [лыжы́]
        5. [ш'ш'и]   10. [д'эн'г'и]

1.6

*A. There was a big fire. When it started up, it caught up the roof (on fire) and immediately there was smoke. Oh there was so much smoke. All the villagers came; it looked like it was in white foam. There were a lot of people I didn't know; they were just shouting, they didn't take anything out (of the house). I went out onto the porch and started throwing off bad (smoking) blocks (of wood). I threw off seven armfuls. I felt faint. My son-in-law came, found hammers, did everything right. I wasn't given anything for the loss.

*B. They are similar sounds. They share the same means of articulation (both are africates), both are voiceless, and the point of articulation for ц is near that of ч.

1.7

* A.

1. [с'а́ду]   6. [из'у́м]
2. [ступл'у́]   7. [сйэл]
3. [сту́п'иш]   8. [йа́рус]
4. [л'эт]   9. [ш'ш'ит]
5. [з'има́]   10. [йу́ный]

*B.

1. voiceless dental stop   10. voiced dental fricative
2. voiced labial stop
3. voiceless velar stop
4. voiceless labial fricative
5. voiceless palatal fricative
6. voiced palatal fricative
7. high front vowel
8. voiceless velar fricative
9. mid back vowel

Chapter 2

2.1

*A.

1. письмо - rule (3) once
2. письме - rule (3) twice
3. структу́ра
4. бро́ви - rule (3) once
5. мо́сте - rule (3) once
6. и́збы
7. уро́к
8. уро́ки rule (3) once
9. кня́зю
10. лю́ди rule (3) once

*B.

1. #кни́г-#
2. #бу́лк-#
3. #звук-#
4. #зонт-'#
5. #во́здух-#
6. #ра́дуг-#

*C.

1. rarely
2. Ukraine

2.2

*A. Unstressed o̱ is pronounced as [ʌ] immediately before the stressed syllable or when it is at the beginning of a word, that is, if it is the first sound of the word. Unstressed o̱ is pronounced as [ъ] everyhwere else in the word as long as it is not under stress.

*B. Unstressed a̱ is pronounced as [ʌ] immediately before the stressed syllable or at the beginning of the word. It is pronounced [ъ] elsewhere in the word when not under stress. That is, unstressed a̱ is reduced to the same sounds and in the same positions as unstressed o̱.

*C.
1. [кʌро́въ]
2. [ча́стъ]
3. [друго́въ]
4. [гърʌдо́к]
5. [ʌдм'ира́л]
6. [стър'ика́]
7. [ско́въръды]
8. [клъдʌво́й]
9. [сто́ръну]
10. [ʌгурцы́]

2.5

*A. Ikan'e involves two sounds, orthographic e̱ and я̱. Since я̱ is phonetically C'+a (пять is [п'ат'] for example, we will need to include this fact in our statement of the environment of the rule that expresses ikan'e. Your rules should look something like:

(1) а, э → и / C' ___ ɤ̆
(2)   э → ь / C' ___

*B   1. уреза́ть   6. уменьша́ть
      2. светово́й   7. связно́й
      3. трезве́ть   8. прямо́й
      4. еди́ный   9. ряды́
      5. свято́й   10. немо́й

*C   1. [чьпуха́]   6. [с'ьр'ибро́]
      2. [т'ьл'ифо́н]   7. [о́чьр'ьд'и]
      3. [б'ьр'гʌво́й]   8. [г'ьрʌи́зм]
      4. [в'исна́]   9. [фклу́б'ь]
      5. [йинва́р']   10. [д'ир'э́вн'ь]

2.6

*A All the words in the right-hand column end in a consonant cluster (two or more consonants together). The word final consonant devoices as expected. In addition the consonant next to the final consonant is also pronounced devoiced. The only exception to this is when the final consonant is a sonorant, as in укоризн. The sonorants are м, н, р, л. Like vowels, these "semivowels" do not become voiceless at the end of a word and consonants next to them also remained voiced.

*B   C   → [-voiced] / ___ C
          [-son]   [-voiced]

Which states that (non sonorant) consonants are pronounced voiceless if next to a voiceless consonant.

*C   1. [муш]   4. [хл'э́бъ]   7. [в'иск]
      2. [б'э́р'ьк]   5. [хл'эп]   8. [д'эн']
      3. [л'убо́ф']   6. [нʌд'э́шт]   9. [п'иро́к]

*D 1. весёлый
    2. здоров
    3. нужд
    4. вождь
    5. молотьбá

    6. ягод много
    7. дождь идёт
    8. денег нет
    9. в коридоре
    10. бумáжка

2.8

*A 1. # л э с á #
    2. # с н э г #
    3. # й á г о д а #

    4. # п' а т' #
    5. # с в' а з' #
    6. # т р' а с т й #

2.10

*A	#óстров#	#подписáт'#	#пэрэшúб#
C→C'	-	подп'исáт'	п'эр'эшúб
akan'e(1)	-	-	-
ikan'e(1)	-	-	п'эр'ишúб
akan'e(2)	óстръв	пъдп'исáт'	-
ikan'e(2)	-	-	п'ър'ишúб
и→ы	-	-	п'ър'ишы́б
C→-voi	óстръф	-	п'ър'ишы́п
C→±voi	-	пътп'исáт'	-
C→C'	-	-	-
	[óстръф]	[пътп'исáт']	[п'ър'ишы́п]
	"island"	"sign"	"fractured"

	#кост'óр#	#окóвыват'#	#жизнэл'ýб#
C→C'	-	-	жизн'эл'ýб
akan'e(1)	кΛст'óр	Λкóвыват'	-
ikan'e(1)	-	-	жизн'ил'ýб
akan'e(2)	-	Λкóвывът'	-
ikan'e(2)	-	-	-
и→ы	-	-	жызн'ил'ýб
C→-voi	-	-	жызн'ил'ýп
C→±voi	-	-	-
C→C'	-	-	жыз'н'ил'ýп
	[кΛст'óр]	[Λкóвывът']	[жыз'н'ил'ýп]
	"campfire"	"bind"	"person who hates life"

	#оплошáт'#	#пэрэт'анýт'#	#гран'#
C→C'	-	п'эр'эт'анýт'	-
akan'e(1)	Λплλшáт'	-	-
ikan'e(1)	-	п'эр'эт'инýт'	-
akan'e(2)	-	-	-
ikan'e(2)	-	п'ьр'ьт'инýт'	-
и→ы	-	-	-
C→-voi	-	-	-
C→±voi	-	-	-
C→C'	-	-	-
	[Λплλшáт']	[п'ьр'ьт'инýт']	[грáн']
	"to blunder"	"to pull over"	"border"

	#сгор'ачá#
C→C'	-
akan'e(1)	-
ikan'e(1)	сгор'ичá
akan'e(2)	сгър'ичá
ikan'e(2)	-
и→ы	-
C→-voi	-
C→±voi	згър'ичá
C→C'	-
	[згър'ичá]
	"in a fit"

*B Give a derivation for each. Here are the underlying forms.

1. #долгожи́тэл'#   4. #прийэ́зд#
2. #бэзкоры́стный#   5. #бэто́н#
3. #разиска́т'#   6. #йа́бэда#

*C 1. код - кот   5. глаз - глас
    2. луг - лук   6. пруд - прут
    3. бог - бок   7. лез - лес
    4. молод - молот   8. лёд - лёт

2.12

*A The spelling of this word has been adapted to the way the word is now pronounced in the standard language. Since stress never fell on the initial syllable, an [o] never was pronounced. Akan'e makes it sound like an a̲, so why not write it that way?

*B Speakers are influenced by how words are spelled. Speakers of this dialect saw written забота, but pronounced it as [зобо́та]. They assumed other   pretonic a̲'s were pronounced o̲.

*C spelling of a̲ for unstressed o̲ and spelling of o̲ for unstressed a̲.

*D Earlier than the 14th century.

*E They knew that akan'e, that slangy, lazy way of pronouncing o̲ was current, probably even in their own speech. They continued to write the o̲, though, and even started writing o̲ in words with original a̲, thinking these must really be o̲'s too.

Chapter 3

3.2

*A We already have a rule that makes unstressed o̲ into ∧ and ъ (akan'e). The proposed rule contradicts akan'e.

*B The rule in (5) must specify that the change occurs only before hard consonants, i.e. the C̲ in (5) is a hard consonant.

*C
1. се́льский
2. сёла
3. тёрн
4. созве́здие
5. ше́рсть
6. искривле́ние
7. искривлённый
8. исте́чь
9. истёк
10. шёрстка

3.4.1

*A   1. #спи́ч/ка#   6. #аккура́т/ный#
       2. #лы́сина# (no fleeting vowel-fv)   7. #знач/'к#
       3. #сэкрэта́рша# (no fv)   8. #рыба́к# (no fv)
       4. #ору́дийэ# (no fv)   9. #цини́зм# (no fv)
       5. #сэм'/йа́#   10. #тигр# (no fv)

3.4.2

*A

1. o	6. o	11. o*	16. e
2. o*	7. o*	12. e	17. e
3. e	8. o*	13. e	18. e
4. o*	9. o	14. и	19. o*
5. o	10. e	15. e	20. e

*changes to e according to the rule in (5)

*B

1. b	6. a
2. a	7. b
3. a	8. b
4. b	9. a
5. b	10. b

3.5

*A   Раньше, хочешь, не хочешь, а замуж надо было идти. Анна Петрокоська говорила: меня обволокли в материну пару, долгие широкие юбки до самого полу, чтобы ног не видно было. А я реву, да не даю в рукава совать.

     Earlier, whether you wanted to or not, you had to get married. Anna P. recounted: I was wrapped in mother's blouse, in long wide skirts to the very floor, so that my legs couldn't be seen. And I howl and don't let them stuff (me) into the sleeves.

хочешь - cekan'e
надо and others - no akan'e
говорила - okan'e
рукова́ - strong okan'e

К венцу врозь везут невесту на своих лошадях и жених на своих, а от венца вместе. На голову невесте-то цветы накладывают восковые белыми цветочками.

They take the bride to the wedding separately on her own horses, and the groom is on his, but from the wedding (they go) together. They put wax flowers with little white petals on the bride's head.

жоних - okan'e
вместе - strange pronunciation of stressed e̱
восковые - okan'e
белыми - again the strange pronunciation of stressed e̱.

Note that the e̱ in CSR seems exceptional too, because it is before a hard consonant and stressed, so ё is expected here in CSR.

Chapter 4

4.2
*A   Letters no longer used: ѣ, i
      Letters still used but used differently today: ъ, я (in the word бѣдныя)

*B   1. ѣ corresponds to modern e̱, i to modern и.
      2. ъ occurs at the <u>end</u> of words
      3. ъ only occurs after prefixes in MR: объяснѝтъ
      4. Adjectives ending in -к (nom sg and nom pl)

4.2.1
*A   OR e̱ equates to e1 (ё)

*B   1. нѣтъ   6. нести
      2. мѣсто   7. стѣна
      3. медъ   8. сѣстъ
      4. береза   9. жена
      5. рѣка   10. смѣхъ

4.2.2

*A The dialectal pronunciation of ѣ as [ê] or [иэ] supports the proposal that this sound was a diphthong in OR. If the northern dialects are conservative then they may well retain the earlier pronunciation.

4.3

*A   TROT (or TRAT)

*B   All have <u>a</u> except Russian and Polish which have <u>o</u>.

*C   TROT

4.4

*A   Old Russian for Modern Russian: ъ - Ø, ѣ - е, ѧ - я, i - и, є - е,
        ж - у, ю - е, ꙗ - я

*B   See how many of these you can get.

4.5

*A   They used to be soft.

4.5.1

*A   This sequence is dissimilation, and goes against the way sounds normally change. The dialect evidence does not support the proposed sequence since there are no instances of (back, hard) velars followed by front vowels, although it is no less reasonable than the one proposed by Shakhmatov, whose explanation also involves dissimilation.

*B These are front vowels and soft consonants are simply fronted varieties of hard consonants (assimilation).

*C These consonants were once preceded by front vowels which caused palatalization of the consonants. The vowels then shifted: пэкъ → (C→C') п'экъ → (э→о) п'окъ → п'ок and пьнтъ → (C→C') п'ьнт'ь → (ьн→ѧ) п'ат'ь → (ѧ→a) п'ат'ь → п'ат'

*D Because it accurately characterizes the situation in modern Russian. Only [и] is pronounced after velars--never [ы]. Why did this rule develop?

No one knows for sure. Shakhmatov suggests rounded velars to solve this problem, but there is no independent evidence that rounded velars existed in Russian at this time. This is an unsolved mystery in Russian.

4.6
*A The ending in the earlier case (it was the locative case) was always stressed.

*B Words in column 1 have stress on the stem, words in column 2 have stress on the stem and end in a velar (пек-, тек, мог-) when cojugated, verbs in column 3 have stress on the ending.

*C   1. -ти/
  2. The combinations гт and кт became ч, as in могти → мочь. The unstressed -и of the ending -ти was lost, leaving a soft т', as in читáти → читáть.
  3. as in:

ProtoSlavic:	[мóгти]
гт / кт → ч:	[мóчи]
unstr. infin. и → Ø:	[моч]

4.7
*A   1. и   4. э   *B   1. [-high, +front]
     2. э,о   5. о,а   2. [-high, -low, -front]
     3. none   6. у,о

*C [front] ([o] is the back (rounded) version of [э])

*D [+front] shifts to [-front]

*E A soft consonant is fronted. [э] is the fronted (nonrounded) variant of [o], so when fronted (soft) consonant was followed by [o], the latter became fronted as well, that is became [э]. The [o] assimilated the fronted quality of the soft consonant.

4.8

*A Jers followed by another jer in the very next syllable were strengthened and retained. Jers not followed by another jer, including all word final jers, were lost.

*B
1. лодъка
2. девушька
3. съвьсѣмъ
4. сънъ
5. отьць
6. окъно
7. довольнъ
8. лѣсъ

4.9

*A

	Москва	девица	цепь	час	меч	учитель
Ст. Оскол	девиса	сепь	час	меч	учитель
Брянск	девиша	шепь	шас	меш	ушитель
Валдай	девица	цепь	час*	меч*	учитель*
Псков	девица	цепь	цас	мец	уцитель
В. Устюг	деви[ц']а	[ц']епь	[ц']ас	ме[ц']	у[ц']итель

*hard [ч]

*B Since Finnish dialects spoken near to where cokan'e occurs in Russian has only one affricate, it has been suggested that this has influenced nearby Russian speakers to reduce their affricates (ч and ц) to one or the other, resulting in cokan'e or chokan'e.

4.10

*A
1. [рот]
2. [лоткъ]
3. [н'ос]
4. [нʌчат']
5. [ул'ицъ]
6. [кто]
7. [л'эс]
8. [д'эн']
9. [пр'ишол]
10. [пр'ишла]

Chapter 5

5.3

*A 1. The acc sg = nom sg masc endings with "inanimate" nouns
    2. These acc sg masc uses the gen sg masc with "animate" nouns

*B It has no ending. All other cases for masc nouns have an overt ending.

*C The vowel letters {а у о э и ы} are used. The letters я ю ё е are never used.

*D Morphological: Prep {стол + э́}, Dat {кисэл' + у́}, Inst {музэ́й + ом}
Orthographic: столе́, киселю́, музе́ем

*E 1. {бэ́рэг + ∅}   3. {мудрэц + о́м}   5. {зу́б + э}
  2. {лэ́бэд' + ∅}   4. {лэ́бэд' + у}   6. {му́ж+ом}

5.5
*A 1. It is {+ а}. Orthographic а < {С + а}, я < {С' + а}, ия < {ий + а}
  2. {газэ́т + а}   {нэдэ́л' + а}   {аллэрги́й + а}
  3. Acc {+ у}   Prep {+ э} and {+ и}
    Gen {+ ы}   Inst {+ ой}
  4. prep and dat

*B
1. долина - nom   4. башня - nom   7. статья - nom
2. долиной - inst   5. башней - inst   8. статьёй - inst
3. долины - gen   6. башни - gen   9. статьи - gen

*C   1. {ли́ний + а}   7. {пэ́с/н' + а}
     2. {ли́ний + ы}   8. {пэ́с/н' + ы}
     3. {кни́г + ы}   9. {пэ́с/н' + ой}
     4. {сэм'/й + у́}   10. {пэ́с/н' + у}
     5. {ступ/н' + о́й}   11. {ку́х/н' + э}
     6. {ли́ний + ой}   12. {ли́ний + у}

5.6
*A   1. {пит'й + о́}   7. {л'уб/'в' + ∅}
     2. {доч + ∅}   8. {пит'/й + а́}
     3. {пло́щад' + и}   9. {ло́шад' + йу}
     4. {свин'/й + а́}   10. {го́р' + о}
     5. {ко́мнат + ы}   11. {учи́тэл' + у}
     6. {двэр' + ∅}   12. {двэр' + йу}

*B The soft sign shows the presence of {С'+й}. This sequence of sounds is found in all cases in the sg of such words.

*C The combination {С' + й} is represented in Russian orthography as <u>Сь</u> <u>(plus vowel letter)</u>, eg., свинья. In the sg of third decl nouns, this combination only occurs in the instr (such as in no. 9 and 12 above). The soft sign occurs in the nom of third decl nouns to show that the final consonant is soft, as in no. 6 and 7 above). Elsewhere in the third decl the front vowel will show this softness, as in no. 3 above.

*D   The gen pl: чтений.

5.7
*A   1. {суш'ш'эств + á}   2. {мор' + á}   3. {здáний + а}

*B

1. reg	5. reg	9. irreg	13. irreg	17. reg
2. reg	6. reg	10. reg	14. irreg	18. irreg
3. reg	7. reg	11. reg	15. reg	19. irreg
4. irreg	8. reg	12. irreg	16. reg	20. reg

*C No normal 3rd decl noun ends in a hard consonant. The words чёрт and сосед almost fit into this category, though.

*D

1. корóв	11. критéриев	21. ýлиц
2. звýков	12. дýшей	22. туч
3. рýнков	13. ситуáций	23. болóт
4. стúлей	14. словарéй	24. ружéй
5. слýчаев	15. богачéй	25. вещéств
6. гроз	16. стáтуй	26. музéев
7. лúчностей	17. авáрий	27. очевúдцев
8. достижéний	18. я́мочек	28. лыж
9. девúц	19. войск	29. свинéй
10. идéй	20. овощéй	30. ключéй

*E
1. {завóд + ов}   2. {морáл' + эй}   3. {душ + Ø}
4. {гэрóй + ов}   5. {дáч + Ø}   6. {крэс/л + Ø}

5.9.1
*A In the 3rd declension (as in ночь: gen ночи, prep ночи, dat ночи);
these nouns are fem, though the neut nouns in -мя also fall into this
declension and have the same syncretic endings: gen, prp, dat: времени.

5.9.2
*A 1. с книгам   2. с книгами   3. с книгама   4. с книгам

Chapter 6

6.1
*A   1. There are two different endings, -ут and -ют.
          2. The same distribution holds as for the first sg: after consonants
          write -ут, after vowels write -ют.

6.2
*A In each the verb forming suffix is absent in conjugation:
{сказ -Ø -й +у}, for example. A dental followed by the present tense
marker {+й} results in mutation by phonological rule.

*B   1. {рабóт -а -й + у}   7. {совэ́т -у -й + у}
          2. {закáз -Ø -й -о + ш}   8. {закрó -Ø -й -о + м}
          3. {начн -Ø -Ø + у}   9. {заказ -Ø -й + у́}
          4. {закрó -Ø -й + у}   10. {п' -Ø -й -о + т}
          5. {рабóт -а -й -о + ш }   11. {совэ́т -у -й -о + ш}
          6. {собир -á -й + у}   12. {забу́д -Ø -Ø + ут}

*C   чтить should conjugate something like золотúть: золочу́,
золотúшь, etc. Thus we expect ччу for 1st sg. Instead the consonant т
is retained in this form: чту, (чтишь, чтят). If mutation is allowed to
occur with this verb, then the resultant root would lose its resemblance
to the infinitive, the double чч being pronounced as one: [чу]. Thus,
though this verb appears to be irregularly conjugated, there is a good
reason for its irregularities.

*D   1. а/а   8. ну/н
        2. а/а   9. Ø/Ø
        3. е/е   10. ва/Ø
        4. Ø/Ø (the н̲ is part of the root)   11. Ø/Ø
        5. Ø/Ø (the ы(→о) is part of the root)   12. Ø/Ø
        6. и/Ø   13. Ø/Ø
        7. ова/у   14. Ø/Ø (я̲ is part of
                                                            the root)

*E   Most Ø/Ø verbs have different stems for the past and present.

6.3
*A   1. {брóс -и + у}   3. {смотр -и + ý}   5. {встрэ́т -и + у}
        2. {брóс -и + ш}   4. {смотр -и + ш}   6. {встрэ́т -и + ш}

*B   1. It never does.
        2. All velars mutated to hushers before front vowels at an earlier
        stage in history.
        3. Second conj is much simpler. The stem is always arrived at by
        removing the infinitive suffix and the preceding suffix, either {э},
        {и}, or {a}.

6.4
*A   It must stand for {Ø}, or some other sound that disappears after й̲.
*B   It must stand for some sound that softens consonants, evidently
{и}, which softens the final consonant of the root and then disappears
after a soft consonant.
*C   Obviously it stands for {и}.
*D   It must be {и}.

*E   It is a difficult task to determine if one imperative ending exists. If
it does, it must have all the qualities given in *A-*D above. An "unstable"
{и} would account for all the phenomena observed above. This sound is
actually heard in говори́ and чи́сти. In встань it palatalizes the final root
consonant then is deleted since it is not stressed nor follows a consonant
cluster. In чита́й the final consonant is already soft, so this suffix has no
effect on verbs of this type. It is simply deleted since it is not stressed nor
follows a consonant cluster.

6.5

*A   1. Standard Russian is based on the central dialects.
2. Most of the dialect shifts can be found in the central dialects.
3. I personally would like to see more logic in the use of verbal aspect, i.e., perfective vs. imperfective. Since the first sg of second conj verbs shows mutation (люблю́), it would be consistent if the third pl also showed mutation (*лю́блят). Fewer unusual suffixes in the first conj would also be nice.

*B She had lived. Berries had grown. She had sung songs, had danced, but no longer after she got married: children came and there was no time.

In October it was warm, though it had snowed in September.

He had earned a lot before the war.

*C   English uses "have" in the past tense plus past participle:
          I had gone by the house.
      French uses "to be" or "have" in the imperfect plus past participle:
          Il avait parlé avec moi.   He had spoken with me.

*D   It is redundant. The person/number suffix is used to indicate person/number *and* present tense.

Chapter 7

7.1

*A   Since the sound {ы} doesn't have any particular stress altering properties, nor do disyllabic suffixes generally have any leverage on stress, we must be dealing with a morphophonemic phenomenon. It is the morpheme {ыва} that is responsible for the shift, not any single sound.

*B

a) root	b) category of root	c) category of word	d) derivation
1. МОР'-	noun	noun	not derived
2. СОВЕТ-	noun	noun	not derived
3. СЛОВАК-	noun	adj	cross-cat.

4. ДЕТ-	noun	noun	intra-cat.
5. СТОЛ-	noun	adj	cross-cat.
6. СОВЕТ-	noun	noun	intra-cat.
7. СТРОЙ-	verb	noun	cross-cat.
8. УЧ-	verb	noun	cross-cat.
9. СТАР-	adj	noun	cross-cat.
10. СОВЕТ-	noun	verb	cross-cat.
11. КРЫ-	verb	verb	not derived
12. УК-	verb	noun	cross-cat.

7.2

*A   1. hard vs. soft д. Historically the first singular ended in -ом which ultimately yielded -у, neither of which caused the preceding д to soften. The second singular ended in -эш, which caused softening. Subsequently this ending became [ош] due to the э → о rule. Morphophonemically, the first sg ending is {-у} which accounts for the hard д. The second singular has the theme vowel {*о}, which is marked to cause preceding consonants to be pronounced soft.

2. Historically the к mutated to ч when followed by a front vowel. Here the front jer of the suffix -ьн was responsible for this mutation. A morphophonemic approach suggests that the adjectival suffix is {*/н}. Before this suffix velars automatically mutate to hushers.

3. The husher seen in дружок is due historically to a following front jer, which was part of the suffix: *другькъ. In strong position this jer shifted to which, falling under stress and before a hard consonant, became о. In morphophonemics, the suffix is {*/к}, which motivates mutation of velars.

4. The vowel in мёртвый was historically a е, which shifted to о, according to the э → о phonological rule. This rule no longer operates in modern Russian. The root of this word therefore is now both {мэрт} and {м'орт}, abbreviated in morphophonemic terms as {м'Орт}.

*B   1. {криК-}   The shift of к to ч is not automatic before this verbal suffix.

2. {наук-} The mutation of velars before this adjectival suffix is automatic.

3. {услов-} Softening of consonants by front vowels occurs phonologically

4. {слуг-} All velars mutate before this suffix, which is {-*и}. In modern Russian velars do not mutate automatically before front vowels, cf. герой, гипноз, etc.

5. {у́лиЦ-} The adjective is explained as in 2. A very restricted morphophonemic rule accounts for the shift of {у́лиЦ} to {у́лиц}.

7.3

*A

1. {а́вгуст-} N
2. {стаН-} N
3. {йск-} N
4. {ры́б-} N
5. {мо́ст-} D

6. {зэм-} D < {зэм + й + á}
7. {двор-} N
8. {пис-} D or {пис'м} N
9. {ры́б-} D
10. {мэ́ст-} N

*B   In all pairs the root final consonant is hard in one partner but soft in the other.

7.4.1

*A   It is the verb forming suffix for second conj verbs.
*B   No new verbs are being formed with this suffix.
*C   Stress always falls on the derived imperfective suffix {-á}.
*D

1. заража́ть
2. отвеча́ть
3. приглаша́ть
4. вставля́ть

5. сооружа́ть
6. разреша́ть
7. упроща́ть
8. округля́ть

7.4.2

*A

1. {слэ́д -ова + т'}   сле́довать
2. {п'йа́нств -ова + т'}   пья́нствовать
3. {тан/ц -ова́ + т'}   танцева́ть
4. {врач -ова́ + т'}   врачева́ть
5. {тоск -ова́ + т'}   тоскова́ть
6. {бэ́дств -ова + т'}   бе́дствовать

7. {брак -ова́ + т'}	браковать
8. {свинц -ова́ + т'}	свинцева́ть
9. {бэсэ́д -ова́ + т'}	бесе́довать
10. {имэн -ова́ + т'}	именова́ть

7.4.3

*A   Though an a/Ø verb, it doesn't take the present tense marker {й}, whose presence would indicate mutation in the present tense. The other strange thing about this verb is that a fleeting vowel occurs in the present t e n s e, though a vowel follows in the next syllable {з/в -Ø -Ø + ý} → зову́. You know another verb that does this. What is it? Hint: it is also an a/Ø verb.

7.4.5

*A

1. слаб	6. захлебну́лся
2. просну́лся	7. поги́б
3. привы́к	8. пры́гнул
4. замёрз	9. дви́нул
5. щёлкнул	10. поддёрнул

*B
1. momentary → perf → ну in past	correct
2. stress location indicates perf → ну in past	correct
3. change of state → imperf → Ø in past	correct
4. static → imperf → Ø in past	correct
5. quick, momentary action → perf → ну in past	correct
6. momentary action → perf → ну in past	correct
7. static → imperf → Ø in past	correct
8. change of state → imperf → Ø in past	correct
9. stress indicates perf → ну in past	correct
10. change of state → imperf → Ø in past	correct

*C Verbal aspect given in *B above. Potixa's characterizations are fairly reliable.

7.4.6

*A Phonological. The shift of <u>и</u> to <u>й</u> sets up the environment for a predictable mutation of dentals and labials.
*B False. It is not a morphophonemic shift.

*C	1. огора́живать	6. допры́гивать
	2. обусла́вливать	7. догова́ривать
	3. залёчивать	8. зата́чивать
	4. недове́шивать	9. выра́щивать
	5. упако́вывать	10. перечи́тывать

7.4.8

*A Since velars do not automatically mutate before the verbal suffix {а}, we can assume that the root morpheme is marked to undergo mutation. Therefore, the morphophonemic representation of these will be {стуК + а́ + т'}, and a morphophonemic rule will shift {стуК-} to {стуч-}. Note that this approach does not refer to historical elements which no longer occur in the language. Historically the suffix a seen in these verbs derives from the long front vowel ѣ which resulted in palatalization of velars. Subsequently ѣ shifted to a (see section 4.5).

*B	(a) verbal suffix	(b) infinitive	(c) alternations
	1. а/Ø	{пла́к -а + т'}	к + й → ч
	2. и/и	{плат -и́ + т'}	т + й → ч
	3. а/а	{рэш -а́ + т'}	none
	4. а/а	{про=свэт -и -а́ + т'}	т + й → ч
	5. а/а	{об=лэгК -а́ + т'}	К → ч by morphophonemic rule
	6. а/и	{трэсК -а́ + т'}	К → ч by morphophonemic rule
	7. ыва/ыва	{у=пак -о́в -ыва + т'}	none
	8. ова/у	{гл'анц -ова́ + т'}	none
	9. Ø/ну/н	{о=слэп -ну + т'}	С → С' before {*о}
	10. ыва/ыва	{раз=иск -ыва + т'}	stress shifts by morphophonemic rule

*C	1. образо́вывать	6. выхола́щивать
	2. спра́шивать	7. пока́зывать
	3. до́игрывать	8. наве́шивать
	4. опра́вдывать	9. зага́дывать
	5. затра́гивать	10. устра́ивать

7.5.2

*A
1. моло́чник
2. иго́льник
3. парово́зник
4. бесе́дчик
5. наёмник
6. обма́нщик
7. паке́тик
8. пиро́жник
9. коте́льщик
10. ходе́бщик

7.5.9

*A
1. вдове́ц
2. глазо́к
3. грибо́к
4. Рижа́нин
5. чертёжик
6. заготовле́ние
7. обогрева́тель
8. разве́дчик
9. ёлочка
10. бесёнок
11. бе́дность
12. ка́менщик
13. зверёнок
14. моги́лщик
15. огово́рщик
16. ослёнок
17. круже́ние
18. опа́сность
19. па́ртиец
20. подру́жка
21. дружо́к
22. голла́ндиец
23. зате́йник
24. творе́ние
25. кни́жность
26. сапо́жник
27. га́лочка
28. дру́жность
29. шту́чка
30. кри́тик

7.5.11

*A
1. нау́ка
2. коне́ц
3. ствол
4. во́дка
5. де́ньги
6. оте́ц
7. оши́бка
8. автомоби́ль
9. биоло́гия

*B
1. ме́стный
2. успе́шный
3. гре́шный
4. гру́стный
5. ме́сячный
6. тетра́дочный
7. культу́рный
8. семе́йный
9. вку́сный
10. доро́жный
11. мы́льный
12. руже́йный

Chapter 8

8.1

*A   1. Я хочу́ пить во́ду, with incorrect stress on the final word sounds like: Я хочу́ пить в аду́.

2. According to Lebedeva, there aren't any.

*B   1. ending - the stem has no vowel, so stem stress is not possible here

2. stem - but you can't tell from this infinitive

3. ending - but this infinitive gives no hints

4. ending - a good candidate for final stress if the nom sg of adjectives has final stress

5. ending - a good candidate for final stress if stress falls on the -ну́ть

6. stem - not a good candidate for final stress; root stress of an infinitive implies stem stress

7. stem - not a candidate for final stress since this nom sg has root stress

8. ending - not predictable

9. ending - a good candidate for final stress since stress falls on the final vowel in the infinitive

*C
1. stem	6. ending
2. stem	7. stem
3. stem	8. stem
4. ending	9. ending
5. ending	10. ending

8.2

*A

1. {снэг + ∅} {снэг -*/'к + ∅} {снэг -*ни́к + ∅} {снэг -ов + о́й}
2. {свэт + ∅} {свэт -а́ + т'} {освэт -л'ак + ∅} {свэт -й + т'}
3. {мо́лот + ∅} {молот -*/'к + ∅} {молот -й +т'} {молот-ов +о́й}

*B The tendency is for stress to fall on the final stressable stem syllable, so:

1. беле́ть
2. темне́ть
3. светле́ть
4. чита́ть
5. влеза́ть
6. мости́ть
7. мягчи́ть
8. крести́ть
9. остри́ть
10. рыбе́ц
11. горде́ц
12. африка́нский
13. долговоло́сый
14. англи́йский
15. ночева́ть
16. истори́ческий*
17. поправле́ние
18. послуша́ние
19. холо́дный
20. рыба́к

*Actually, one might guess *истори́ческий, but the e̲ of this suffix is not stressable. Discussion below.

*C
1. пара́д
2. кинжа́л
3. виногра́д
4. лейтена́нт
5. фо́рма
6. культу́ра
7. систе́ма
8. мимо́за
9. капу́ста
10. миксту́ра
11. колыма́га
12. кукуру́за
13. желе́зо
14. коле́но
15. боло́то
16. полоте́нце
17. кре́сло
18. взро́слый
19. могу́чий
20. неле́пый
21. угрю́мый
22. открове́нный
23. знамени́тый
24. подо́бный
25. блаже́нный
26. равня́ть
27. хвата́ть
28. отрица́ть
29. кувырка́ть
30. запряга́ть

*D
1. стака́нчик
2. у́жинать
3. дежу́рить
4. обезде́нежеть
5. карма́нчик
6. подколе́нный
7. замёрзнуть
8. ме́сячина
9. овра́жистый
10. сою́зничество

8.3
*A
1. молодча́га
2. черепа́ха
3. городи́ще
4. молото́к
5. золоти́ть
6. воротничо́к
7. насторожи́ть
8. голода́ть
9. голоси́ть

*B 1. Ø 3. a 5. Ø 7. a 9. Ø
    2. a 4. Ø 6. a 8. a 10. a

8.5 *A
1. землянин
2. персиянин
3. рижанин
4. ростовчанин
5. римлянин
6. харьковчанин
7. древлянини
8. полянин
9. соборянин
10. каторжанин

*B
1. волжанин
2. россиянин
3. армянин
4. угличанин
5. крестьянин
6. парижанин
7. варшаванин
8. мирянин

*C
1. оленёнок
2. болтун
3. проектант
4. дурак
5. трясучий
6. копировать
7. копировальный
8. увеличитель
9. грязуха
10. акустический
11. плавучий
12. зайчонок
13. мышонок
14. консультант
15. здоровьяк
16. скрипач
17. плакун
18. рекламировать
19. папуша
20. осведомитель

8.6.1

*A
1. стипендия
2. академия
3. компания
4. невралгия
5. педиатрия
6. эмбриология
7. эмбриолог
8. фобия
9. руссификация
10. паталогия

*B
1. плавание
2. настаивание
3. осматривание
4. образование
5. следование
6. достижение
7. положение
8. учение
9. ослабление
10. исполнение

*C   Both have unpredictable stress according to this system: покáяться has strong stem stress which should be retained with the weak suffix {-ний}. The same is true for послýшать. Why do you think the stress has shifted in the derived forms?

8.6.2

*A 1. ábедничество - s   6. леснúчество - s
    2. мýжество - о   7. госудáрство - s
    3. произвóдство - о   8. стройтельство - s
    4. сопéрничество - s   9. мáстерство - о
    5. монáшество - s   10. óбщество - о

8.6.3

*A 1. ёжик   6. солдáтик   11. вагóнчик
    2. тáзик   7. пакéтик   12. донóсчик
    3. рýблик   8. зýбчик   13. сигнáльчик
    4. акадéмик   9. развéдчик   14. танцóвщик
    5. фонáрик   10. мизúнчик   15. заговóрщик

derived from: ёж, таз, рубль, акадéмия, фонáрь, солдáт, пакéт, зуб, развестú, мизúнец, вагóн, доносúть, сигнáл, танцевáть, заговорúть

8.6.4

*A 1. солидáрность   6. молчалúвость   11. доставúтель
    2. трéпетность   7. всáсываемость   12. заполнúтель
    3. мелодúчность   8. болóтистость   13. опрыскиватель
    4. грóмкость   9. усилúтель   14. предáтель
    5. похóжесть   10. заместúтель   15. собирáтель

8.6.5

*A 1. размáлывать   6. перечúтывать   11. опечáтывать
    2. снúзывать   7. окáпывать   12. обрабáтывать
    3. целовáть   8. отбрáсывать   13. прóбовать
    4. жáловать   9. тосковáть   14. рáбствовать
    5. даровáть   10. подпúсывать
                                            15. свидéтельствовать

8.6.6

*A

1. четверго́вый	6. ро́зовый	11. ту́ндровый
2. дождёвый	7. пятако́вый	12. дворо́вый
3. съе́здовый	8. леднико́вый	13. костро́вый
4. ножево́й (irreg)	9. шёлковый	14. ки́товый
5. берёзовый	10. ла́мповый	15. дворцо́вый

*B

1. ара́бский	6. купе́ческий	11. коре́йский
2. кана́дский	7. оте́ческий	12. алба́нский
3. бо́жеский	8. славя́нский	13. мона́шеский
4. сосе́дский	9. апте́карский	14. кавка́зский
5. дру́жеский	10. дуна́йский	15. све́тский

8.6.7

*A

1. лесни́чество	5. чуло́чек
2. чуда́чество	6. телёночек
3. садо́вничество	7. мину́точка
4. уда́рничество	8. крючо́чек

8.7.1

*A

1. ме́стный	6. посло́вичный
2. па́мятный	7. публи́чный
3. со́вестный	8. фабри́чный
4. возду́шный	9. символи́чный
5. ло́дочный	10. единогла́сный

8.7.3

*A

1. лове́ц	6. краса́вец	11. коне́ц
2. земледе́лец	7. горде́ц	12. боре́ц
3. зубе́ц	8. европе́ец	13. змеебо́рец
4. трезу́бец	9. кузне́ц	14. хитре́ц
5. лука́вец	10. укра́инец	15. америка́нец

8.7.4 *A

1. мона́шек	6. сни́мок
2. дру́жка	7. поку́пка
3. кни́жка	8. сыно́к
4. сапожо́к	9. прове́рка
5. де́вочка	10. голосо́к

8.7.5

*A The imperfective маха́ть (машу́, ма́шешь) has an ordinary root. The suffix -ну is weak and, therefore, should not recieve the stress in this word. It does. One suspects the stress of this word is due to the fact that it is perfective, since most perfective -нуть verbs have finál stress.

*B   (Valencies are given in parentheses.)

1. хрома́ть (o)   11. посягну́ть (w)
2. зама́зать (s)   12. су́нуть (o)
3. опозда́ть (o)   13. защити́ть (o)
4. лысе́ть (o)   14. изобрази́ть (w)
5. старе́ть (o)   15. удо́брить (s)
6. цари́ть (o)   16. прису́тствовать (o)
7. буди́ть (o)   17. насле́довать (o)
8. мы́слить (s)   18. волнова́ть (w)
9. оцени́ть (o)   19. организова́ть (w)
10. пры́гнуть (s)   20. жа́ждать (s)

8.8

*A   1. бе́лая, бела́, бе́ло, бе́лы
      2. вокза́ла, вокза́лы, вокза́лов
      3. везу́, везёшь, везу́т, везла́, везли́
      4. ве́тви, ве́тви, ветве́й
      5. пье́су, о пье́се, пье́сы, пье́сами
      6. гаража́, в гараже́, гаражи́, гараже́й
      7. гру́бое, груба́, гру́бо, гру́бы
      8. боло́та, боло́та, боло́т, боло́тах
      9. ста́ну, ста́нешь, ста́нут, ста́ла, ста́ли
      10. пою́, поёшь, пою́т, пе́ла, пе́ли
      11. куплю́, ку́пишь, ку́пят, купи́л, купи́ла, купи́ли
      12. да́ра, да́ром, дары́, даро́в
      13. зу́ба, зу́бом, зу́бы, зубо́в
      14. письма́, о письме́, пи́сьма
      15. сро́чная, сро́чное, сро́чен, сро́чна, сро́чно, сро́чны
      16. скамья́, скамью́, скамьи́, о скамье́, скамьи́
      17. клюю́, клюёшь, клюю́т, клева́л, клева́ла, клева́ли

8.8.1

*A
1. года́ (see no. 3)
2. во́йны (see no. 4)
3. звезду́, звёзды (see no. 4)
4. ме́лочь, ме́лочи, мелоче́й (see no. 5)
5. острово́в (see no. 3)
6. ключа́ (see no. 2)
7. вдо́вам (see no. 4)
8. си́лу, си́лой (see no. 1)
9. бана́н, бана́ны (see no. 1)
10. городо́в (see no. 3)

8.8.2

*A
1. кра́сный, кра́сен, красна́, кра́сны (AC - see no. 5)
2. смешно́й, смешо́н, смешна́, смешны́ (BB - see no. 2)
3. ста́рый, стар, стара́, ста́ры (AC - see no. 5)
4. физи́ческий (A∅ - see no. 1)
5. жа́ркий, жа́рок, жарка́, жа́рки (AC - see no. 5)
6. ни́зкий, ни́зок, низка́, ни́зки (AC - see no. 5)
7. живо́й, жив, жива́, жи́вы (BC - It's not BB, see no. 2, so it must be BC)
8. го́рдый, горд, горда́, го́рды (AC - see no. 5)
9. волше́бный, волше́бен, волше́бна, волше́бны (AA - see no. 5)
10. сне́жный, сне́жен, сне́жна, сне́жны (AA - see no. 5)

8.8.3

*A

1. ступи́ть	ступлю́	сту́пишь	ступи́ла
2. постро́ить	постро́ю	постро́ишь	постро́ила
3. смягчи́ть	смягчу́	смягчи́шь	смягчи́ла
4. ви́деть	ви́жу	ви́дишь	ви́дела
5. понима́ть	понима́ю	понима́ешь	понима́ла
6. трясти́	трясу́	трясёшь	трясла́
7. проси́ть	прошу́	про́сишь	проси́ла
8. реши́ть	решу́	реши́шь	реши́ла
9. поста́вить	поста́влю	поста́вишь	поста́вила
10. положи́ть	положу́	поло́жишь	положи́ла

8.9

*A
1. AA
2. AA - foreign: BB unlikely
3. BB
4. AA - BB impossible
5. AA
6. BB

7. AA - foreign -BB unlikely
8. BB
9. AA - BB impossible
10. BB
11. BB
12. BB

*B
1. AB
2. BB
3. AA
4. AA
5. AA
6. AB
7. AA
8. AB
9. BB
10. AA

*C
1. BC
2. AC
3. BC
4. AC

*D
1. AB
2. AC
3. AB
4. BB
5. AC
6. AC
7. AC
8. AC
9. AC
10. AC
11. BA
12. BC
13. BB
14. AB
15. BB
16. BB
17. BA
18. CB
19. AB
20. AC

*E
1. номера, номеров, номерами
2. образ, образом, образах
3. колокол, колоколе, колоколов
4. кондуктору, кондукторов, кондукторах
5. голос, голоса, голосов

*F
1. мораль, морали, морали, моралей
2. мелочь, мелочи, мелочи, мелочей
3. часть, части, части, частей
4. мыслью, мысли, мыслей
5. церковь, церкви, церкви, церквей

*G
1. AB 2. BB 3. AA 4. CC 5. CA 6. AC

*H.

nom sg	acc sg	prep sg	nom pl	gen pl	pattern
большо́й	большо́й	большо́м	больши́е	больши́х	BØ
певе́ц	певца́	певце́	певцы́	певцо́в	BB
мост	мост	на мосту́	мосты́	мосто́в	AB
па́спорт	па́спорт	па́спорте	паспорта́	паспорто́в	AB
бога́ч	богача́	богаче́	богачи́	богаче́й	BB
сла́вный	сла́вный	сла́вном	сла́вные	сла́вных	AA
ключ	ключ	ключе́	ключи́	ключе́й	BB
о́бласть	о́бласть	о́бласти	о́бласти	областе́й	AC
ко́рень	ко́рень	ко́рни	ко́рни	корне́й	AC
ветвь	ветвь	ве́тви	ве́тви	ветве́й	AC
бровь	бровь	бро́ви	бро́ви	брове́й	AC
го́лубь	го́лубя	го́лубе	го́луби	голубе́й	AC

*I

1. мышо́ночек мышо́ночка мышо́ночки
2. ка́мень (masc.) ка́мня ка́мни
3. по́езд (nom pl. поезда́) по́езда
4. молоде́ц молодца́ молодцы́
5. свисту́н свистуна́ свистуны́
6. морози́лка морози́лки мороози́лки
7. орнитоло́гия орнитоло́гии -
8. пригота́вливать
9. значо́к значка́ значки́
10. дру́жба дру́жбы -
11. лицо́ лица́ ли́ца
12. гость го́стя го́сти
13. коза́ козы́ ко́зы
14. аборда́ж аборда́жа аборда́жи
15. мост (на мосту́) мо́ста мосты́

16. благоче́стие благоче́стия -
17. моложа́вость моложа́вости -
18. бага́ж багажа́ багажи́
19. слова́рь словаря́ словари́
20. плечо́ плеча́ пле́чи

*J   1. Это интересная <u>поговórка</u>. У русских много <u>поговóрок</u>.
      2. У меня нет <u>ключа́</u>. Все <u>ключи́</u> были на <u>столе́</u>.
      3. Мне нравится эта изба́. Все другие <u>и́збы</u> сгорели.
      4. <u>Купцы́</u> гуляли в <u>саду́</u>. Там собрались все <u>се́мьи</u>.
      5. Сколько <u>карма́нов</u> в этом костюме? Нет ни одного <u>карма́на</u>.
      6. Это приятное село́. Здесь все <u>сёла</u> красивые.
      7. Это большая гора́. Мы сегодня едем в <u>го́ры</u>.
      8. Такие красивые <u>голоса́</u>! У нее тоже красивый <u>го́лос</u>.
      9. Он нашел старый буква́рь. А что он нашел в <u>букваре́</u>?
      10. Если он троглодит, тогда и она <u>троглоди́тка</u>.

*K   Вода была <u>лошадя́м</u>[1] по <u>гру́ди</u>[1], с <u>необыкнове́нной</u>[2] силой
рвалась между <u>бе́лых</u>[3] <u>камне́й</u>[4], которые в иных <u>места́х</u>[5]
<u>видне́лись</u>[24] на <u>у́ровне</u>[7] <u>воды́</u>[8], и <u>образо́вывала</u>[9] около ног
<u>лошаде́й</u>[1] пеняциеся, шумя́щие <u>стру́и</u>[10]. <u>Ло́шади</u>[1] удивля́лись[11]
<u>шу́му</u>[12] воды, <u>подыма́ли</u>[13] <u>го́ловы</u>[14], настора́живали[9] уши, но
<u>ме́рно</u>[2] и осторо́жно[2] <u>шага́ли</u>[13] против <u>тече́ния</u>[15] по <u>неро́вному</u>[2]
дну. <u>Седоки́</u>[13] <u>подбира́ли</u>[13] <u>но́ги</u>[14] и <u>ору́жие</u>[16]. Пехо́тные[2]
<u>солда́ты</u>[17], <u>буква́льно</u>[18] в одних <u>руба́хах</u>[17], <u>поднима́я</u>[19] над <u>водо́ю</u>[8] <u>ру́жья</u>[8], на которые <u>наде́ты</u>[6] были узлы с <u>оде́ждой</u>[6], <u>уси́лием</u>[16]
<u>стара́лись</u>[13] <u>противостоя́ть</u>[11] <u>тече́нию</u>[15].

      Как скоро <u>перепра́ва</u>[6] кончилась, <u>генера́л</u>[17] вдруг
<u>вы́разил</u>[20] на своем <u>лице́</u>[8] какую-то <u>заду́мчивость</u>[6] и
<u>серьёзность</u>[17], <u>поверну́л</u>[26] <u>ло́шадь</u>[1] и поехал по широкой,
окруженной <u>ле́сом</u>[22] поляне.

      В <u>лесу́</u>[23] <u>видне́ется</u>[24] пеший человек в <u>черке́ске</u>[17], <u>друго́й</u>[25],
третий... Кто-то из <u>офице́ров</u>[17] <u>говори́т</u>[21]: «Это <u>тата́ры</u>[17]».

1. 3rd decl without suffix: AC likely
2. (о) root, suffix in -*/н: stress on stem
3. nom is бе́лый: all adjs have fixed stress in long form

4. 1st decl ending in a soft cons without suffix: AC likely
5. AB likely for neut nouns with stem stress in sg
6. (s) root
7. AC pattern has word initial stress in sg
8. <u>B</u> in sg = nom, gen, prep, dat, instr with end stress
9. ыва always precede by stress
10. If the nom sg is either струя́ or стру́я stress will be on the root in the nom pl. (It's струя́.)
11. has derived imperfective suffix а́/а́, which is strong
12. (o)
13. (o) + (o)
14. nom sg in -а́ or -я́ = BA
15. polysyllabic suffix {-э́ний} is strong on initial syllable
16. suffix {-ий} is weak
17. polysyllabic root -- strong
18. strong suffix
19. (w)+(o)
20. prefix вы- with perfective verbs is always stressed
21. (w)+(w)
22. A in sg = fixed stem stress throughout the sg paradigm (exception: 23)
23. Loc-2 ending -у́ is always stressed
24. This is a difficult one. вид is (s) -- ви́деть. виднеется is < {вид -*/н -э +й +o+ тс'а}. The nonvocalic principle (sec. 8.7.1) allows stress to fall to the right of / if the stem is verbal. Here the root and stem are verbal.
25. nom sg adj ending -ой is always stressed
26. вернуть is a nonprefixed perfective with stem ending in consonant (sec. 7.4.5)

APPENDIX 2
Valencies and Grammatical Categories of 451 Roots

Roots are in the form as given in Gribble, except that the acute mark is added to polysyllabic strong and ordinary roots to indicate stress. Where more than one syllable of the root may receive stress, both are marked. The roots given here are among the most widely used, forming about 25,000 words in Russian, based on the count in Kuznecova and Efremova and to the frequency rates given by Zasorina.

Column 1: roots, Column 2: accentual valencies, Column 3: grammatical category of the root, Column 4: words whose stress is exceptional given the valency of the root.

Root	Valency	Category	Exceptions
Б/Р	w	v	
БАВ	s	v	
БЕД	w	n	беднéть
БЕЛ	o	a	
БИЙ	w	v	
БИР	w	v	
БЛУД	w	v?	блуд
БОДР	o	a	
БОЙ	w	v	бой
БОЛ	w	v	боль
БОЛÓТ	s	n	
БОР	o	v	
БОРОД	w	n	
БРЕД	o	n	бредовóй
БРОД	o	v	
БРОС	o	v	брóсить
БУКВ	o	n	
БУЛ/К	o	n	
БУМÁГ	s	n	
БУР	o	n	буровóй
БЫ	o	v	
ВАГ	o	n	
ВАГÓН	s	n	
ВАЛ	o	n	
ВАР	o	v	
ВЕД	s	n	
ВЕД	w	v	
ВЕЗ	w	v	
ВЕЙ	s	v	
ВЕР	s	v	
ВЕРТ	o	v	
ВЕРХ	o	n	верховóй
ВЕС	s	v	весовóй
ВЕСЁЛ	o	a	
ВЕСТ	o	n	вестовóй
ВЕТ	s	v	
ВÉЧЕР	o	n	
ВИД	s	v	видáть
ВИЗГ	o	n	
ВИЙ	w	v	
ВИН	w	n	
ВИС	w	v	вíснуть
ВКУС	o	n	
ВЛАД	w	v	
ВОД	w	n	
ВОД	o	v	
ВОЗ	o	v	
ВОЛ	o	n	
ВОЛК	o	n	
ВОЛН	w	n	
ВОЛОК	w	v	волочíть
ВÓЛОС	o	n	
ВОРÓТ	o	v	вóрот,ворóта
ВОСК	o	n	
ВРАЧ	w	n	
ВРЕД	w	n	
ВСТРЕТ	s	v	
ВУЛКÁН	s	n	
ВЬЮГ	s	n	
ВЯЗ	o	v	

ГАД	o	v		ДВОР	w	n	
ГАЗÉТ	s	n		ДЕВ	s	n	
ГАС	o	v		ДЕЙ	s	v	
ГЕРÓЙ	s	n		ДЕЛ	s	v	делéц
ГИБ	s	v		ДЕРГ	o	v	
ГЛАВ	w	n		ДЁРГ	s	v	
ГЛАД	s	a		ДИК	o	a	
ГЛАЗ	o	n		ДОБР	o	a	
ГЛУБ	w	n		ДОЖД	o	n	
ГЛУП	o	a		ДОЛГ	o	n	одолжúть
ГЛУХ	w	a		ДОРОГ	w	a	
ГЛЯД	w	v		ДОРÓГ	s	n	
ГНЕЗД	w	n		ДРОГ	w	v	
ГОВОР	w	v	гóвор	ДРУГ	o	n	
ГОД	w	a		ДУЙ	s	v	
ГОЛОВ	w	n		ДУМ	s	v	
ГОЛОД	o	n		ДУР	w	a	
ГÓЛОС	o	n	голосúть	ДУХ	o	n	
ГОН	o	v		ДЫМ	o	n	дымúть
ГОР	w	n		ДЫР	w	n	
ГОРБ	w	n	гóрбить	ЕД	s	v	
ГОРД	o	a		ЕДЍН	o	a	
ГÓРОД	o	n		ЕЗД	s	v	ездóк
ГОРÓХ	s	n		ЕЛ	s	n	
ГОР	s	n	горéть	ЁМ	s	n	
ГОСТ	w	n		Ж/М	o	v	
ГОТÓВ	s	a		Ж/Г	o	v	
ГРАН	w	n	грань	ЖАЛ	o	n	
ГРЕБ	w	v		ЖАР	s	n (w--colloq.)	
ГРЕЙ	s	v		ЖЕЛÉЗ	s	n	
ГРЕХ	w	n		ЖЕН	o	n	женá
ГРИБ	w	n		ЖЕРТВ	s	n	
ГРОБ	o	n	грóбить	ЖИВ	w	v/a	
ГРОЗ	w	n	грозовóй	ЖИР	o	n	жировóй
ГРУБ	o	a		ЖУРНÁЛ	s	n	
ГРУЗ	o	n	грзовóй	З/Р	w	v	
ГРУСТ	o	n	грустúть	ЗÁВЍСТ	o	n	
ГРЫЗ	w	v		ЗАКÓН	s	n	
ГРЯЗ	o	n		ЗВЕЗД	w	n	
ГУБ	w	v		ЗВЕР	o	n	
ГУД	w	n		ЗВОН	w	v	звон
ГУЛ	w	v		ЗВУК	o	n	звучáть
ДА	w	v		ЗДОРÓВ	s	a	
ДАВ	o	v		ЗЕЛÉН	o	a	
ДАР	o	n		ЗЕМ	w	n	
ДВИГ	s	v	движóк	ЗН(А)	w	v	

Root			Derived	Root			Derived
ЗО́ЛОТ	o	n	золоти́ть	КРОВ	o	n	
ЗУБ	o	n		КРОХ	w	n	кроши́ть
ИГ/Л	w	n		КРУГ	o	v	
ИГР	w	n/v		КРУП	w	a	
ИД	w	v		КРУТ	w	a	
ИСЧЕЗ	o	v		КРЫ	s	v	
КАЗ	o	v		КУЛАК	w	n	
КАЗАК	w	n		КУП	o	v	
КАЛ	w	v		КУР	o	v	
КАПУ́СТ	s	n		КУС	o	v	
КАРМА́Н	s	n		ЛЕ́БЕД	o	n	
КАРТИ́Н	s	n		ЛЕГ	w	v	
КАТ	o	v		ЛЕГ/К	w	a	
КАЧ	w	v		ЛЕП	o	v	
КВАРТИ́Р	s	n	квартирова́ть	ЛЕС	o	n	лесно́й
КИД	o	v		ЛЕТ	w	v	лётный
КИП	w	v		ЛЕЧ	w	v	
КИС	o	a		ЛИЙ	w	v	
КЛАД	w	v	клад	ЛИК	w	n	
КЛЕЙ	s	n		ЛОВ	o	v	
КЛОН	o	v		ЛОГ	o	v	
КЛЮЧ	w	n		ЛО́К/Т	o	n	
КНИГ	s	n		ЛОМ	o	v	
КОВ	w	v		ЛОПА́Т	s	n	
КОЖ	s	n		ЛО́ША́Д	o	n	
КОЛ	o	v		ЛУП	o	v	
КОЛЕС	w	n		ЛУЧ	w	n	
КО́ЛОКО́Л	o	n		ЛЫС	o	a	
КОЛО́Т	o	v		ЛЮБ	o	v	любова́ться
КОЛ/Ц	w	n		МАЗ	s	v	
КОН	w	n		МАЛ	o	a	
КОНЦЕ́РТ	s	n		МАН	o	v	
КОП	o	v		МАС/Л	s	n	
КОПТ	w	v		МАХ	o	v	махну́ть
КОРМ	o	n		МЕД	o	n	медо́вый
КОРО́В	s	n		МЕЖ	w	n	
КОРОТ	w	a		МЕЛ	o	a	
КОС	w	a		МЕН	o	v	
КОС	w	n	коси́ть	МЕР	s	n	
КОСТ/Р	w	n		МЕРЗ	o	v/a	
КОСТ	o	n		МЕРТВ	o	a	
КОТ/Л	w	n		МЕС	o	v	
КРАС	w/s	a/v		МЕСТ	o	n	
КРЕП	w	a		МЕТ	o	v	
КРЕСТ	w	n	крести́ть	МЕЧТ	w	n	
КРИВ	w	a		МИР	s	n	мири́ться

МОГ	o	v	
МОЗГ	o	n	мозговой
МОЗО́Л	s	n	
МОЛ	o	v	
МОЛОД	w	a	
МОЛОК	w	n	
МО́ЛОТ	o	n	
МОРО́З	s	n	
МОТ	o	v	
МУК	s	n	
МЫ	s	v	
МЫСЛ	s	n	
НАГЛ	o	a	
НАЧН	w	v	
НЕС	w	v	
НИЗ	o	n	
НИМ	w	v	
НОВ	o	a	
НОГ	w	n	
НОЖ	w	n	
НО́МЕР	o	n	
НОС	o	v	
НОЧ	o	n	ночева́ть
НЫР	w	v	
ОБИ́Д	s	n	
ОБЩ	o	a	
ОГ/Н	w	n	
ОК/Н	w	n	
ОСНО́В	o	n	основно́й
ОСТР	o	a	
О́СТРОВ	o	n	островой
ОЧК	w	n	
ПАД	s	v	пасть
ПАЛ	w	v	пал
ПАР	o	n	па́рить
ПАС	w	v	
ПАХ	o	v	
ПЕВ/ПОЙ	w	v	
ПЕК	w	v	
ПЕС/К	w	n	песо́чек
ПЕСТР	o	a	
ПЕЧА́Л	s	n	
ПЕЧА́Т	s	n	
ПИЙ	w	v	
ПИЛ	w	n	
ПИС	o	v	

ПИТ	o	v	
ПИХ	o	v	
ПЛАВ	s	v	
ПЛЕТ	w	v	
ПЛОД	w	n	
ПЛОТ	o	a	
ПЛОХ	w	a	
ПЛЫ	w	v	
ПОБЕ́Д	s	n	победи́ть
ПОГО́Д	s	n	
ПОЛЗ	o	v	ползти w
ПОЛН	o	a	испо́лнить etc.
ПОЛ	o	n	полево́й
ПОЛЬЗ	s	v/n	
ПРАВ	s	n	
ПРАЗД/Н	s	a	
ПРОС	o	v	
ПРОСТ	w	a	
ПРУД	w	n	
ПРЫГ	s	v	прыжо́к
ПРЯД	s	n	
ПРЯТ	s	v	
ПУГ	w	v	
ПУСК	o	v	
ПУСТ	o	v	
ПУТ	s	v	
ПЫЛ	o	n	пыли́ть
РАБ	w	n	
РАБО́Т	s	n	
РАВ/Н	o	a	
РАД	s	a	
РАЗ	w	n	
РВ	w	v	
РЕД	o	a	
РЕЗ	s	v	резну́ть
РЕК	w	n	
РЕМО́НТ	s	n	
РЕШ	w	v	
РИС	w	v	
РОД	o	n	роди́ть
РУБ	o	v	
РУК	w	n	
РЫБ	o	n	
РЫ́Н/К	s	n	
РЯД	o	n	
САД	o	n	

САПОГ	w	n		СУК	w	n	
СА́ХАР	s	n		СУХ	w	a	
СВЕЖ	o	a		СЫП	w	v	
СВЕТ	o	n	световóй	ТАН/Ц	s	n	танцевáть
СВИСТ	o	n		ТАСК	o	v	
СВОБО́Д	s	n		ТВЕРД	o	a	
СЕВ	s	n		ТВОР	w	v	
СЕК	w	v		ТЕК	w	v	
СЕЛ	w	n		ТЕМ/Н	o	a	
СЕРД	o	v		ТЕП/Л	o	a	
СИД	w	v		ТЕРП	o	v	
СИЛ	s	n	силовóй	ТИР	w	v	
СИН	o	a		ТОК	o	v	
СКАК	o	v		ТОК	o	n	
СКУК	o	n		ТОЛК	o	n	толковáть
СЛ	w	v		ТОЛСТ	o	a	
СЛАБ	o	a		ТОП	o	v	
СЛАВ	s	n		ТОПТ	o	v	
СЛЕД	o	n	следи́ть следовóй	ТОРГ	w/s	v/n	(торговáть, торгóвец)
СЛЕП	w	a		ТО́РМОЗ	o	n	тормози́ть
СЛУГ	w	n	служи́ть	ТРАВ	w	n	трави́ть
СЛУХ	s	n		ТРУБ	w	n	
СМЕЙ	o	v		ТРУД	w	n	труди́ться
СМОТР	o	v		ТРУС	s	n	
СНЕГ	o	n		ТРЯС	w	v	
СОБ	w	n		ТУГ	w	a	
СОЛ	o	n	соляной	ТУМА́Н	s	n	
СОС	w	v		ТУП	w	a	
СОЮ́З	s	n		ТЯГ	s	n	
СПАС	w	v		У́ЖА́С	o	n	ужасну́ть
СРОК	s	n		УК	o	v	
СТАВ(Н)	s	v	постанóвка	У́ЛИЦ	s	n	
СТАР	o	a		УЛЫБ	w	v	
СТОЙ	w	v		УМ	w	n	
СТОЛ	w	n		УХ	o	n	
СТО́РОЖ	o	n	сторожи́ть	ФОРМ	s	n	
СТОРОН	w	n	сторони́ться	ФРАЗ	s	n	
СТРАН	w	n		ХВАТ	o	v	
СТРАХ	o	n	страховáть	ХВОСТ	w	n	
СТРЕЛ	w	n		ХИТР	o	a	
СТРОЙ	s	v		ХЛОП	s	v	
СТУК	o	n	стучáть	ХОД	o	v	
СТУП	o	v		ХО́ЛОД	o	n	холоди́ть
СТЫД	w	n		ХРАБР	o	a	
СУД	w	n	суди́ть	ХРАН	w	v	

ЦВЕТ	w	n	
ЦЕН	w	n	цени́ть
ЧАС	o	n	часово́й
ЧАСТ	o	n	
ЧЕРН	o	a	
ЧЁС	s	n	
ЧИН	o	v	
ЧИН	w	v	
ЧИСЛ	w	n	чи́слить
ЧИСТ	o	a	
ЧИТ	w	v	
ЧУД	w	v	чу́до
ЧУЖ	w	a	
ШАГ	o	n	шагну́ть
ШЕЛК	o	n	
ШИБ	w	a	
ШИЙ	w	v	
ШУМ	o	n	
ШУТ	w	n	шути́ть
ЩИП	o	v	
Я́БЛОК	s	n	
ЯВ	o	v	
Я́ГОД	s	n	
ЯЗЫК	w	n	
ЯСН	o	a	

APPENDIX 3
PRINCIPLES AND DEFINITIONS

Affricate	A manner of articulation whereby the air flow is stopped completely then allowed to continue, creating a stop-turning-into-a-husher effect
Allomorph	See Morphophoneme
Allophone	See Phoneme
Akan'e	The pronunciation of <u>o</u> and <u>a</u> as reduced sounds when not stressed
Alternation	An observed shift from one sound to another within a single morpheme
Analogy	A sound or morphemic shift due to the preponderance of one form over another in a given paradigm
Assimilation	The process of one sound becoming more like another due to its proximity to the other sound
Base Form	The initial form of a word upon which derivations act
Basic Form	The form of a word from which other stress patterns can be predicted, infinitive, nom sg, or nom sg long form
Common Slavic	The ancestor language of all the Slavic languages, spoken from about 3000 BC to arount 500 BC
Crosscategory	The formation of a word of one grammatical category on the basis of a stem or root of a different grammatical category: учи́ть (verb) - уче́ние (noun).

Deadjectival	Derived from an adjectival stem
Denominal	Derived from a noun stem
Deverbal	Derived from a verbal stem
Dental	A sound made with the teeth as part of the point of articulation
Derivation	The process of developing one form, such as the phonetic form, from another form, such as the phonological, by means of established rules
Derivationally Strong	Syllables receiving stress in derivation become accentually strong in regard to further derivation
Devoicing	The process of pronouncing a consonant voiceless
Dissimilation	The process of one sound become less like another due to its proximity
Disyllabic	Containing just two syllables
Epenthesis	The adding of an extra sound, such as л in люблю
Fleeting vowel	A vowel which occurs in at least one form of a paradigm; but which is absent in other forms, usually when another vowel follows.
Fricative	Manner of articulation whereby the air flow is restricted creating a hushing sound
Grammatical category	Refers to the class of the root or stem: noun, verb, adjective, or Adverb
Hard	See Velarized

Ikan'e	The pronunciation of <u>о, а, я, э</u> as [и] or [ь] when not stressed
Inflection	Having to do with the addition of conjugational or declensional endings onto words
Intracategory	The formation of a word based on a stem or root of the same grammatical category
Jer	A reduced vowel, either <u>ъ</u> or <u>ь</u> found in old Russian writings. Pronounced "yer"
Labial	A sound made by using the lips or a lip as the point of articulation
Labio-dental	A sound produced by using both teeth and lips, such as [в]
Lexical	Having to do with roots and their meanings
Lingua Franca	A language used by many nations as a common means of communicating
Manner of Articulation	The method by which the air flow is disrupted, such as stopping the air flow completely, or restricting it greatly to cause noise
Monosyllabic	Containing one syllable
Morpheme	A unit of sound that bears either lexical or grammatical meaning
Morphophoneme	A morpheme which may have an effect on the pronunciation of a contiguous morpheme. Allomorphs are morphophonemically determined variants of morphophonemes

Nonderived	The word exists independently of any derivational suffix
Nonvocalic	Does not contain a vowel
Nonvocalic Principle	If stress falls on a /, it will fall to the right by one syllable if the stem is verbal, otherwise it falls to the left by one syllable
Obstruent	A consonant other than a sonorant
Okan'e	The pronunciation of unstressed o̱, and occasionally a̱, as [o]
Old Church Slavic	A south Slavic language spoken from about 800 AD to about 1100 AD The earliest written forms of Slavic are in OCS
Old Russian	A language spoken from about 800 AD to about 1300 AD
Orthography	Normal spelling using letters from the Cyrillic alphabet
Palatal	A hushing sound produced by raising the tongue toward the palate
Palatalized	A sound produced whereby the spine of the tongue is further forward and higher than in the "hard" or velarized pronunciation of that sound
Paradigm	Usually a distinct set of endings, such as the endings for the sg or pl, or both for a given decl
Penultimate	The next to last, in accentuation: the syllable right before the stressed one

Phoneme	A sound unit whose substitution into a word alters the meaning of the word. Allophones are phonologically determined variants of phonemes
Phonetics	The discriptions of sounds in various environments
Phonology	The study of communicative (oral) sounds and how they are altered in speech
Polysyllabic	Containing more than one syllable
Point of Articulation	The place in the oral cavity where the air flow is disrupted or redirected
Posttonic	A syllable after the stress
Pretonic	A syllable before the stress
Primary Stress Rule	Stress can be assigned just to one syllable per word
Root	The unit that bears the fundamental lexical meaning of a word
Rounded	Manner of articulation whereby the lips are rounded
Soft	see Palatalized
Sonorant	Any one of the sounds [л], [м], [н], [р], or their palatalized counterparts, and [й]
Stem	The root and any attached suffixes
Stop	Manner of articulation whereby the air flow is stopped completely

Strong Position	Reference is to where a jer occurs in a word. It is strong if under stress or before a weak jer. Jers in weak position are those at the end of a word and those that are not followed by another jer
Theme vowel	In most 1st conj verbs, the vowel -o- occurring right before the person/number ending. The verbal suffix -и- functions as a theme vowel throughout the paradigm of 2nd conj verbs
Tonic	Syllable which is stressed
Truncation	The deletion of one or more morphemes or part of a morpheme
Underlying Form	See Base Form
Valency	The accentual weight of a given morpheme, strong, weak, or ordinary
Velar	A sound made with the soft or back of the hard palate as the point of articulation
Velarized	The process of pronouncing an otherwise soft consonant hard, that is, retracting the tongue toward the back of the mouth
Voice	When the vocal chords are vibrating during the pronunciation of a given sound, that sound is said to be voiced. Voiceless sounds are produced with vocal chords at rest.
Voiceless	See Voice
W+W principle	Stress falls the second of weak adjacent syllables if the second syllable is not nominal If it is nominal, then stress falls on the first weak syllable

Weak Position   See Strong Position

Yodicized   The process of pronouncing a [й] at the beginning
                       of a vowel sound

BIBLIOGRAPHY

Аванесов, Р. И. 1972. *Русское литературное произношение.* Москва: Просвещение.

Аванесов, Р. И. и Орлова, В. Г. 1965. *Русская диалектология.* Москва: Наука.

Академия наук СССР. 1980. *Русская грамматика.* Москва: Наука.

Алексеев, А. А. 1986. «Почему в древней руси не было диглоссии». *Литературный язык древней руси.* Ленинград: Ленинградский университет.

Арват, Н. Н., и Скиба, Ю. Г. 1977. *Древнерусский язык.* Киев: Вища Школа.

Channon, R. 1972. *On the Place of the Progressive Palatalization of Velars in the Relative Chronology of Slavic.* The Hague: Mouton.

Coats, H. S. 1976. *Stress Assignment in Russian, Vol I: Inflection.* Edmonton, Alberta: Linguistic Research, Inc.

Coats, H. S. and Lightner, T. M. "Transitive Softening in Russian Conjugation." *Language* 51/2, 338-341.

Coats, H. S. and D. K. Hart. 1989. "The Assignment of Stress in Russian Nouns." *Linguistic Analysis,* 19:3-4, 123-175.

Даль, Владимир. 1978. *Толковый словарь живого великорусского языка, том 1-4.* Москва: Русский язык.

Garde, P. 1976. *Histoire de l'accentuation slave, vol. 1-2.* Paris: Institut des Etudes Slaves.

Гринкова, Н. П. и Чагашева, В. И. 1957. *Практические занятия по диалектологии.* Ленинград: Госучпедгиз.

Зализняк, А. А. 1977. *Грамматический словарь русского языка.* Москва: Русский язык.

_____ 1985. *От праславянской акцентуации к русской.* Москва: Наука.

Засорина, Л. Н. 1977. *Частотный словарь русского языка.* Москва: Русский язык.

Горбачевич, М. 1986. *Нормы современного русского литературного языка.* Москва: Просвещение.

Дыбо, В. А., Замятина, Г. И., и Николаев, С. Л. 1990. *Основы славянской акцентологии.* Москва: Наука.

Feldstein, R. 1993. "The Nature and Use of the Accentual Paradigm as Applied to Russian." *Journal of Slavic Linguistics, 1/1*, 44-60.

Gribble, C. E. 1989. "Omisssion of the Jer Vowels in Early East Slavic Manuscripts." *Russian Linguistics, 13*, 1-14.

Gribble, C. E. 1981. *Russian Root List.* Columbus, Ohio: Slavica.

Halle, M. 1971. *The Sound Pattern of Russian.* The Hauge: Mouton.

Hamilton, W. S. 1980. *Introduction to Russian Phonology and Word Structure.* Columbus, Ohio: Savica.

Hart, D. K. 1987. "A Minimal Rule Approach to Teaching First-year Russian Conjugation and Verb Stress." *Russian Language Journal, XLI, no.138-139*, 19-29.

Иванов, В. В.1990. *Историческая грамматика русского языка.* Москва: Просвещение.

Иванов, В. В., Сумникова, Т. А., и Панкратова, Н. П. 1990. *Хрестоматия по истории русского языка.* Москва: Просвещение.

Kantor, M. and Smith R. 1975. "A Sketch of the Major Developments in Russian Historical Phonology." *Folia Linguistica, VII:3/4*, 389-400.

Касаткин, Л. Л., ред. 1989. *Русская диалектология*. Москва: Просвещение.

Kilbury, James. 1976. *The Development of Morphophonemic Theory*. Amsterdam: John Benjamins.

Klepko, V. 1964. *A Practical Handbook on Stress in Russian*. New York: Staphograph.

Колесов, В. В. 1972. *История русского ударения*. Ленинград: Ленинградский университет.

_____ 1980. *Историческая фонетика русского языка*. Москва: Высшая школа.

Кондрашов, Н. А. 1986. *Славянские языки*. Москва: Просвещение.

Кузнецова, А. И. и Ефремова Т. Ф. 1986. *Словарь морфем русского языка*. Москва: Русский язык.

Кузнецова, О. Д. 1985. *Актуальные процессы в говорах русского языка*. Ленинград: Наука.

Лебедева, Ю. Г. 1986. *Звуки, ударение, интонация*. Москва: Русский язык.

Levin, M. I. 1978. *Russian Declension and Conjugation: A Structural Description with Exercises*. Columbus, Ohio: Slavica.

Lightner, T. M. 1972. *Problems in the Theory of Phonology*. Edmonton, Alberta: Linguistic Research, Inc.

Lunt, H. 1987. "On the Relationship of Old Church Slavic to the Written Language of Early Rus'." *Russian Linguistics, 11*, 133-162.

Mahota, W. 1993. "The Genitive Plural Endings in the East Slavic Languages." *Journal of Slavic Linguistics, 1/2*, 325-342.

Марков, В. И. 1974. *Историческая грамматика русского языка--именное склонение.* Москва: Высшая школа.

Матусевич, М. И. 1976. *Современный русский язык: фонетика.* Москва: Просвещение.

Meillet, A. 1965. Le slave commun. Paris: Champion.

Мельниченко, Г. Г. 1984. *Хрестоматия по русской диалектологии.* Москва: Просвещение.

Micklesen, L. R. 1974. "The Common Slavic Verbal System." *American Contributions to the VII International Congress of Slavists.* University of Michigan, 241-273.

Nandriş, G. and Auty, R. 1965. *Old Church Slavonic Grammar: I-II.* London: Athalone Press.

Ожегов, С. И. 1983. *Словарь русского языка.* Москва: Русский язык.

Панов, М. В. (ред.). 1968. *Фонетика современного русского литературного языка: народные говоры.* Москва: Наука.

Потиха, З. А. 1970. *Современное русское словообразование.* Москва: Просвещение.

Розенталь, Д. Е. и Теленкова, М. А. 1981. *Словарь трудностей русского языка.* Москва: Русский язык.

Shakhmatov, A. A. 1957. Историческая морфология русского языка. Москва: Учпедгиз.

Shevelov, G. Y. 1965. A Prehistory of Slavic. New York: Columbia University Press.

Shapiro, M. 1986. "The Russian System of Stress." *Russian Linguistics,* *10,* 183-204.

Swan, O. E. 1984. "The Morphophonemics of the Russian Imperative." *Russian Linguistics, 8,* 39-47.

Townsend, C. E. 1980. *Russian Word Formation.* Columbus, Ohio: Slavica.

Фасмер, М. 1986. *Этимологический словарь русского языка, том 1-4.* Москва: Прогресс.

Федянина, Н. А. 1976. *Ударение в современном русском языке.* Москва: Русский язык.

Филин, Ф. П. 1979. *Русский язык, энциклопедия.* Москва: Советская энциклопедия.

Vlasto, A. P. 1986. *A Linguistic History of Russian to the End of the Eighteenth Century.* Oxford: Clarendon Press.

Хабургаев, Г. А. 1974. *Старославянский язык.* Москва: Просвещение.

Янко-Триницкая, Н. А. 1982. *Русская морфология.* Москва: Русский язык.

Янович, Б. И. 1986. *Историческая грамматика русского языка.* Минск: Университетское.